Best Books for Beginning Readers

Related Titles

Helping Students Learn to Write Poetry: An Idea Book
for Poets of All Ages
Joyce C. Bumgardner
0-205-26169-8

Connecting Informational Children's Books with Content Area Learning
Evelyn B. Freeman and Diane Goetz Person
0-205-26753-X

The Right Book, the Right Time: Helping Children Cope
Martha C. Grindler, Beverly D. Stratton, and Michael C. McKenna
0-205-17272-5

Developing Reading and Writing through Author Awareness:
Grades 4–8
Evelyn Krieger
0-205-17355-1

Poetry Across the Curriculum: An Action Guide
for Elementary Teachers
Aaren Yeatts Perry
0-205-19807-4

Children's Books in Children's Hands: An Introduction
to Their Literature
Charles Temple, Miriam Martinez, Junko Yokota, and Alice Naylor
0-205-16995-3

For more information or to purchase a book, please call 1-800-278-3525.

In loving memory of my sister,
Barbara Maxwell Buchman

Contents

Preface

An essential ingredient in the acquisition of initial literacy skills and the development of a love of reading is the reading of a wide variety of books at the appropriate level of difficulty. Novice readers need books that captivate them but that are not too difficult for them to read on their own or with a little help. The purpose of *Best Books for Beginning Readers* is to provide a descriptive listing of books for novice readers and to present methods for matching children with books that are on the appropriate level of challenge. In addition, *Best Books for Beginning Readers* explores techniques for using books to develop beginning reading skills.

Chapter 1 explains the benefits of wide reading for novice readers and explains how books were chosen and arranged by levels of difficulty. Chapter 2 explores techniques for using books with novice readers. Techniques include reading to children, reading along with children, and providing various kinds of assistance to children so they can read books that might be a bit too difficult for them to read entirely on their own. Chapter 3 discusses easy-to-apply procedures that may be used to ensure that children are given books that are neither too easy nor too difficult.

Chapter 4 is the core of *Best Books for Beginning Readers*. It provides a listing and brief description of more than 1,000 high-quality children's books that can be read by beginning readers. These books are arranged in order of difficulty, beginning with those that can be read simply by using illustrations and moving up to those that have brief chapters and contain 500 to 1,000 words or more.

Appendix A presents the Primary Readability Index, a device that was used to estimate the difficulty level of books included in *Best Books for Beginning Readers* and that you might use to judge the difficulty level of those beginning readers not listed. Appendix B contains a word- and passage-reading inventory designed to estimate the reading ability of beginning readers. Yielding the same levels as those provided by the Primary Readability Index, it is designed to help you determine what level of materials your novice readers can handle. Appendix C lists sets of beginning readers produced by educational publishers. Generally, these are brief booklets designed to provide practice for novice readers.

To assist you in locating appropriate books, *Best Books for Beginning Readers* features four indices. In addition to featuring separate author, title, and subject indices, a skills index is provided to help you locate books that might be used to reinforce specific decoding and comprehension skills as well as locate models and possible topics for writing.

Although this book was written primarily for classroom teachers and remedial tutors, it may also be used by librarians as they add to their picture book and easy reader collections and make recommendations to parents and teachers of novice readers. Parents and grandparents will also find *Best Books for Beginning Readers* useful as they seek out books for children and grandchildren who are in the beginning stages of learning to read.

ACKNOWLEDGMENTS

Many thanks to Virginia Lanigan of Allyn and Bacon for her enthusiastic support of this project. I am grateful to Kris Lamarre, her assistant, who so capably handled all the myriad details that led up to publication. I would also like to extend my appreciation to the following reviewers whose suggestions were both thoughtful and perceptive and helped me see ways in which I might improve the manuscript: Jami Craig, Countryside Elementary School; Rebecca J. Downing, Pleasant Ridge Elementary School; and Stephanie Moretti, Menlo Park School. Thanks, also, to Norma Kable, whose illustrations enliven the selections in the Primary Reading Passages Inventory and to Lynda Griffiths of TKM Productions for her careful copyediting.

Chapter 1

Children's Books for Beginning Readers

As a classroom teacher, I knew intuitively that the best way to foster children's growth in reading was to entice them to read, read, read. From my earliest days of teaching, a classroom library was an essential part of my reading program. As a parent, I watched as my four children developed initial reading skills. I had my doubts about the value of the workbook pages they brought home, but it was crystal clear that being read to and reading on their own were vital elements in the development of their basic literacy skills.

DEVELOPMENT OF READING

As director of the Reading Clinic at Southern Connecticut State University, I noticed that some children made more progress than others, even though each child was assigned a knowledgeable instructor who was closely supervised. Of course, some children worked harder than others or had less serious problems, so that explains their superior progress. However, a number of children who had serious difficulties were instructed four, five, or even more semesters and had a different teacher each semester. Since progress varied from semester to semester, sometimes dramatically so, that suggests that some teachers were more effective than others. In searching through records and observational notes that I kept on each teacher, I found that in addition to being well prepared, flexible, and enthusiastic, the most effective teachers "made the match." They supplied children with lots of books that matched both the children's interests and levels of reading ability. Students who read widely on the appropriate levels of difficulty generally made excellent progress. Those who did not read widely or who were given materials that were too hard or too easy made limited progress or virtually no progress at all.

An analysis of successful intervention programs for children struggling to learn to read yielded a similar finding. A major characteristic of the best programs is extensive reading of appropriate books. Marie Clay (1993), one of the founders of Reading Recovery, which may well be the most successful reading program for young children ever devised, comments: *"The teacher must be the expert chooser and sequencer of the texts for a Reading Recovery pupil—this is critical"* (p. 13, emphasis in original). Indeed, Reading Recovery teachers are provided with a bibliography of hundreds of children's books arranged in order of estimated difficulty.

Although all students gain when they read on their own, those who are the farthest behind gain the most. By one estimate, young, above-average readers gain as much as one extra year's growth in reading ability, as measured by standardized reading tests, when they engage in at least 60 minutes of reading each day (Paul, 1996). This includes reading done at home and in school. Instead of gaining one year, which is the normal expectation, average readers gain two years. And, according to this commercially sponsored study, below-average readers gain two and one-half years.

One reason some students make slow progress in reading is because they read less. According to Paul (1996), the bottom 25 percent of readers read only one-quarter as much as the top 25 percent. Even slight increases in the time spent reading lead to gains in reading achievement (Anderson, 1996). In one study, students showed significant gains when they engaged in as little as 10 minutes of free reading each day (Fielding, Wilson, & Anderson, 1986).

The amount of reading one does in the early grades has a payoff in later grades. For example, the number of minutes a day a child spends reading in the early grades helps determine how well he or she reads in grades 5 and 6 (Anderson, 1996).

DEVELOPMENT OF OVERALL LITERACY

Wide reading not only fosters improved reading but it also improves other literacy skills. Krashen (1993) comments, "Reading is a powerful means of developing reading comprehension ability, writing style, vocabulary, grammar, and spelling" (p. 22). In fact, in many studies, reading was as effective as direct instruction in improving reading, writing, spelling, and overall language development. As Krashen explains, reading does not, by itself, produce the highest level of competence. "Rather, it provides a foundation so that the highest levels of competence may be reached" (p. 1).

PURPOSE OF THIS BOOK

Despite the importance of wide reading in developing a love of reading and literacy skills, there is no readily accessible extensive annotated listing of beginning books arranged according to level of difficulty. *Best Books for Beginning Readers* is a compilation of more than 1,000 high-quality children's books that might be used to teach or improve reading skills of children who are in the early stages of learning to read. Books are arranged in order of difficulty, from the emergent or very beginning level up through the first half of second grade.

HOW THE BOOKS WERE CHOSEN

Many of the books listed on these pages were chosen on the basis of using them with children or observing teachers use of them with children. Recommendations were solicited from children, teachers, librarians, and parents. A number of professional texts were also consulted. In addition, I examined every picture book and easy reader in more than a dozen libraries, several bookstores, and the collection of the Children's Book Council. Publishers' and book distributors' catalogs were also searched. Selection criteria included the following:

- The book is interesting.
- The book is worthwhile.
- The book has a natural flow.
- The book is positive.
- The book is accurate.
- The book is graphically appealing.
- The book is somewhere on a beginning reading level—that is, emergent, first, or beginning second-grade level.

Omitted were books that were stilted, boring, violent, or inaccurate and books that lacked overall appeal. Also omitted were instructional books or books that are part of libraries for beginning readers created by educational publishers. However, a listing of libraries of books at the beginning levels is provided in Appendix C. These books provide valuable practice but often lack the sparkle and variety of children's trade books.

The more than 1,000 books listed represent some of the finest books published. Some, such as *Millions of Cats* (Gag, 1928), *Ask Mr. Bear* (Flack, 1932), or *Are You My Mother?* (1960), are classics. Despite their age, they are still in print and still in demand. Side by side with these classics are attractive, intriguing books, such as *Toby, Where Are You?* (Steig, 1997), *Little Cloud* (Carle, 1996), or *Shrinking Mouse* (Hutchins, 1997), that have been published within the past year. Many of the books chosen have won prestigious awards or are recommended by Reading Rainbow or other highly respected sources. Unfortunately, despite an extensive search, there are undoubtedly some fine books that have not been included. If you are aware of any such books, please send me your recommendations so that they may be considered for the next edition.

Most of the books listed in *Best Books for Beginning Readers* are in print and may be obtained from bookstores, publishers, or distributors. However, about 50 books that are not now in print are included in the listings. These are books that have a special value in promoting literacy. They cover a vital topic or reinforce a skill in a unique way. Books that are out of print are often available from school and public libraries. In addition, a number of children's books that are out of print for a time are reissued in their original form or with new illustrations.

DIFFICULTY LEVEL OF BEGINNING READING BOOKS

Books designed for young children vary enormously both in subject matter and level of difficulty. While most books for young children feature talking animals, pets, playing with friends, family life, and school, others deal with such serious subjects as homelessness and the death of a grandparent. Difficulty level ranges from those that require no reading (the books have no words; the stories are told entirely through pictures) to those that require the reading ability of an average fifth- or sixth-grade student. Although dealing with content interesting to young children, most picture books are designed to be read by adults to children. Only about one picture book in twenty is easy enough to be read by children in grade 1 or 2. It was from this 5 percent that *Best Books for Beginning Readers* were chosen.

Following are descriptions of the levels of difficulty as well as examples of books for each category. Levels are arranged from easiest to most challenging.

DESCRIPTION OF LEVELS

Picture Level

At the picture level, each page illustrates a single word or phrase with a drawing or photo. The word *lion*, for instance, is accompanied by a drawing of a lion; the word *three* is accompanied by the numeral three and three cats. The text is so fully and clearly depicted that no reading is required. Picture level + means that the reader may not be able to identify one or more of the illustrations. An unfamiliar animal such as a yak may be depicted, or an illustration may be ambiguous. The reader may not know whether a mule, a donkey, a pony, a horse, or a colt is being shown and would need to be able to read at least the initial consonant of the caption to know that it is a donkey because the caption begins with a *d*. Examples of picture-level books include:

Numbers by Guy Smalley. The numbers 1 to 10 are illustrated: 1 dog, 2 apples, 3 boats, and so on.

Colors by John Burningham. Color words are illustrated with objects drawn in the target color.

Up to Ten and Down Again by Lisa Campbell Ernst. The numbers 1 to 10 are illustrated: 1 duck, 2 cars, 3 dogs, and so on.

See Figure 1.1 for an example of a picture-level selection. The selection is excerpted from the Primary Reading Passages Inventory in Appendix B.

Caption/Frame Level

The text of the book is illustrated so that the reader can use pictures to identify most but not all of the words. Caption-level books frequently feature frame sentences, which are easy sentences, such as *I can* _____, *I am* _____, or _____ *can swim*, that are repeated throughout the text. The name of the object, animal, or person that completes the frame is usually depicted. There is one sentence and one illustration per page. In a caption + text, the reader may not be able to identify one or more of the items depicted. Examples of caption-level texts include:

Cat on the Mat by Brian Wildsmith. Drawings accompanying the frame sentence "The _____ sat on the mat " show a variety of animals sitting on a mat.

Figure 1.1
Example of Picture-Level Selection

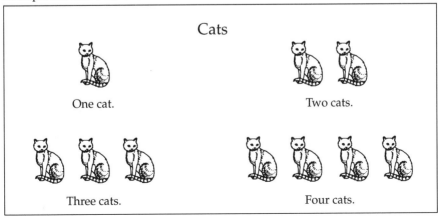

Cats

One cat.

Two cats.

Three cats.

Four cats.

My Barn by Craig Brown. The farmer repeats "I like the sound _____" and says the sound that each farm animal makes.

The Cat Sat on the Mat by Alice Cameron. Drawings accompanying the text frame "The cat sat on the _____" show the cat sitting in an assortment of places.

See Figure 1.2 for an example of a caption/frame-level selection. The selection is excerpted from the Primary Reading Passages Inventory in Appendix B.

Easy Sight-Word Level

The easy sight-word level is similar to the caption level, but more reading is required. Up to 35 different words might be used, nearly all of which would be found on the Primary High-Frequency Word List, which is presented in Figure A.2 in Appendix A. It is a list of the 500 words most frequently found in children's library and school books (Zeno, Ivens, Millard, & Rajduvvuri,

Figure 1.2
Example of Caption/Frame-Level Selection

I see a seal.

I see a seal in the zoo.

1995). At this level of difficulty, there would only be about 4 to 6 words per 100 not on the Primary High-Frequency Word List. The text is brief and would generally be less than 100 words in length. There is 1 illustration per page and 1 or 2 lines of text per page. The illustrations generally depict some or much of the text but may be simply supportive. Examples of easy sight-word level books include:

Brown Bear, Brown Bear, What Do You See? by Bill Martin

Bugs by Patricia and Fredrick McKissack

Who Is Who? Patricia McKissack

See Figure 1.3 for an example of a sight-word level selection. The selection is excerpted from the Primary Reading Passages Inventory in Appendix B.

Figure 1.3
Example of Sight-Word Level Selection

The Red Kangaroo

Hop! Hop! Hop! The red kangaroo likes to hop. The red kangaroo can hop over you. It can hop ten feet.

Beginning Reading A

Selections are approximately 100 to 150 words long and contain 35 to 50 different words. There may be less repetition and less predictability than on the easy sight-word level. There is usually one illustration and from 1 to 4 or more lines of print per page. There would be approximately 7 or 8 words per 100 not on the Primary High-Frequency Word List. Examples of beginning reading A books include:

The Ant and the Dove by Mary Lewis Wang

The Foot Book by Dr. Seuss

Sleepy Dog by Harriet Ziefert

See Figure 1.4 for an example of a beginning A selection. The selection is excerpted from the Primary Reading Passages Inventory in Appendix B.

Beginning Reading B

Selections are approximately 150 to 200 words long and contain more than 50 different words. There is usually 1 illustration and from 1 to 5 or more lines of print per page. There would be approximately 9 or 10 words per 100 not on the Primary High-Frequency Word List. Examples of beginning reading B books include:

And I Mean It Stanley by Crosby Bonsall

The Cake that Mack Ate by Rose Robart

Jason's Bus Ride by Harriet Zieffert

See Figure 1.5 for an example of a beginning B selection. The selection is excerpted from the Primary Reading Passages Inventory in Appendix B.

Beginning Reading C

Selections are approximately 200 to 250 words long and contain a varied vocabulary. There is usually 1 illustration and from 1 to 6 or more lines of print per page. There would be approximately 11 or 12 words per 100 not on the Primary High-Frequency Word List. In addition to being longer, selections at this level are more complex. Plots are more involved and informational books are more detailed. Examples of beginning reading C books include:

Little Bear's Visit by Else Holmelund Minark

Clifford the Small Red Puppy by Norman Bridwell

Yoo Hoo, Moon! by Mary Blocksma

Figure 1.4
Example of Beginning A Selection

The Tallest Animal

The giraffe is the tallest animal of all. A baby giraffe is six feet tall. When it is fully grown, a giraffe can be 18 feet tall.

The giraffe's long neck and long legs make it tall. Its legs are six feet long. And so is its neck. The giraffe has the longest legs and longest neck of any animal. Giraffes eat a lot of food. With their long necks, giraffes can eat from the tops of trees.

Figure 1.5
Example of Beginning B Selection

Ben

Ann was sad. Ben had climbed up a tree. Ben is her cat. "Come down, Ben!" Ann ordered. "Come down right away!" Ben did not come down. He just climbed to a higher branch.

Ann did not know what to do, so she called her mom at the office. Her mom is a vet. "Put a dish of milk at the bottom of the tree," her mom said. Ann did just that. When Ben saw the dish of milk, he climbed down the tree as fast as he could.

See Figure 1.6 for an example of a beginning C selection. The selection is excerpted from the Primary Reading Passages Inventory in Appendix B.

Figure 1.6
Example of Beginning C Selection

Johnny Appleseed

John looked strange. He wore a tin pan for a hat, and he was dressed in rags. Even so, people liked John. He was kind to others, and he was kind to animals.

John loved apples. He left his home and headed West about 200 years ago. He wanted everyone to have apples. On his back he carried a pack that was full of apple seeds. At that time, there were few apple trees in many parts of our country. Traveling from place to place, John planted his apple seeds. As the years passed, the seeds grew into trees. After planting hundreds and hundreds of apple trees, John came to be called "Johnny Appleseed."

Beginning Reading D

Selections are approximately 250 words or longer and contain a more varied vocabulary and longer sentences than the previous level. Books may be 48 or more pages long and are frequently divided into brief chapters. There is usually 1 illustration per page, but pages may have 10 or more lines of print. Illustrations are supportive but may not explicitly depict text. The book may incorporate a few words not in the reader's listening vocabulary and may contain 1 or 2 unfamiliar concepts. There would be approximately 13 or 14 words per 100 not on the Primary High-Frequency Word List. Examples of beginning reading D books include:

Henry and Mudge, the First Book by Cynthia Rylant

Frog and Toad at Home by Arnold Lobel

Feed Me by William Hooks

See Figure 1.7 for an example of a beginning D selection. The selection is excerpted from the Primary Reading Passages Inventory in Appendix B.

Grade 2A

Selections are similar to the type found in beginning reading D books. However, there is a noticeable increase in the proportion of words not on the Primary High-Frequency Word List. There may also be a greater proportion of words not in the students' listening vocabulary. There is usually 1 supportive illustration and up to 20 lines of print per page. There would be approximately 15 to 20 words per 100 not on the Primary High-Frequency Word List. Examples of grade 2A books include:

Bread and Jam for Frances by Russell Hoban

Thank You, Amelia Bedelia by Peggy Parish

Stone Soup by Ann McGovern

See Figure 1.8 for an example of a Grade 2A selection. The selection is excerpted from the Primary Reading Passages Inventory in Appendix B.

To make the eight levels of difficulty more understandable, Table 1.1 shows each of the categories in terms of grade-level equivalents and Reading Recovery levels. Although the reading levels of the books are expressed as being on a k-emergent level or somewhere on a first- or second-grade level, this does not mean that books have to be used on the designated grade level. Books are categorized according to difficulty level rather than the grade level on which they might be used. Some children in first grade, for instance, may be able to handle books on a second-grade level. Others may

Figure 1.7
Example of Beginning D Selection

Puppy Tails

Bob gets a new puppy almost every year. The puppy is not Bob's to keep. Bob only has the puppy for a year and then he must give it back.

Bob is in a club known as Puppy Tails. The boys and girls in Puppy Tails raise puppies for Seeing Eye. Seeing Eye trains guide dogs for blind people. A puppy is not ready for guide dog training until it is at least 14 months old. The boys and girls in Puppy Tails take care of the puppies until they are grown up enough to be taught by Seeing Eye.

Bob feels sad when the year is up and he has to give his puppy back to Seeing Eye. He will miss his pup. But in a way, Bob feels happy, too. He knows that his pup will help someone in need.

need books on a k-emergent level. And some kindergarten children will be able to read books on an advanced first- or second-grade level. On the other hand, some slow-progress students in grades 2 and 3 may need books at the lowest levels of difficulty. In the annotations, interest level is indicated so that you can consider both reading level and maturity level when selecting books.

Figure 1.8
Example of Grade 2A Selection

Clowns

What do you like best about the circus? Many boys and girls like the clowns best of all.

Clowns wear funny costumes. Clowns might wear shoes that are so big that you could put two feet in one shoe. Their baggy pants and extra-large shirts may also be many sizes too big for them. And a clown king may wear a crown that is so big it covers his ears.

Clowns do funny tricks. They pretend that they are throwing pails of water at each other. But all that comes out are bits of paper. They may also drive tiny cars. It looks funny to see a very tall clown climb out of a very small car.

It is not easy to be a clown. Circus clowns spend much of their time on trains traveling to towns and cities around the country. Clowns also spend many hours painting their faces and practicing their tricks. Although being a clown is hard work, it is fun. It is fun to make children and grown-ups laugh.

Table 1.1
Comparison of Beginning Reading Levels

Best Books Level	Grade Equivalent	Reading Recovery Level
Picture	K-Emergent	1
Caption	K-Emergent	2–3
Easy sight word	1.0–1.1	4–8
Beginning A	1.2–1.3	9–11
Beginning B	1.4–1.5	12–14
Beginning C	1.6–1.7	14–17
Beginning D	1.8–1.9	18–20
Grade 2A	2.0–2.49	-----

DETERMINING DIFFICULTY LEVEL OF BEGINNING READING BOOKS

Traditionally, the difficulty level of children's books has been determined by the use of a readability formula. Based on a calculation of the number of hard words in a selection and the average sentence length, the formula yields an estimated difficulty level. The Spache (Spache, 1974), Wide Range (Harris & Jacobson, 1982), and Fry (1977) instruments have been used widely to estimate the difficulty level of beginning-level textbooks and children's books. Some publishers of children's books list the estimated readability levels on the covers or front pages of their books.

Readability formulas are valid indicators of the grade level of a book. They are effective devices for estimating whether a book is on a first-, second-, or third-grade level. However, formulas are not useful for making fine discriminations (Chall, Bissex, Conard, & Harris-Sharples, 1996). To determine whether a book is on a picture, caption, or easy sight-word level, it is necessary to look at the book's illustrations, the relationship between the text and the illustrations, the format of the text, the type of language used, the concepts explored, and other factors not directly measured by current formulas. Recently, several subjective scales have been created to discriminate among levels of difficulty at the beginning stages of reading. Teachers in New Zealand created a readability system that assigns levels to books according to a number of factors, including:

- Content
- Length
- Children's assumed background of experience
- Story structure and style
- Language structure
- Size and type of print
- Amount, placement, and usefulness of illustrations of text (Learning Media, 1994)

These characteristics were used to grade books in the Ready to Read series, a set of books used to teach beginning reading in New Zealand. Books were categorized into nine levels: emergent, early 1, early 2, early 3, early 4, fluency 1, fluency 2, fluency 3, and fluency 4. Adapting New Zealand's Ready to Read system, Reading Recovery has classified hundreds of children's books into 20 levels, ranging from a very beginning or picture-reading level to end of first grade (Peterson, 1991). A partial listing of leveled books can be found in Chapter 6 of *Bridges to Literacy: Learning from Reading Recovery* (Deford, Lyons, & Pinnell, 1991). Also adapting the Ready to Read system, Weaver (1992) created a scheme for placing books into nine levels, ranging in difficulty level from grades 1 through 3. One problem with all of these scales is that they are difficult to apply without specific training. In addition, they consider only subjective factors.

To get as valid a readability estimate as possible for beginning books, I constructed the Primary Readability Index. This index uses both objective and subjective factors to estimate the difficulty level of beginning reading books. The key objective factor that determines the difficulty level of early reading materials is vocabulary or the difficulty that the novice reader will experience pronouncing the words in a book. Stories that use a few common words should prove easier to read than those that use a variety of words, including some that do not occur with high frequency. Vocabulary difficulty is measured by counting the number of words that do not appear on the Primary High-Frequency Word List, which is presented in A.2 of Appendix A. The Primary High-Frequency Word List is a compilation of the 500 words that occur with the highest frequency in first-grade textbooks and children's books that are on a first-grade level. The total number of words and the total number of different words were also calculated at the easiest levels. In addition, subjective factors, such as background knowledge and language development needed to read a particular book, relationship of pictures to text, and format were assessed. Directions for applying the Primary Readability Index along with technical information about its construction are presented in Appendix A.

The difficulty level of a text depends, in part, on how it is to be read. The reading can be independent, guided, or shared. In *independent* reading, children read on their own. They are given no assistance before or during reading. In order for a book to be on the independent level, the reader should know at least 98 to 99 percent of the words. In *guided* reading, the teacher typically builds needed background information and goes over any words that may be unfamiliar in meaning or that may be in the child's listening/speaking vocabulary but are unfamiliar in print. In order for a book to be on the guided level, the reader should know at least 95 percent of the words. In *shared* reading, both the teacher and the student read the book. The proportion that each reads can vary considerably. For a difficult book, the teacher might read most of the text and have the student read easy repeated sentences. For an easier text, the teacher might read half and the student might read half.

Chapter 2

Ways of Using Children's Books in the Reading/Writing Program

The most important reason for including children's books in any reading program is to instill a love of reading in children. Through broad exposure to a variety of the best that has been written, children learn that reading can be satisfying and informative. The key is to provide children with many books that they can read with ease. Other important ingredients include giving children choices so that they can select books or other reading materials that are appealing to them and setting aside time each day for children to read whatever they want to read. This need only be 15 or 20 minutes a day. Giving children a chance to talk about books also fosters an interest in reading.

TIPS FOR MOTIVATING READING

Intrinsic motivation works best. Students will read more if they enjoy reading and if the circumstances surrounding reading are pleasant and positive. Round-robin oral reading can ruin a good story, as can quiz-type questions and endless worksheets. However, reading with a small group of friends, having one's personal response to a book valued, and engaging in dramatizations and other extensions add to the enjoyment of reading.

Have available a wide assortment of books that students want to read and can read. Even the liveliest discussion and the most creative activities can't make boring books interesting or overly difficult books easy. Capitalize on students' individual interests. Also, allow students to make choices whenever possible. Even in the early grades, students' interests vary. The book on sharks that is so interesting to one student may be viewed as being deadly dull by a second youngster.

Providing a wide range of books is important. The more books that are available—whether they be in a school or a public, home, or classroom library—the more children read. In one study, increasing the supply of books by 20 percent increased circulation by 10 percent (Houle & Montmarquette, 1984). Also consider obtaining multiple copies of the most popular and the most useful books so that students can read with a partner or in small sharing groups.

Creating a Reading Center

Atmosphere is also an important factor in motivating young children to read. Morrow (1982) found that creating attractive reading centers enticed children in the early grades to visit these areas during free-choice times. If the reading areas were inviting, most children chose a reading activity. If the reading areas were not attractive, most children chose other activities. The reading centers should have an area rug and comfortable places to sit or recline, such as a rocking chair, a sofa, overstuffed pillows, and beanbag chairs. Although readily accessible, the area should be quiet and private, enclosed on three sides. Books should be attractively displayed. At least some of the books should have their covers facing outward so that they attract students. Posters, puppets, felt boards, stuffed animals, and tape recorders with head sets should be placed in the center (Morrow, 1993). A computer with CD-ROM versions of books will certainly prove to be a popular attraction in the center. Changing displays, adding new books, and planning special activities for the center will help maintain its appeal throughout the school year.

Arranging Books

Books may be arranged in a variety of ways: by theme, genre, title, author, or some sort of combination of these elements. You may also want to arrange books by difficulty level. A convenient way to indicate difficulty level is to use colored dot stickers.

Reading Aloud

Reading aloud also fosters wide reading. Children whose parents read to them read more (Neuman, 1986), as do children whose teachers read to them (Morrow & Weinstein, 1982, 1986). Reading aloud has a double benefit. Hearing books read encourages children to read on their own. Young children often want to read books that have been read to them (Gutkin, 1990). In addition, reading to children develops language and builds background so that students are better prepared to read independently.

Modeling Voluntary Reading

Modeling voluntary reading also encourages children to read on their own. Children read more when they see their parents and teachers read for pleasure. Talking about books is also an important ingredient for promoting voluntary reading. Research reveals that children who voluntarily read at least 30 minutes a day often have someone at home with whom they can discuss their reading and who makes suggestions about what they might read next (Guthrie, Schafer, Wang, & Afflerbach, 1995).

Discussing books with friends and classmates can be motivational, too. As Wilson (1992) notes, "Reading becomes something that students do because of friendship, because their friends read. More important, sharing their thoughts and feelings about books becomes part of the intellectual currency of their social relationships within the classroom. Reading becomes part of the culture of the classroom" (p. 163).

Setting Aside Time for Reading

Because of the importance of voluntary reading, many teachers set aside time each day for free reading. Originally called Sustained Silent Reading (SSR), the name has been changed by some to Self-Selected Reading. Because of the benefits of discussing books or reading with a group or partner, students should not be required to be silent during free-reading time. During SSR, everyone, including the teacher, reads or discusses what they are reading. Students can read alone or with a friend or in a small group. They can read along with an audio tape or a CD-ROM version of a book. If they choose to do so, they can discuss their reading with a friend or a small group.

Children should be allowed to read whatever they want, whether it be a children's book or magazine or something from the electronic media. Reading materials should be readily accessible. It is helpful for young children if books that the teacher read to them that day or within the past week are available. Even children in the earliest stage of reading can participate. They can read books on the picture or caption level, read along with a friend, or read along with an audio tape or CD-ROM version.

Reading at Home

By all means, encourage students to take books home to read. Time for sustained reading during the school day is limited. Reading at home provides the additional practice that is so important for developing fluency. The hope is that students will continue reading at home a book that they started in class.

Organizing the Program

As with any other classroom activity, SSR works best when children are involved in creating the ground rules. An effective set of ground rules might include the following:

- Each student is involved in reading.
- The teacher reads.
- Books to be read should be chosen before the session starts.
- Students should choose two or three books, in case the original selection is not satisfactory.
- A timer is used.
- No book reports or other assignments are required. (Gunning, 1996)

It takes some children a while to adjust to SSR. You might start with sessions that last for just 10 minutes and work up to 20- to 30-minute sessions.

Using Children's Books Instead of Workbooks

In a study conducted by Anderson (1984), it was estimated that children in the early grades completed more than 1,000 workbook pages a year. What's more, the quality and effectiveness of the workbook exercises were often questionable (Osborn, 1984). Although the workbooks of the 90s are clearly better than those of the 80s, 1,000 pages a year is obviously too many. In many instances, time spent on workbook pages would be more profitably spent reading children's books. Instead of assigning workbook pages, encourage children to read materials of their own choosing. In addition to being more interesting and more satisfying, reading children's books also provides more effective practice. There is no better way of reinforcing reading skills than through actual practice with the real thing.

INSTRUCTIONAL USES FOR CHILDREN'S BOOKS

In addition to being a source of pleasure and satisfaction, children's books can also be a vehicle for instruction. In fact, today's basal reading series, which are the main vehicles for delivering reading instruction, are composed primarily of selections from children's books. Dick and Jane have been replaced by a host of characters created by the best children's authors. Children's books can be used to teach and reinforce sight vocabulary, phonics, context clues, and comprehension; foster fluency; develop background of information, vocabulary, and language; serve as models for writing; and develop concepts in math, science, and social studies. Children's books can be used instead of content textbooks or along with them. As Pat Lauber (1996), a well-known children's author who specializes in science books, explains, a children's book offers the voice and vision of an individual author who is attempting to convey feeling as well as information. As she puts it, "A good trade book sparks interest and makes learning pleasurable."

The description of many of the books in the annotated listing (Chapter 4) contains suggestions for using the books for instructional purposes. These books are also categorized in the Skills Index according to skills that they reinforce. This does not mean that they should be used to teach or reinforce skills, however. It just means that they provide especially effective instructional opportunities for teaching and reinforcing sequencing, drawing conclusions, comparing and contrasting, or some other skill, should you choose to use them in that way. The books, of course, can simply be read for enjoyment or information. Even when there is no instruction, students still benefit from wide reading. Background of information is expanded, vocabulary is developed, and fluency is enhanced simply by reading.

PRESENTING BOOKS

As noted earlier, the difficulty level of a book depends, in part, on the way the book is presented or used. Books that are too difficult for children to read on their own can be read to them. Books that are easy can be read independently. In between are various kinds of assistance that the teacher can provide. The various ways to present books are discussed next. The methods are arranged according to degree of assistance and teacher involvement, starting with the highest degree, which is reading to students.

Reading to Children

Before reading to the children, the teacher might discuss the title and cover illustrations with them and ask them to predict what the book might be about. As the teacher reads, she or he points out interesting passages, clarifies confusing parts, explains hard words, and might discuss the outcome of students' predictions and have them change their predictions or make new ones, if necessary. After the oral reading, the story is discussed. The teacher is careful to limit discussion and explanations so that the flow of the story can be maintained.

Shared Reading

Sometimes known as the grandmother's lap or big book method, shared reading is based on the way grandparents and parents read to children (Holdaway, 1979). As the adult reads, the child follows along, looking at illustrations and maybe even print. Using a big book so that a group of students can see the print, the teacher reads a selection, pointing to each word as she reads it aloud. Just as in reading aloud to children, there is a preliminary discussion, predictions are made, interesting or confusing parts are discussed during the reading, and there is a discussion after the reading. During subsequent shared readings of the same big book, students are invited to join in. At first, they may read a brief phrase or sentence that is repeated many times during the story. As they become more familiar with the text, they might read longer or more difficult portions. On their own or with a partner, students might read a regular-sized version of the big book or a tape-recorded version.

Choral Reading

With the teacher as the leader, a whole group reads a story together. This version of shared reading works especially well with highly repetitive text such as that found in *Chicken Little*, *The Three Little Pigs*, and other traditional tales, poems, or songs.

Recorded Reading

The students view and read along with a CD-ROM version of a story displayed on a video screen or read along as a book is read on an audio tape. Reading along with a story shown on a computer screen is easier if the words are highlighted as they are being read. Reading along with a tape-recorded version is somewhat more difficult because the reader must be able to track the words as they are being read. Novice readers' rate of reading is well below the average rate of speaking, so if you are recording tapes for your students, read at a slower pace than you normally would. If you are using commercially produced tapes, play them at below-average speed on a tape player on which the speed of playback can be regulated. Students who are unable to read because of a documented reading disability may qualify for books taped for the blind. Talking Books, a service sponsored by the National Library Service for the Blind and Physically Handicapped (Library of Congress), provides taped versions of periodicals and popular adult and children's books for the blind and physically disabled, including people with organic reading disabilities. (For more information, write to Recorded Books for the Blind. The address is in Appendix D.)

Echo Reading

As its name suggests, the teacher reads a sentence of a story and then the student reads the sentence. This technique works best with brief selections.

Paired Reading

The teacher, a parent, or a child who is a more proficient reader teams up with a student. (Paired reading is different from partner or buddy reading in which two students of similar reading ability read a book together.) The student picks the book to be read. The book chosen should be one that the student would be unable to read on his or her own. After a preliminary discussion of the title and cover illustration, the teacher and student read the book out loud together. During this simultaneous reading, the teacher adjusts his or her reading rate so it matches that of the student. When the student feels able to read a portion on his or her own, the child signals the teacher by raising his or her left hand. When the child wants the teacher to resume reading with him or her, the child raises his or her right hand. The teacher automatically provides assistance when the student stumbles over a word or is unable to read the word within five seconds. The help provided is swift, direct, and nonevaluative. The teacher simply says the word and has the student say it. The reading then continues. Quick correction reduces the student's anxiety and maintains the flow of the activity (Topping, 1987, 1989). The teacher also praises the child periodically.

In England, where paired teaching has been implemented extensively, students tripled their gains, achieving in one year what usually takes three years (Topping, 1987, 1989). When peer tutors are used, the tutors usually gain as much or more than the children being tutored. Explaining the success of paired teaching, Topping (1987) states,"The *reading together* aspect, coupled with the availability of virtually immediate support, frees many children from word by word decoding and enables them to read much more fluently"p. 611).

Parents often help their children by listening to them read. Although this has proved to be effective in boosting reading achievement, parents tend to react more negatively to errors and are more critical than teachers or professional tutors (Topping, 1987). When parents were provided with adequate training, paired reading proved to be an excellent method for giving help. For one thing, paired reading increases the amount of reading children do. In addition, it

> gives children some peaceful private attention from their parents which may not otherwise be available. Perhaps, most significantly, the technique gives parents a clear, coherent, straightforward, and enjoyable way of helping their children which is designed to be self reinforcing so parents shouldn't get confused, worried, or bad tempered about reading. (Topping, 1987, p. 611)

Instructed Reading

Through building background, clarifying unfamiliar concepts, and going over potentially difficult vocabulary, including words that students know when they hear them but might not recognize when they encounter their printed forms, teachers can make a difficult book more accessible. As noted earlier, the level at which a student can read a book, if given assistance, is known as the instructional level. The instructional level is the point at which the students can read at least 95 percent of the words. (Reading Recovery level is 90 percent. However, Reading Recovery children are given one-on-one instruction by highly trained specialists.) If there are more than 5 words out of 100 that are unknown, there is simply too much preparation required, more than the student can be expected to grasp at one time. At the instructional level, children can understand 75 percent of what they read.

The degree of reading preparation varies. In the typical lesson, the teacher builds background necessary for an understanding of the story and introduces words that the student might find difficult. In a book such as *The Three Billy Goats Gruff*, the teacher might discuss what billy goats are and what a troll is. Because *bridge, hillside*, and *stream* are important words in the story but novice readers might not recognize them in print, the written forms of the words would be presented.

When students are struggling with their reading and writing, the teacher might provide a more intensive form of preparation known as a *picture* or *text walk–through*. Having previewed the book in terms of the child's capabilities, the teacher "walks through" the book with the child, pointing out the title and author, and using illustrations to present an overview of the text. The child is invited to relate the text to other books he or she has read or relevant experiences that he or she has had. The teacher may review from the text unfamiliar terms, expressions, or syntactic structures. These may be pointed out in the text and the student may be asked to repeat them (Clay, 1991). The basic purpose of this orientation is to prepare the child for a successful reading of the text. A sample walk-through lesson is presented next.

Introducing a Book Using the Walk-Through Technique

• *Step 1: Analyze the Text.* Note the concepts, background information, words, or language structures that might be barriers for the prospective reader. In the book *Leo the Late Bloomer* (Kraus, 1971), the phrase *late bloomer* would most likely be unfamiliar to the child. To understand the story, the reader would need to have a concept of a *late bloomer* and having *patience*.

• *Step 2: Introduce the Title and Topic.* Discuss the title and help the student relate the topic to his or her own background of experience. Do not dwell on the identity of the author or illustrator or spend too much time in discussion, as this will detract from the main purpose, which is a successful reading of the text. When introducing *Leo the Late Bloomer*, for instance, read the title and ask the child to point to Leo on the cover and the flowers that are blooming. Discuss what it means to say that "flowers are blooming."

• *Step 3: Highlight the Story.* Walk the student through the story, page by page, so that he or she acquires an overview of the tale. Knowing the gist of the story and who the main characters are, the student will be better able to use contextual and other clues to achieve a successful reading. As you walk the student through the story, preview words, concepts, and language structures that you think he or she might have difficulty understanding. Paraphrase key portions of the text that contain difficult items. Then help the student point out these items. For instance, after paraphrasing the page on which the expression *late bloomer* is used, discuss how a person might bloom and what a late bloomer might be. Then ask the student to point to the words *late bloomer* on the page. Also have the student point to the words *patience* and *watched* on that page. These are words that would be in the child's listening/speaking vocabulary, but not likely in his or her reading vocabulary. As you walk through the text, paraphrasing the story, have the student point out other words that might be hard for him or her to read (e.g., *sloppy, television, neatly, sentence*). Go through the entire text, except for the last page, in this way. Instead of displaying the last page, ask the student to tell what he or she thinks Leo will say when he speaks his first sentence. Although the student will know most of the story before reading the book, he or she will still have the enjoyment of finding out how the story of Leo ends.

• *Step 4: Read the Story.* Generally, the first reading of a story is silent but a student in the very beginning stages of learning to read might read softly to himself or herself (Fountas & Pinnell, 1996). Soft oral reading fades away as silent reading takes its place. Encourage the student to read the story on his or her own, but provide guidance and support as needed.

• *Step 5: Discuss the Story.* Start with the student's purpose for reading, which, in this example, was to find out what Leo said. Discuss, too, what things Leo learned to do when he finally bloomed.

• *Step 6: Reinforce the Use of Skills/Stategies.* Praise the student for his or her use of strategies: "I like the way you used the meaning of the story to help you read *thought* and I like the way you used the picture to help you read *television.*

• *Step 7: Reread the Story.* Encourage the student to reread the story, perhaps for a different purpose. For instance, the student might read to find out how the author showed that many months passed before Leo bloomed; he or she might do this by reading portions of the story to show that new seasons had arrived. The student might also read the story to a child in a lower grade or a younger brother or sister. You might also arrange for an oral rereading of a segment of the text to assess the student's reading. As the child reads, note whether the selection seems to be on the appropriate level and also analyze his or her performance to see what strategies the child is using to decode words and what strategies may still need work. Does the student use context, picture clues, and sounding out to decipher difficult words? Are these strategies used in integrated fashion?

Independent Reading

The most challenging reading for students is that which they do on their own. Although assisted and instructed reading are important, independent reading is the most essential component of a reading program. Students simply will not develop to their fullest potential unless they spend a significant amount of time reading on their own. In order to be able to read a book independently, students should know nearly all the words in the selection to be read. There should only be 1 or 2 words out of 100 that they do not know. Easy reading of this type fosters fluency so that the stop-and-go reading of the novice becomes much smoother, thus allowing the student to focus on the message. Series books such as *Frog and Toad, Fox, Henry and Mudge,* and *Curious George* are excellent for building speed and ease of reading.

One way to ease students into independent reading is to encourage them to read with a partner. In partner or buddy reading, the two students can read chorally or take turns reading a page. With the support and encouragement of a partner, students will often read books that they may have been reluctant to try on their own.

On occasion, students should be allowed to try reading on their own those books that are beyond their independent levels. Interest in a subject and enriched background might enable them to cope with a book that normally would be too difficult for them to handle. However, students who consistently select books that are too difficult for them may need some guidance.

EVALUATING PROGRESS

Evaluating students' progress is essential. Through evaluation, you can assess the effectiveness of your reading program and make adjustments to improve its quality. Evaluation requires that you match assessment with goals. If your goal is to foster overall growth in reading, you might periodically assess students' growth by having them orally read to you a typical book at their levels. Follow the procedures described for the Primary Reading Passages Inventory, which is located in Appendix B. If the book is brief (fewer than 200 words), have the students read the whole text. For longer books, have them read a 100- to 200-word sample. Note the strategies the children use to decode difficult words. Also ask them to retell the story. Assess the quality of their retelling. Does it incorporate the essentials of the selection? How well organized is the retelling? Instead of requesting a retelling, you can ask questions about the selection. Or you can combine both procedures. In addition to determining students' progress, periodic assessment of their oral reading will also help you see whether the books they are reading are on the appropriate level of difficulty and whether the students are ready to move up to the next level. Try to assess students once every one or two weeks. Tapes of students' oral reading recorded periodically and observations also provide valuable information about students' progress.

If your goal is to foster wide reading and a love of reading, keep a record of the number and types of books that students read. Through observation, also note whether the students seem to enjoy reading: Do they have favorite books and authors? Do they like to talk about their reading? When they have free time, do they choose reading activities? In their conversations and in classroom discussions, do they mention stories or books that they particularly like?

Maintaining a portfolio is also an excellent way to assess progress. A portfolio might include samples of students' writing, sample projects completed, a list of books read, tapes of oral reading, and other samples of students' work. In addition, records of observations and completed checklists can provide helpful assessment information.

Chapter 3

Matching Children with Books

When given the opportunity to select books, Pam, a first-grader, chose *Fox on the Job,* an enjoyable book recommended by the highly popular TV show *Reading Rainbow.* There was only one problem. Pam is reading on a beginning A level. *Fox on the Job* is on a beginning D level. Pam should be reading brief selections composed primarily of the most common words and heavily supported by illustrations. *Fox on the Job* is a chapter book, contains a fair number of words that would be difficult for Pam to read, and provides only a moderate amount of picture support. The gap between Pam's skills and what is required to read *Fox on the Job* is too wide to be bridged.

Why is Pam choosing books that are too difficult? Having gotten off to a slow start in reading, Pam may not realize that the book is too difficult. She may believe that reading is supposed to be hard and that books usually contain lots of difficult words. There is also a social factor at work. Pam's friends are adept readers and can handle chapter books such as the *Fox* series with ease. Pam, quite naturally, is anxious to read the kinds of books that her friends enjoy.

The first step in developing children's ability to choose books wisely is to create an environment that encourages children to be proud of their own individual abilities and to respect the abilities of others. Differences in abilities and interests need to be affirmed. The ability to read higher-level books should not be a status symbol; rather, students should be rewarded for doing their best and respecting the abilities and achievements of others.

Along with establishing an atmosphere that encourages respect for differences, the teacher should provide a wide range of materials on the appropriate levels of difficulty (Fielding, 1996). A special attempt should be made to acquire plenty of books for students who are making slow progress. Spending additional time reading will help these youngsters catch up. Recognizing that some beginning readers will need extra practice, I have tried to include at least 100 books on each level and was successful for all but the Picture and the Caption levels.

DEVELOPING BOOK SELECTION CRITERIA

To foster students' ability to choose books, help them develop criteria for selecting books that are easy as well as ones that are challenging. Also help them identify books that are simply too difficult. Explain to students that they should choose books that are comfortable for them to read. Urge them to select books that look interesting but that do not have too many hard words. Model the book selection process. Show how you might go about choosing an easy book and a challenging one. To find an appropriate-level book, students might ask themselves the following questions:

- Does the book seem interesting?
- Does the book seem to be like the ones I usually read? Does it have about the same number of words? Does it have about the same number of pictures?
- Can I read most of the words or figure out most of the ones I don't know?
- When I try reading a page or two, does my reading seem smooth or do I have to stop a lot to try to figure out words? (Fielding, 1996)

Review your student's book selections from time to time. Have conferences with those who are having difficulty with book selection, evidenced by consistently choosing books that are either too hard or too easy. Have students who consistently make wise choices explain how they do so. Also recommend to individual students those books that are at the appropriate level and that touch on topics in which they are interested.

To avoid stigmatizing slow-progress readers, try to obtain easy books that are of such high interest that everyone wants to read them. This helps unite students of varied reading abilities because it provides them with common literacy experiences. Another way of encouraging slow-progress readers to read appropriate-level books is to have them read books in preparation for reading them to younger children. A slow-progress second-grader, for instance, might practice reading an easy first-grade book in preparation for reading it to a first-grade or kindergarten child or a younger brother or sister.

DETERMINING STUDENTS' LEVELS

In order for students to get the most out of their reading, it is essential that they read materials that are on the appropriate level. Students have three reading levels: independent, instructional, and frustrational. As its name suggests, the *independent level* is the point at which students can read on their own, without any help from teachers, parents, or peers. They recognize at least 99 percent of the words and comprehension is nearly perfect.

At the *instructional level*, students can read at least 95 out of 100 words and they recall at least 75 percent of what they read. If given instructional assistance, they can read with confidence and competence.

At the *frustration level*, the material is simply too difficult for students to read, even with assistance. Students miss 10 or more words out of 100 and/or remember only half of what they read. Students may exhibit lip movement during silent reading, may be easily distracted, or may engage in hair twisting, grimacing, or other stress-signaling behaviors (Johnson, Kress, & Pikulski, 1987).

If students are going to read on their own, they or you should select independent-level books. If they will be given help with their reading, instructional-level books should be chosen. When in doubt, be conservative. It is better to give a student a book that is too easy than one that is too hard. Reading easy books builds speed and fluency; reading books that are too hard creates frustration and a sense of failure.

Students' reading levels can be determined in a number of ways. The most widely accepted placement device is the informal reading inventory. The idea behind the informal reading inventory is to have students begin with easy material and read increasingly difficult material so that you find the level that has the right fit. There are a number of commercially produced inventories; however, these typically provide only four levels at the beginning stages: preprimer, primer, first, and second. This text divides beginning reading into eight levels. Commercial inventories will put you in the right ballpark, but you will need to do some additional assessing to obtain a more exact placement. To assist you in obtaining a more precise placement, the Graduated Word Lists and the Primary Reading Passages Inventory are presented in Appendix B. Either of the two will provide reasonably valid placement information. However, using both measures will yield more reliable estimates and will also provide more information about your students' reading abilities. After students have been assigned a level, check the accuracy of their placement by observing their reading. If books on the assigned level seem too difficult, move students down a level. If they seem too easy, move students up a level.

Chapter 4

Annotated Listing
of Best Books

The books presented in this chapter are listed in order of difficulty from picture level through grade 2A. Annotations contain the title, author's name, publisher, year of publication, and number of pages. If the pages in the book were numbered, that information was used to indicate number of pages. If the pages were unnumbered, as is the case with most picture books, the number of pages containing text and or illustrations was counted. Publishers' addresses and phone numbers are listed in Appendix D. Where available, the publisher's ordering address and phone number, rather than the editorial address and phone number, are provided.

The annotations also contain an overview of the book, and, for some books, suggestions for using the book with students. In addition, an estimated interest level (designated IL) is supplied. For older students who are making slow progress, you may want to seek out books that have an interest level that extends up to 8, 9, or 10 years of age. Students make the most progress in reading when their reading materials match both their interests and their abilities. Books that are especially appealing and highly readable are starred and are noted in the annotations as being highly recommended.

Annotations also indicate if books are available in paperback, audiotape, or big-book format. If a book is out of print, that is noted. The status of books is subject to change. Some books now in print may be out of print by the time you read this text. In addition, books that were available only in regular-size hardback form when this list was compiled may since have been published in paperback, big-book, or audiotape format. It should also be noted that information about big-book format and availability of audiotapes is difficult to track down. Big books and/or audiotapes may be available but are not indicated for some titles.

PICTURE LEVEL

Burningham, John. *Colors*. Crown, 1985, 24 pp. Each of the color words is depicted with a humorous scene. IL: 5–7.
Theme/subject: Colors

Burton, Marilee Robin. *Tail Toes Eyes Ears Nose*. HarperCollins, 1989, 28 pp. Judging from parts of animals shown, the reader must guess the animal. IL: 5–7. Available in paperback.
Theme/subject: Characteristics of animals

Cohen, Caron Lee. *Three Yellow Dogs*. Greenwillow, 1986, 28 pp. Three yellow dogs run home. IL: 5–7. Out of print.
Theme/subject: Dogs; Humor

Ernst, Lisa Campbell. *Up to Ten and Down Again*. Lothrop, Lee & Shepard, 1986, 23 pp. During a picnic, a series of objects are sighted: one duck, two cars, three dogs, four boys, five girls, and so on. As the picnic breaks up, the items are shown in descending order. IL: 5–7.
Theme/subject: Counting; Picnic

Hoban, Tana. *Count and See*. Simon & Schuster, 1972, 40 pp. Pictures of objects from 1 to 15, 20, 30, 40, 50, and 100 are accompanied by the number in numerals and words. IL: 5–7.
Theme/subject: Counting

Inkpen, Mick. *Kipper's Book of Weather*. Harcourt, 1994, 16 pp. Kipper, a small dog, is shown in rain, sun, snow, ice, fog, wind, and hail. The book ends with Kipper viewing a rainbow. Contains just eight words. IL: 5–7.
Theme/subject: Weather

Smalley, Guy. *Colors*. Camex Books, 1989, 22 pp. This book illustrates colors: pink pig, brown bear, orange pumpkin, and so on. IL: 5–7.
Theme/subject: Numbers; Colors

Smalley, Guy. *Numbers*. Camex Books, 1989, 22 pp. This book illustrates the numbers 1 to 10: 1 dog, 2 apples, 3 boats, and so on. IL: 5–7.
Theme/subject: Numbers

Wood, Leslie. *Dig, Dig*. Oxford, 1988, 16 pp. Various kinds of digging are shown and the only word presented is *dig*. IL: 5–7. Paperback.
Theme/subject: Digging

PICTURE-LEVEL PLUS

Arnosky, Jim. *Crinkleroot's 25 Mammals Every Child Should Know*. Bradbury, 1994, 25 pp. After a brief description of mammals, labeled drawings of 25 common mammals are presented. IL: 5–8.
Theme/subject: Animals; Mammals

* Brown, Rick. *What Rhymes with Snake?* Tambourine, 1994, 24 pp. In this lift-the-flap book, the reader lifts one flap to find a rhyming picture and lifts a second flap to find the word that names the rhyming picture. Lifting the picture of a hen, for

example, the reader finds a picture of a pen. Lifting the *h* from the word *hen*, the reader uncovers the word *pen*. Reader may need help identifying crane and goose. Provides practice in using and substituting initial consonants, as well as patterns, rhyming, and initial consonants. Highly recommended. IL: 5–7.
Theme/subject: Language games and activities

Davenport, Zoe. *Animals.* Ticknor & Fields, 1995, 10 pp. This book labels drawings of common animals and some of the animal's body parts. Part of Words for Everyday series. IL: 5–7.
Theme/subject: Animals

Davenport, Zoe. *Garden.* Ticknor & Fields, 1995, 10 pp. This book labels drawings of objects and creatures found in a garden. Part of Words for Everyday series. IL: 5–7.
Theme/subject: Gardens

Feder, Jane. *Table–Chair–Bear: A Book in Many Languages.* Ticknor & Fields, 1995, 27 pp. Common objects and their names are depicted in English and 12 other languages. Reader may need help recognizing *shelf* and reading "Please come in." IL: 5–7.
Theme/subject: Multicultural; Language study

Gardner, Beau. *Guess What?* Lothrop, Lee & Shepard, 1985, 21 pp. Shown a part of an animal, the reader is invited to guess the animal's identity. Reader might need intial consonant as well as picture clues to identify animals' names. Provides practice in drawing conclusions based on visual clues. Actively engages reader. IL: 5–7.
Theme/subject: Animals; Games and activities

Grundy, Lynn N. *A Is for Apple.* Ladybird Books, 1980, 26 pp. Apple, ball, elephant, and other common items are depicted and accompanied by the name of the item and the letter the item begins with. For example, a drawing of a mouse is accompanied by *m* and *mouse*. Reader may need help identifying the panda. IL: 5–7.
Theme/subject: Alphabet

Hutchins, Pat. *1 Hunter.* Greenwillow, 1982, 22 pp. A hunter hunts animals but fails to see them until they all gather in one place and frighten him off. IL: 5–7. Available in paperback.
Theme/subject: Counting; Humor

Marshall, Janet. *Look Once, Look Twice.* Ticknor & Fields, 1995, 52 pp. The reader is shown a letter that contains the pattern of an object and also represents the beginning sound of that object. Corn on the cob, for instance, is represented by a *c* composed of rows of corn. The object and its name are shown on the reverse page. The reader might need to use initial consonants to help read labels for pictures initially or as a cross-check. Many children will need help identifying the iris, macaw, and viper. IL: 5–7.
Theme/subject: Games and activities; Visual patterns

Paterson, Bettina. *My First Wild Animals.* HarperCollins, 1989, 24 pp. Drawings and one-word captions depict a variety of wild animals. Contains 24 words. Out of print
Theme/subject: Animals.

Tafuri, Nancy. *Who's Counting?* Greenwillow, 1986, 22 pp. A curious puppy counts animals: 1 squirrel, 2 birds, 3 moles, and so on, until it counts 10 puppies eating. Reader may need to use initial consonants plus illustrations to identify the mole and tadpoles. IL: 5–7. Available in paperback (Mulberry).
Theme/subject: Counting

Wallwork, Amanda. *No Dodos*. Scholastic, 1993, 24 pp. The numbers 0 through 10 are depicted with endangered animals. Reader may need help identifying some of the endangered animals. IL: 5–7.
Theme/subject: Counting; Endangered animals

Weiss, Nicki. *Sun–Sand–Sea–Sail*. Greenwillow, 1989, 29 pp. A family's trip to the beach is depicted. Each illustration is labeled with a one- or two-word caption. Some pictures may be difficult to interpret (e.g., parents, sidestroke). Reader may need to use initial consonants plus illustrations to read captions. IL: 5–7.
Theme/subject: Family; Beach

Wood, Jakki. *Animal Parade*. Bradbury Press, 1993, 26 pp. The parade of elephants starts with an aardvark, an antelope, and other animals whose names begin with *a* and proceeds through the rest of the letters of the alphabet. Each illustration of an animal is accompanied by the name of the animal. Reader may need help identifying some of the animals: kookaburra, kiwi. IL: 5–7.
Theme/subject: Animal names; Alphabet book

CAPTION/FRAME LEVEL

Asch, Frank. *Little Fish, Big Fish*. Scholastic, 1992, 16 pp. Opposites are shown: little house–big house, little cat–big cat, little boat–big boat, little elephant–big elephant. Foldout pages are used to display long items. IL: 5–7.
Theme/subject: Word study: opposites

Asch, Frank. *Short Train, Long Train*. Scholastic, 1992, 24 pp. Opposites are shown: short train–long train, short nose–long nose, short walk–long walk, short car–long car, short tail–long tail. Foldout pages are used to display long items. IL: 5–7.
Theme/subject: Word study: opposites

Asch, Frank, & Vagin, Vladimir. *Here Comes the Cat*. Scholastic, 1989, 28 pp. Mice in hot-air balloons, on bikes, underwater, and on foot spread the news: "Here comes the cat." The cat appears pulling a giant wheel of cheese. The text appears in both English and Russian. Only four different words are used: *here, comes, the, cat*. Fosters predicting what will happen when the cat comes. IL: 5–8. Available in paperback.
Theme/subject: Cats

Brown, Craig. *My Barn*. Greenwillow, 1991, 20 pp. As each farm animal makes its characteristic sound, the farmer says that he likes the sound it makes: "I like the sound Moo MMMMOOOhhh Mooooh MMoooo... the sound a cow makes." This is an excellent choice for partner, shared, or choral reading of repeated parts. IL: 5–7.
Theme/subject: Farm animals; Animal sounds

* Cameron, Alice. *The Cat Sat on the Mat*. Houghton Mifflin, 1994, 30 pp. Looking through cutouts on every other page, the reader guesses where the cat sat: on the mat, the car, the step, and so on. Provides reinforcement for the *-at* pattern (repeating: The cat sat on the___) and can also be used for predicting where the cat sat. Highly recommended. IL: 5–7.
Theme/subject: Pets: cats

* Carle, Eric. *Have You Seen My Cat?* Scholastic, 1987, 24 pp. A boy searching for his lost cat seeks help from people around the world who point him to a series of wild cats: a lion, a panther, a tiger, a puma, and so on. The last person he asks points him to his lost cat, who has just had kittens. Very easy reading. Highly recommended. IL: 5–7. Available in paperback.
Theme/subject: Pets: lost

Coxe, Molly. *Whose Footprints?* Crowell, 1990, 36 pp. A mother and her daughter examine footprints in the snow and ask: "Whose footprints?" The creature who made the footprints is shown on the reverse page. IL: 5–7. Out of print.
Theme/subject: Snow; Footprints

Falwell, Cathryn. *Clowning Around.* Orchard, 1991, 30 pp. Shows how scrambled letters can be put together to construct common words. Words are illustrated. IL: 5–8. Out of print.
Theme/subject: Word study: formation of words

Gomi, Taro. *My Friends.* Chronicle Books, 1990, 32 pp. A little girl learns to walk, run, march, hide, smell, kick, sing, and climb from the animals. But she learns to play and love from friends. Provides possible writing topic and format: I learned ___ from my friend ___. IL: 6–8. Available in paperback.
Theme/subject: Friends; Learning from others

Gomi, Taro. *Who Hid It?* Millbrook Press, 1991, 22 pp. Readers find hidden objects by closely examining illustrations. Fosters practice in interpreting pictures and actively engages the reader. Available in paperback. IL: 6–7.
Theme/subject: Games and activities; Hidden objects

Grejniec, Michael. *What Do You Like?* North-South Books, 1992, 28 pp. Two children tell what they like: rainbows, playing, flying, music, cats, fruit, and their mothers. They ask readers what they like and love. Provides a possible writing topic and format: What I like. Available in paperback. IL: 5–7.
Theme/subject: Personal preferences

Kalan, Robert. *Rain.* Greenwillow, 1978, 18 pp. Brief captions and illustrations depict a changing sky and rain. IL: 5–7. Available in paperback (Mulberry).
Theme/subject: Rain

Koch, Michelle. *Just One More.* Greenwillow, 1992, 29 pp. Singular nouns and their irregular plurals are depicted: *child, children; moose, moose, ox, oxen; knife, knives; tooth, teeth.* IL: 6–8.
Theme/subject: Language study: plurals

Lillie, Patricia. *Everything Has a Place.* Greenwillow, 1993, 22 pp. A little girl sees that everything has a place: a cow in a barn, a bird in a nest, a bowl in a cupboard, a baby on a lap, and a family in a house. IL: 5–7.
Theme/subject: Family

Maris, Ron. *My Book.* Puffin, 1983, 30 pp. Gate, door, book, and other objects are labeled in this lift-the-flap book. Contains just 17 words. IL: 5–7. Available in paperback.
Theme/subject: Home

McMillan, Bruce. *One, Two, One Pair.* Scholastic, 1991, 30 pp. Captions and photos depict pairs of objects related to ice skating. Uses just four different words. Fosters the ability to group objects into pairs. IL: 5–7.
Theme/subject: Ice skating

McMillan, Bruce. *Beach Ball—Left, Right.* Holiday House, 1992, 28 pp. A little boy's beach ball becomes airborne and is seen in many settings until it finally drops back onto the sea and floats back to the boy. Developing the concept of left and right, each left-hand page has the word *left* printed on it, and on each right-hand page is the word *right.* IL: 5–7.
Theme/subject: Concept of left and right; Beach

McMillan, Bruce. *Mouse Views, What the Class Pet Saw.* Holiday House, 1993, 30 pp. A pet mouse wanders around a school. What he sees is shown from the mouse's point of view. Readers are invited to guess what the objects are. Fosters careful analysis of pictures and using visual clues to come to a conclusion, and promotes active engagement. IL: 5–7.
Theme/subject: Games/activities; Guessing identity of objects based on visual clues

McMillan, Bruce. *Sense Suspense.* Scholastic, 1994, 30 pp. Looking at such color photos as a child licking a lollipop, smelling flowers, and feeling a piece of ice, the reader is asked to tell what sense is being used. Caption answers are given in the back of the book. IL: 5–7.
Theme/subject: Senses

Rathmann, Peggy. *Good Night, Gorilla.* Putnam, 1994, 34 pp. Zoo animals sneak home with their keeper and attempt to sleep in his room. The reader might need to use initial consonants to verify captions and may not recognize the armadillo. IL: 6–8.
Theme/subject: Sleep; Humor

Rotner, Shelley, & Kreisler, Ken. *Faces.* Simon & Schuster, 1994, 24 pp. All kinds of faces are shown: smiling, thinking, talking, smelling, hearing, feeling. The book also focuses on parts of faces: ears, mouths, eyes, and noses. IL: 5–7.
Theme/subject: Physical appearance; Individuality of people

Rubinstein, Gillian. *Dog In, Cat Out.* Ticknor & Fields, 1993, 28 pp. Illustrations and captions depict various scenes in which the dog is outside and the cat is inside and vice versa. Uses just four different words: *dog, cat, in, out.* IL: 5–8.
Theme/subject: Pets: cats and dogs

Sawicki, Norma Jean. *The Little Red House.* Lothrop, Lee & Shepard, 1989, 20 pp. Child retrieves little houses nested in larger houses until reaching one in which there is a teddy bear. Lends itself to predicting what child will find. IL: 6–7.
Theme/subject: Toys: teddy bear

Smalley, Guy. *Sizes.* Camex, 1989, 22 pp. This book illustrates a number of sizes arranged as opposites: little–big, long–short, large–small, huge–tiny. IL: 5–7.
Theme/subject: Word study: opposites; Sizes

Tafuri, Nancy. *Have You Seen My Duckling?* Greenwillow, 1984, 24 pp. Mother duck searches for her missing duckling. Contains only the words: *Have you seen my duckling?* IL: 5–7.
Theme/subject: Lost child

* Wildsmith, Brian. *Cat on the Mat.* Oxford, 1982, 16 pp. A cat sitting on a mat is joined by a dog, a goat, a cow, and an elephant. At that point, the mat is so crowded that the cat chases the other animals away. Reinforces the short vowel *-at* pattern. Paperback. Highly recommended. IL: 5–7.
Theme/subject: Humor; Crowding

Wildsmith, Brian. *What a Tail!* Oxford, 1983, 16 pp. The reader is introduced to the tails of a variety of animals. IL: 5–7. Paperback.
Theme/subject: Animals: tails
Wildsmith, Brian. *Toot, Toot.* Oxford, 1984, 16 pp. Animals make their characteristic sounds as they prepare to take a train ride. Paperback. IL: 5–7.
Theme/subject: Animal sounds

CAPTION-LEVEL PLUS

Avery, Maryann Watson, & Avery, Donald M. *What Is Beautiful?* Tricycle, 1995, 20 pp. This book focuses on different parts of faces and portrays them as being beautiful: beautiful eyes, nose, mouth, dimples, beard. It ends with a page that contains a mirror and asks: "What is beautiful about you?" IL: 6–8.
Theme/subject: Self-esteem; Physical appearance
Ayliffe, Alex. *Slither, Swoop, Swing.* Viking, 1992, 24 pp. Illustrations depict animals as they swing, slither, pounce, dive, run, cling, and scratch. Reinforces clusters. IL: 5–8. Out of print.
Theme/subject: Animals: movement
Bernal, Richard. *Night Zoo.* Contemporary, 1989, 18 pp. A variety of animals are seen sleeping. Students might need help identifying herons and gazelles. IL: 5–7.
Theme/subject: Sleep: animals
Bond, Michael. *Paddington's Opposites.* Viking, 1991, 32 pp. This book illustrates 15 common opposites. Most illustrations feature Paddington Bear and do an especially good job of conveying the meanings of the words depicted. This is one of the best of the many oppposite books. Students might need to use phonics, especially initial consonants, as a complement to picture clues, to decipher words. IL: 5–7.
Theme/subject: Word study: opposites
Carroll, Kathleen Sullivan. *One Red Rooster.* Houghton Mifflin, 1992, 21 pp. Farm animals and blue birds make their characteristic sounds: four white sheep went bleat, bleat, bleat; nine yellow chicks went peep, peep, peep. IL: 5–7. Available in paperback.
Theme/subject: Counting; Animal sounds
Crowther, Robert. *Who Lives in the Country?* Candlewick, 1992, 12 pp. In this lift-the-flap book, the reader is asked to tell who lives in the hive, shed, woods, tree, and other places. The answer is under the flap. Readers may need help with the words *bulrushes, water-mill,* and *hayloft.* Reinforces drawing a conclusion based on visual clues. IL: 5–7.
Theme/subject: Animals: homes, habitats
Mandel, Peter. *Red Cat, White Cat.* Holt, 1994, 24 pp. Illustrations and two-word captions depict a variety of cats: white cat, red cat, short cat, tall cat, farm cat, town cat. Readers may need help with some words (*bold, stout*). IL: 5–7.
Theme/subject: Opposites
Marzollo, Jean. *Ten Cats Have Hats.* Scholastic, 1994, 20 pp. This counting book displays from 1 to 10 animals or objects and items that belong to them: three pigs have wigs. Some illustrations may need to be interpreted. IL: 5–7.
Theme/subject: Counting

McMillan, Bruce. *One Sun*. Holiday House, 1990, 30 pp. Two-word captions and color photos depict a day at the beach. Reader may need to use initial consonants along with pictures to read captions. Part of Terse Verse series. IL: 5–7. Available in paperback.
Theme/subject: Beach

McMillan, Bruce. *Play Day: A Book of Terse Verse*. Holiday House, 1991, 30 pp. With color photos and two-word verses, this book depicts children at play and their toys: bear chair, fat bat. Readers might need to use initial consonants to help verify identity of photos. Reinforces rhyme and word patterns. IL: 5–7.
Theme/subject: Play

Miller, Margaret. *Whose Hat?* Greenwillow, 1988, 36 pp. Shown a hat, the reader is asked to answer the question: "Whose hat?" The answer is shown in pictures and text on the reverse page. The reader may need help identifying the words *chef, construction worker,* and *cow hand.* Reinforces using visual clues to draw conclusions. Promotes active engagement. IL: 5–7.
Theme/subject: Occupations

Miller, Margaret. *Who Uses This?* Greenwillow, 1990, 37 pp. This book shows pictures of a hammer, garden tools, and other items and asks: "Who uses this?" Answers are shown in captioned illustrations on the reverse pages. IL: 5–7.
Theme/subject: Tools

Miller, Margaret. *Whose Shoe?* Greenwillow, 1991, 36 pp. The book shows baby shoes, clown shoes, horse shoes, and other shoes and asks: "Whose shoe?" Answers are presented on reverse pages. Reader might need help with the words *angler* and *ballet dancer.* IL: 5–7. Fosters using visual clues to draw a conclusion. Promotes active engagement.
Theme/subject: Clothing: shoes

Pienkowski, Jan. *Weather*. Simon & Schuster, 1975, 22 pp. Many weather words are illustrated. IL: 5–7. Available in paperback.
Theme/subject: Weather

Tafuri, Nancy. *Spots, Feathers, and Curly Tails*. Greenwillow, 1988, 28 pp. A portion of a farm animal is shown and the reader is asked to identify the animal: "What has a curly tail?" Reinforces drawing a conclusion based on picture and printed information. Promotes active engagement. IL: 5–7.
Theme/subject: Animals: farm

Turner, Gwenda. *Opposites*. Viking, 1992, 24 pp. Fairly easy opposites are illustrated. Reader may need help with the word *parcel* and might need to use intitial consonants to help verify identity of photos and read captions. IL: 5–7.
Theme/subject: Opposites

SIGHT-WORD LEVEL

* Accorsi, William. *Billy's Button*. Greenwillow, 1992, 20 pp. The reader is invited to locate Billy's button on each page. All pages have a number of buttons, but only one button has four holes, which indicates that it is Billy's. Very easy reading. Fosters visual discrimination of illustrations and reinforces initial *b.* Highly recommended. IL: 5–7.
Theme/subject: Games/activities: Finding hidden items

Agee, John. *Flapstick.* Dutton, 1993, 20 pp. Silly rhymes are completed by lifting a flap. Reinforces rhyming. IL: 5–7.
Theme/subject: Riddles

Anderson, Peggy Perry. *Time for Bed, the Babysitter Said.* Houghton Mifflin, 1987, 32 pp. Joe refuses to go to bed until the babysitter uses the magic word *please*. Reinforces short *e* words. IL: 5–7.
Theme/subject: Bedtime; Babysitters

Appelt, Kathy. *Elephants Aloft.* Harcourt, 1993, 28 pp. Two elephants take a trip in a hot-air balloon to see their Aunt Rwanda. Illustrations are accompanied by one-word captions: *in, out, across, around, over, under.* IL: 5–7. Very easy reading.
Theme/subject: Travel: hot-air balloon

* Aruego, Jose, & Dewey, Ariane. *We Hide, You Seek.* Greenwillow, 1979, 30 pp. Playing hide-and-go-seek, a clumsy rhino finds the other animals through luck or accident rather than skill. He locates the hidden animals by accidentally stepping on a tail, chasing buterflies, sneezing, and digging for gerbils. Very easy reading. Highly recommended. IL: 5–7. Available in paperback (Mulberry).
Theme/subject: Games: hide-and-go-seek; Humor

Asch, Frank. *Baby in the Box.* Holiday House, 1989, 28 pp. A baby in a box is joined by a fox and an ox. The baby, fox, and ox knock down some blocks but help clean up. Reinforces short *o* pattern. IL: 5–7. Out of print.
Theme/subject: Babies; Humor

Asch, Frank. *Moonbear's Books.* Simon & Schuster, 1993, 12 pp. Moonbear likes to read all kinds of books: happy books, sad books, tall books, thin books, and thick books. Part of Moonbear series. Very easy reading. IL: 5–7.
Theme/subject: Reading

Asch, Frank. *Earth and I Are Friends.* Harcourt, 1994, 28 pp. A little boy makes known his feelings for nature by declaring "The Earth and I are friends" and showing how he and the Earth do things together. IL: 5–7.
Theme/subject: Nature

Barton, Byron. *Where's Al?* Houghton Mifflin, 1972, 30 pp. A boy and his lost dog are reunited after his dog has a series of humorous misadventures. IL: 5–7.
Theme/subject: Pets: lost

Beck, Ian. *Five Little Ducks.* Holt, 1992, 24 pp. One by one each of the five ducks disappears. Although there is a fox around, the ducks safely reappear. Reinforces short-vowel patterns. IL: 5–7.
Theme/subject: Counting; Animals: ducks; Mother and babies

Berenstain, Stan, & Berenstain, Jan. *Inside Outside Upside Down.* Random House, 1968. 27 pp. A bear in a box gets a ride on a truck. IL: 5–7.
Theme/subject: Humor

Berenstain, Stan, & Berenstain Jan. *Bears on Wheels.* Random House, 1969, 32 pp. This humorous counting book shows varied number of bears on a variety of wheels. Bright and Early Books series. Reinforces number words. Very easy reading. IL: 5–7.
Theme/subject: Counting; Humor

Carle, Eric. *Do You Want to Be My Friend?* HarperCollins, 1976, 30 pp. Addressing what seems to be a horse tail, a mouse asks, "Do you want to be my friend?" A number of tails then appear, until finally, there is one that belongs to a a mouse, who replies, "Yes." The two friends then hide from a snake. Very easy reading.

IL: 5–7. Available in paperback.
Theme/subject: Friendship

Casey, Patricia. *My Cat Jack.* Candlewick Press, 1994, 24 pp. Jack the cat stretches, yawns, laps, pounces, purrs, and tries acrobatics. IL: 5–7.
Theme/subject: Animals: cats

Christelow, Eileen. *Five Little Monkeys Jumping on the Bed.* Clarion, 1989, 32 pp. Five energetic little monkeys jumping on the bed keep Mama awake and the doctor busy. Repeated lines provide opportunities for choral or shared reading. Part of Five Little Monkey series. IL: 5–8. Available in paperback and on audiotape.
Theme/subject: Play; Mischievous behavior

Clarke, Gus. *EIEIO: The Story of Old MacDonald Who Had a Farm.* Lothrop, Lee & Shepard, 1992, 24 pp. Tired of all the animals on his farm, old MacDonald sells them and turns the farm into a camping site. The song lends itself to choral reading or singing. Reinforces -at pattern. IL: 5–8.
Theme/subject: Humor; Humorous version of traditional song

Cousins, Lucy. *What Can Rabbit See?* Tambourine, 1991, 16 pp. The reader is invited to lift the flaps to find out what rabbit, who has new glasses, can see in the hedge, the grass, the stable, the hutch, and the sky at night. Fosters predicting what the rabbit can see. IL: 5–7.
Theme/subject: Glasses; Senses: vision

Cousins, Lucy. *Maisy Goes to School.* Candlewick, 1992, 36 pp. At school, Maisy plays in the playhouse, paints pictures, writes a story, dresses up, and dances like a ballerina. Tabs and lift the flaps add to the reader's involvement. IL: 5–7.
Theme/subject: School; Dancing

Cox, Mike, & Cox, Chris. *Flowers.* Aro, 1979, 22 pp. A little girl takes flowers to her grandmother. Contains just 10 different words. Reading Research 10-Word series. Very easy reading. IL: 5–7. Available in paperback.
Theme/subject: Grandparents; Gifts

Crews, Donald. *School Bus.* Greenwillow, 1984, 32 pp. A fleet of school buses carry students to school and back home again. IL: 5–7. Available in paperback (Mulberry).
Theme/subject: Transportation: school buses

Crume, Marion. *Do You See Mouse?* Silver Burdett, 1995, 28 pp. Unable to find a place to hide during a game of hide-and-seek, Mouse stays in back of Turtle, who is "It". Not expecting Mouse to be in back of him, Turtle is unable to find Mouse. Repeated lines provide opportunities for choral or shared reading. Reinforces easy long *e* words and short *i* patterns and sight words. IL: 5–7. Available in paperback.
Theme/subject: Play; Games: hide-and-seek

Dale, Penny. *The Elephant Tree.* Putnam, 1991, 28 pp. Elephant's friends help him find a tree that he can climb. IL: 5–7. Out of print.
Theme/subject: Friendship

De Regniers, Beatrice Schenk. *Going for a Walk.* HarperCollins, 1961, 1993, 24 pp. A little girl greets a number of animals but when she says hi to a little boy, the two decide to play together. Very easy reading. Repeated lines provide opportunities for choral or shared reading. IL: 5–7.
Theme/subject: Friendship; Making friends

* Duffy, Dee Dee. *Barnyard Tracks*. Boyds Mill Press, 1992, 29 pp. Reading about a sound and seeing tracks, the reader is asked: "Who's there?" Repeated lines provide opportunities for choral or shared reading. Fosters active engagement and drawing conclusions based on clues. Highly recommended. IL: 5–7.
Theme/subject: Farm animals; Escape from danger

Florian, Douglas. *A Winter Day*. Greenwillow, 1988, 22 pp. Captioned text shows and tells how a family spends a winter day. Readers might need to use intitial consonants to help verify identity of illustrations. IL: 5–8.
Theme/subject: Seasons: winter

Farjeon, Eleanor. *Cats Sleep Anywhere*. Harper Collins, 1996, 16 pp. Poem and illustrations show various places where cats might sleep. IL: 5–8.
Theme/subject: Pets: cats; Poem

Ginsburg, Mirra. *The Chick and the Duckling*. Simon & Schuster, 1972, 24 pp. A chick imitates a duckling as the duckling walks, digs, and catches a butterfly, but the chick runs into difficulty when it tries to swim. Repeated lines provide opportunities for choral or shared reading. Reinforces *-ing* ending. IL: 5–8. Available in paperback.
Theme/subject: Being oneself; Humor

Ginsburg, Mirra. *Asleep, Asleep*. Greenwillow, 1992, 22 pp. The birds, the foxes, the fish, and the woods are asleep. Everyone and everything is asleep, except a small child and the wind. Finally, the child falls asleep. The lullaby lends itself to choral reading. IL: 5–7.
Theme/subject: Sleep; Lullaby

Gomi, Taro. *Where's the Fish?* Morrow, 1977, 24 pp. The reader is invited to locate the fish in each illustration. Uses just nine different words. Very easy reading. IL: 5–7.
Theme/subject: Games/activities; Finding hidden items

Greene, Carol. *Snow Joe*. Children's Press, 1982, 30 pp. Joe has fun in the snow. Uses just 15 different words. Very easy reading. Reinforces long *o* pattern words. IL: 5–8. Available in paperback.
Theme/subject: Playing; Snow

Greene, Carol. *Hi, Clouds*. Children's Press, 1983, 31 pp. A boy and a girl looking at the sky see shapes of creatures and objects in the clouds: cloud dog, cloud fish, cloud sheep, cloud frog, and even a cloud covered wagon. IL: 5–7.
Theme/subject: Clouds: seeing objects in

Greene, Carol. *Shine, Sun!* Children's Press, 1983, 30 pp. A girl shows the many ways in which she enjoys the sun. IL: 5–7. Available in paperback.
Theme/subject: Sun

Grindley, Sally. *Four Black Puppies*. Lothrop, Lee & Shepard, 1987, 22 pp. Four black puppies wake up, get into lots of mischief, and then go back to sleep once more. Provides a possible discussion and writing topic for readers: telling about funny things one's pets have done. IL: 6–7.
Theme/subject: Pets: puppies

Hague, Michael. *Teddy Bear, Teddy Bear*. Morrow, 1993, 16 pp. In this action rhyme, Teddy Bear is asked to do such things as turn around, touch the ground, and show his shoe. Repeated lines provide opportunities for choral or shared reading. Very easy reading. IL: 5–7.
Theme/subject: Bedtime; Action rhymes

Hall, Kristen, & Flaxman, Jessica. *Who Says?* Children's Press, 1990, 29 pp. Singing at the direction of a musical conductor, animals make their customary sounds: cow moos, dog barks, horse neighs. The conductor becomes increasingly distressed at the cacophony. Repeated lines provide opportunities for choral or shared reading. IL: 5–7. Available in paperback.
Theme/subject: Animal sounds; Humor

Hall, Nancy. *The Mess.* Children's Press, 1990, 29 pp. A young boy cannot go outside to play until he cleans up the mess he made. IL: 5–7. Available in paperback.
Theme/subject: Cleaning up

Henkes, Kevin. *SHHHH.* Greenwillow, 1989, 20 pp. The house is quiet as everyone is asleep except for the little girl who wakes everyone up. IL: 5–7.
Theme/subject: Family; Sleep; Humor

Hoban, Tana. *One Little Kitten.* Greenwillow, 1979, 22 pp. Black-and-white photos and brief captions depict a day in the life of a kitten. IL: 5–7. Available in paperback (Mulberry).
Theme/subject: Pets; Cats: kittens

Hutchins, Pat. *Rosie's Walk.* Simon & Schuster, 1968, 30 pp. When Rosie the hen goes for a walk, the fox following her has a series of misadventures. Reinforces short *o* patterns. IL: 5–8. Available in paperback.
Theme/subject: Humor; Escaping from enemies

Hutchins, Pat. *What Game Shall We Play?* Greenwillow, 1990, 22 pp. Duck and Frog hunt up their friends and ask each, "What game shall we play?" Owl has a very wise suggestion. IL: 5–7.
Theme/subject: Playing

Inkpen, Mick. *Kipper's Book of Opposites.* Harcourt, 1994, 16 pp. Kipper, a small dog, demonstrates a number of oppposites: *in–out, slow–fast, day–night.* Part of Kipper series. IL: 5–7.
Theme/subject: Opposites

Issacsen-Bright & Holland, Margaret. *No, No, Joan.* Willowwisp Press, 1986, 24 pp. A cat's curiosity leads her into mischief. Repeated lines provide opportunities for choral or shared reading. Very easy reading. IL: 5–7. Out of print.
Theme/subject: Pets: cats; Pets: misbehaving

Jonas, Ann. *Now We Can Go.* Greenwillow, 1986, 23 pp. A small child packs a bag for a trip and includes a book, a teddy bear, a hat, and a variety of toys. Provides a possible writing topic: what students would pack. IL 5–7.
Theme/subject: Trip: packing; Prized possessions

Jonas, Ann. *Where Can It Be?* Greenwillow, 1986, 30 pp. In this lift-the-flap book, a little boy searches for his most prized possession—his blanket. Fosters predicting. IL: 5–7.
Theme/subject: Prized possessions: blanket

Keats, Ezra Jack. *Kitten for a Day.* Four Winds, 1974, 30 pp. A puppy pretends to be a kitten. IL: 5–7. Available in paperback.
Theme/subject: Pets; Humor; Being oneself

Kopper, Lisa. *Daisy Thinks She's a Baby.* Knopf, 1994, 23 pp. The real baby becomes resentful when the family dog acts like a baby, especially when it gets cuddled by the baby's mother. But the real baby is delighted when the the dog has puppies. Repeated lines provide opportunities for choral or shared reading. IL: 5–8.
Theme/subject: Pets; Having puppies; Babies; Pets and babies

Kraus, Robert. *Whose Mouse Are You?* Simon & Schuster, 1970, 28 pp. A litttle mouse explains that he is nobody's mouse because his mother is in a cat, his father is in a trap, his sister is far away, and he has no brother. However, he rescues his parents, his sister returns, and a little brother is born. Fosters making predictions. Available in paperback. IL: 6–7.
Theme/subject: Family; New addition to family

Lillegard, Dee. *Where Is It?* Children's Press, 1984, 30 pp. A little boy searches everywhere for his red baseball cap. He is just about to give up the search when his baby brother crawls in wearing the red cap. Fosters predicting. Provides possible writing topic for students: objects they have lost. IL: 5–8.
Theme/subject: Familes: younger siblings; Babies; Lost and found objects

Lindgren, Brabo. *Sam's Ball.* Morrow, 1983, 28 pp. Sam and Kitty learn to play together with Sam's ball. Part of Sam series. Reinforces short *a* patterns. IL: 5–7.
Theme/subject: Pets: kitten; Playing

Mansell, Dom. *My Old Teddy.* Candlewick Press, 1991, 24 pp. Because her old teddy has been repaired so many times, a little girl's mother buys her a new one. The little girl likes the new teddy but loves the old teddy better. Repeated lines provide opportunities for choral or shared reading. IL: 5–7. Available in paperback.
Theme/subject: Toys: teddy bears

Maris, Ron. *Is Anyone Home?* Greenwillow, 1985, 30 pp. In this lift-the-flap book, a young boy opens a series of doors, sometimes with surprising results. Fosters predicting to find out who is behind the door. IL: 5–7.
Theme/subject: Farm; Grandparents

* Martin, Bill, Jr. *Brown Bear, Brown Bear, What Do You See?* Holt, 1967, 24 pp. In this highly popular children's book, a bear and other creatures are asked to tell what they see. Highly repetitive and predictable text provides opportunities for choral or shared reading. Highly recommended. IL: 5–7.
Theme/subject: Animals; Color words

Matthias, Catherine. *Out the Door.* Children's Press, 1982, 31 pp. A little girl goes to school on a rainy day, works and plays, and then comes home again. By this time, the sun is shining. IL: 5–7. Available in paperback.
Theme/subject: Weather: rainy day; School

Matthias, Catherine. *Over-Under.* Children's Press, 1984, 29 pp. On a playground, a little boy demonstrates high-frequency words such as *over, under, in, out, above,* and *below.* As he explains, "I am always somewhere doing something." IL: 5–7.
Theme/subject: Playing: playground

McKissack, Patricia C. *Who Is Who?* Children's Press, 1983, 30 pp. Although similar in many ways, the twins, Bobby and Johnny, have differing likes and dislikes. Fosters comparison/contrast. IL: 5–7. Available in paperback.
Theme/subject: Family: peers; Twins: individuality

McKissack, Patricia. *Who Is Coming?* Children's Press, 1986, 31 pp. A little monkey in Africa runs from a snake, a crocodile, a leopard, a lion, an elephant, and a hippo, but not a tiger. There are no tigers in Africa. IL: 5–7. Available in paperback.
Theme/subject: Escape from enemies

McKissack, Patricia, & McKissack, Fredrick. *Bugs!* Children's Press, 1988, 30 pp. A boy and a girl find bugs everywhere. Reinforces short *u* patterns. IL: 5–7.
Theme/subject: Science: insects

Morris, Ann. *Tools.* Lothrop, Lee & Shepard, 1992, 32 pp. Full-color pictures and brief captions depict tools for working, eating, cleaning, farming, and school. Tools are seen in settings around the world. Readers might need to use initial consonants to help verify identity of photos. IL: 6–8.
Theme/subject: Tools

Morris, Ann. *I Am Six.* Silver Press, 1995, 28 pp. This book shows a class of six-year-olds, the class animals (a snake and a hamster) and the children reading, writing, counting, singing, walking, talking, giggling, and taking a trip to the zoo. Provides a model for a class experience story. IL: 5–6. Available in paperback.
Theme/subject: School: interests and activities of children

Namm, Diane. *Little Bear.* Children's Press, 1990, 24 pp. Little Bear won't eat anything but honey. Very easy reading. Uses just 16 different words. IL: 5–7. Available in paperback.
Theme/subject: Eating habits: picky eater

Namm, Diane. *Monsters!* Children's Press, 1990, 28 pp. Monsters slip into a boy's bedroom. Although the boy suspects they are there, he can't find them. IL: 5–8.
Theme/subject: Monsters

Packard, Mary. *Surprise!* Children's Press, 1990, 24 pp. A boy tries to guess what is in a gift box. Very easy reading. Uses just 16 different words. Fosters predicting. IL: 5–7. Available in paperback.
Theme/subject: Gifts

Paparone, Pamela. *Five Little Ducks.* North-South, 1995, 26 pp. The ducks go up a hill, but one fails to come back. This happens day after day until none of the ducks comes back. They all return when the mother duck goes to the top of the hill and quacks. This book lends itself to partner, shared, or choral reading. Reinforces short vowel patterns. IL: 5–7.
Theme/subject: Animals: ducks; Mother and babies

Peek, Merle. *Roll Over! A Counting Song.* Clarion, 1980, 24 pp. Each time a little boy in bed rolls over, 1 of the 10 imaginary animals falls out until he has the bed to himself. Because the six-line verse is repeated 10 times, it lends itself to choral singing or reading. Reinforces short *i* pattern. IL: 5–7. Available in paperback.
Theme/subject: Traditional song; Counting

Perkins, Al. *The Ear Book.* Random House, 1968, 28 pp. Ears can be used to hear the toot of a flute, the boom of a drum, the tap of feet, and the pop of popcorn. Reinforces short vowel patterns. IL: 5–9.
Theme/subject: Ears; Senses: hearing

Petrie, Catherine. *Joshua James Likes Trucks.* Children's Press, 1982, 32 pp. Joshua James likes all kinds of trucks. Reinforces short *u* pattterns. IL: 5–7. Available in paperback.
Theme/subject: Trucks

Pomerantz, Charlotte. *Where's the Bear?* Greenwillow Books, 1984, 32 pp. A group of people look for the bear and finally find it at the end of the story. Fosters predicting where the bear is. IL: 5–7. Available in paperback (Mulberry).
Theme/subject: Animals: bears

Poulet, Virginia. *Blue Bug's Beach Party.* Children's Press, 1975, 32 pp. Blue Bug cleans up the beach in preparation for a party. Part of Blue Bug series. Reinforces short *u* pattterns. Very easy reading. IL: 5–7. Out of print.
Theme/subject: Litter; Cleaning up; Environment

Poulet, Virginia. *Blue Bug's Circus*. Children's Press, 1975, 32 pp. After failing at several roles for a circus, Blue Bug becomes a clown. Reinforces short vowel patterns. Very easy reading. IL: 5–7. Out of print.
Theme/subject: Circus; Using one's talents
Raffi. *Wheels on the Bus*. Crown, 1988, 28 pp. Traditional song celebrates a bus ride through a small town. This book lends itself to choral singing or reading. Part of Raffi Songs to Read series. IL: 5–8. Available in paperback.
Theme/subject: Song; Transportation: bus
Raffi. *Five Little Ducks*. Crown, 1989, 30 pp. One by one, each of the five ducks disappears. Although there is a fox around, the ducks safely reappear. Reinforces short vowel patterns. Repeated lines provide opportunities for choral or shared singing or reading. IL: 5–7.
Theme/subject: Animals: ducks; Mother and babies; Counting
* Raschka, Chris. *Yo! Yes!* Orchard, 1993, 32 pp. Two lonely boys become friends. Very easy reading. Reinforces short vowel patterns. Highly recommended. IL: 6–9.
Theme/subject: Friendship; Making friends
Rayner, Mary. *Ten Pink Piglets*. Dutton, 1994, 22 pp. In this song, 10 piglets fall off the wall one by one. Repeated lines provide opportunities for choral singing or reading. IL: 5–10.
Theme/subject: Traditional song; Counting
Rees, Mary. *Ten in a Bed*. Little, Brown, 1988, 24 pp. In this traditional song, children roll over and, one by one, fall out of bed. Repeated lines provide opportunities for choral singing or reading. IL: 5–8.
Theme/subject: Traditional song; Sleeping; Counting
Reese, Bob. *Crab Apple*. Aro, 1979, 20 pp. A crab apple is crabby with every creature that it meets, but is surprised when a worm crabs at it. Reinforces short *a* and *u* patterns. Uses only 10 different words. Part of Reading Research 10-word series. Very easy reading. IL: 5–7. Available in paperback.
Theme/subject: Moods: grouchiness
Reese, Bob. *Little Dinosaur*. Aro, 1979, 20 pp. A little dinosaur grows up. Uses only 10 different words. Part of Reading Research 10-word series. Very easy reading. IL: 5–7.
Theme/subject: Dinosaurs
Reese, Bob. *Sunshine*. Aro, 1979, 20 pp. Although Sunshine can be a nuisance because she barks so much, the family becomes upset when Sunshine disappears. Uses only 10 different words. Part of Reading Research 10-word series. Very easy reading. IL: 5–7. Available in paperback.
Theme/subject: Dogs: barking
Reese, Bob, & Reese, Brittany. *For Keeps*. Aro, 1993, 20 pp. A little girl who cages a bird lets it go free when she sees that it is unhappy. Uses only 10 different words. Part of Reading Research 10-word series. Very easy reading.
Theme/subject: Animals: setting free
Rose, Agatha. *Hide and Seek in the Yellow House*. Viking, 1992, 24 pp. A mother cat has difficulty keeping track of the whereabouts of her kitten. Repeated lines provide opportunities for choral or shared reading. IL: 5–7. Available in paperback.
Theme/subject: Animals: cats; Parenting

Ruane, Joanna. *Boats, Boats, Boats.* Children's Press, 1990, 28 pp. Captions and illustrations describe a variety of boats. IL: 5–7. Available in paperback.
Theme/subject: Transportation: boats
Shaw, C. G. *It Looked Like Spilt Milk.* HarperCollins, 1947, 30 pp. This book describes what a cloud might look like—rabbit, angel, mitten—as it changes shape. Readers might need to use intitial consonants to help verify identity of photos. Illustrations don't always clearly indicate identity of some of the hard words. IL: 5–7. Available in paperback.
Theme/subject: Clouds
Shebar, Sharon Sigmond. *Milk.* Aro, 1979, 20 pp. The king and his knights enjoy milk. Uses only 10 different words. Part of Reading Research 10-word series. Very easy reading. IL: 5–7. Available in paperback.
Theme/subject: Food: milk
Smith, Mavis. *Fred, Is that You?* Little, Brown, 1992, 20 pp. In this lift-the-flap book, a duck searches for his friend Fred. Repeated lines provide opportunities for choral or shared reading. Reinforces short *e* pattern words. IL: 5–7.
Theme/subject: Friendship; Lost person
Snow, Pegree. *A Pet for Pat.* Children's Press, 1984, 32 pp. Pat has fun with her new pet. Reinforces short *e* pattern words. IL: 5–7. Available in paperback.
Theme/subject: Pets: dog; Acquiring pet; Caring for pet
Steig, William (1997). *Toby, Where Are You?* HarperCollins, 1997, 24 pp. Toby, the ferret, hides from his parents. They look everywhere but can't find him.
Theme/subject: Family life: parents and children
Steptoe, John. *Baby Says.* Lothrop, Lee & Shepard, 1988, 24 pp. Older brother lets baby play with his blocks. Very easy reading. IL: 5–8. Available in paperback (Mulberry).
Theme/subject: Family: siblings, babies
Stobbs, William. *Gregory's Dog.* Oxford, 1987, 16 pp. Gregory teaches his dog to obey commands. Very easy reading. IL: 5–7. Paperback.
Theme/subject: Pets: training
Stott, Dorothy. *Kitty and Me.* Dutton, 1993, 12 pp. In this very simple lift-the-flap book, which is a companion to *Puppy and Me,* children have fun with a kitten. IL: 5–7.
Theme/subject: Pets: dogs
Stott, Dorothy. *Puppy and Me.* Dutton, 1993, 12 pp. In this very simple lift-the-flap book, which is a companion to *Kitty and Me,* children have fun with a puppy. IL: 5–7.
Theme/subject: Pets: dogs
Tafuri, Nancy. *Early Morning in the Barn.* Greenwillow, 1983, 21 pp. This book shows the sounds that farm animals make early in the morning. Promotes use of phonics skills to decode animal sounds. IL: 5–7. Available in paperback (Mulberry).
Theme/subject: Animal sounds
Tafuri, Nancy. *Rabbit's Morning.* Greenwillow, 1985, 24 pp. During his morning run, rabbit sees a variety of animals. Very easy reading. IL: 5–7.
Theme/subject: Exploring one's environment
Tafuri, Nancy. *Do Not Disturb.* Greenwillow, 1987, 21 pp. During the day, a family has fun on its camping trip, but at night, the many sounds made by the forest animals keep everyone awake. Promotes use of phonics skills to decode animal

sounds. IL: 5–8.
Theme/subject: Family life: camping trip

Tafuri, Nancy. *The Ball Bounced*. Greenwillow, 1989, 22 pp. A bouncing ball sets in motion a chain of activities that ends up with a baby laughing. IL: 5–7.
Theme/subject: Babies; Toys: ball

Tafuri, Nancy. *This Is the Farmer*. Greenwillow, 1994, 24 pp. The farmer's kiss starts a chain of events that ends with the milking of a cow. IL: 5–7.
Theme/subject: Farm life

Wildsmith, Brian. *My Dream*. Oxford, 1986, 16 pp. A little girl dreams that she is riding a tiger, sitting on a whale, lifting an elephant, and climbing a giraffe's neck. IL: 5–7. Paperback.
Theme/subject: Dreams

* Williams, Sue. *I Went Walking*. Harcourt, 1989, 30 pp. As a little boy goes walking, he notices a lot of animals looking at him. At the end of his walk, he notices that the animals have been following him. Highly recommended. IL: 5–7. Available in paperback.
Theme/subject: Animals; Walking

Winder, Jack. *Who's New at the Zoo?* Aro, 1979, 20 pp. A boy asks animals who's new at the zoo. Uses only 10 different words. Part of Reading Research 10-word series. Very easy reading. IL: 5–7. Available in paperback.
Theme/subject: Zoo

Winter, Susan. *I Can*. Kindersley, 1993, 21 pp. A young boy tells about all the things he can do that his little sister can't: dress and feed himself, give himself a bath, swim without waterwings, stand on his head. But when he imagines monsters in the night, he snuggles up to her. Repeated lines provide opportunities for choral or shared reading. Fosters development of comparing and contrasting. IL: 5–8.
Theme/subject: Growing up; Becoming independent

Wolcott, Patty. *The Cake Story*. Addison-Wesley, 1974, 20 pp. When someone eats bear's cake, the other animals bake him another one. Uses only 10 different words. Very easy reading. IL: 5–7. Out of print.
Theme/subject: Helping others

Wolcott, Patty. *My Shadow and I*. Addison-Wesley, 1975, 24 pp. A boy has fun with his shadow. Uses only 10 different words. Very easy reading. IL: 5–7. Out of print.
Theme/subject: Shadows

Wong, Olive. *From My Window*. Silver Burdett Press, 1995, 32 pp. Looking down on the street, a young boy sees snow and a friend, which "made me want to run down, down, down, and out of the building to play." Repeated lines provide opportunities for choral or shared reading. IL: 5–8. Available in paperback.
Theme/subject: Friendship; Play; Snow

Wood, Leslie. *The Frog and the Fly*. Oxford University Press, 16 pp. Tickling a frog from the inside, a fly that has been swallowed escapes. IL: 5–7. Paperback.
Theme/subject: Escaping from enemies

Wylie, Joanne, & Wylie, David. *A Fishy Alphabet Story*. Children's Press, 1983, 24 pp. The reader learns about the alphabet by catching fish in alphabetical order. An ABC fish is caught first, and then a DEF fish, and so on. Reinforces alphabetical order. IL: 5–7. Available in paperback.
Theme/subject: Alphabet

SIGHT-WORD PLUS

Anholt, Catherine, & Anholt, Laurence. *Bear and Baby.* Candlewick Press, 1990, 16 pp. Baby and Bear go everywhere together, and if it's stormy weather, they hide together. IL: 5–7.
Theme/subject: Friendship

Bang, Molly. *Yellow Ball.* Morrow, 1991, 22 pp. A yellow ball that floats out to sea is carried to a new home. Suggests a possible writing topic: lost objects. IL: 5–7. Available in paperback.
Theme/subject: Sea; Toys

Barton, Byron. *Machines at Work.* HarperCollins, 1987, 30 pp. Workers use machines to knock down a building, bulldoze a tree, load a truck, and build a road. Reader may need help identifying the words *rubble* and *bulldoze.* IL: 5–8.
Theme/subject: Machines; Construction

Benjamin, Cynthia. *Footprints in the Snow.* Scholastic, 1994, 29 pp. When the snow falls and the wind blows, the animals head for home, as does a little girl. IL: 5–7. Available in paperback.
Theme/subject: Snow; Home

Gardner, Beau. *Have You Ever Seen . . . ? An ABC Book.* BGA, 1986, 26 pp. The book asks questions that incorporate the sound correspondence being presented: "Have you ever seen an Alligator with Antlers? A Banana with Buttons?" Readers may need to use decoding skills to help interpret some pictures: inchworm, oatmeal, spaghetti. Reinforces beginning sounds and their spellings. IL: 5–7. Available in paperback.
Theme/subject: Games; Activities; Silly questions; Beginning sounds

Mahurin, Tim. *Jeremy Kooloo.* Dutton, 1995, 29 pp. Jeremy Kooloo, a furry white cat, spills a carton of milk after drinking four glasses of milk. Sleepy and full, he lies down for a nap. Ask readers what is special about this story, and they might notice that the story is told in such a way that the words appear in alphabetical order. Provides possible writing activity: composing a story in alphabetical order. IL: 5–8.
Theme/subject: Pets: cat; Word games

Morris, Ann. *Hats Hats Hats.* Lothrop, Lee & Shepard, 1989, 26 pp. Color photos and captions depict a variety of head coverings used in the United States and other countries. IL: 5–9. Available in paperback (Mulberry).
Theme/subject: Clothing: hats; Other cultures

Serfozo, Mary. *Joe Joe.* Simon & Schuster, 1993, 27 pp. Joe Joe, a small boy, bangs a stick on a fence, bongs a garbage can, clangs, claps, hops, stops, splashes, squishes, slips, and drips. Reinforces consonant clusters. IL: 5–7.
Theme/subject: Playing

Titherington, Jeanne. *Pumpkin Pumpkin.* Greenwillow, 1986, 21 pp. Jamie plants a pumpkin seed and tends it as it grows into a full-sized pumpkin ready for carving. IL: 5–7.
Theme/subject: Gardening; Pumpkins

BEGINNING A

Allen, Julia. *My First Job.* Aro, 1987, 20 pp. A boy completes a variety of chores around the home and is proud of his performance. Reinforces short *a* patterns. Provides a model for students for writing about jobs they perform. IL: 5–8. Available in paperback.
Theme/subject: Chores

Ancona, George, & Ancona, Mary Beth. *Handtalk Zoo.* Simon & Schuster, 1989, 32 pp. Children demonstrate sign language as they tour a zoo. Reinforces long *o* patterns. Introduces sign language. IL: 6–8.
Theme/subject: Zoo; Sign language

Asch, Frank. *Just Like Daddy.* Simon & Schuster, 1981, 30 pp. In preparation for a fishing trip, Child Bear does everything just like Daddy, but catches a big fish just like Mommy does. Because of repeated sentences, this book lends itself to shared or choral reading. IL: 5–7.
Theme/subject: Parents; Fishing

Auster, Benjamin. *I Like It When.* Raintree, 1990, 24 pp. The youngest in the family tells what he likes and doesn't like about common situations. Could be model for a piece of writing on the same topic. IL: 5–8. Available in paperback.
Theme/subject: Personal preferences

Barton, Byron. *Bones, Bones, Dinosaur Bones.* Crowell, 1990, 30 pp. This book shows how dinosaur bones are located, dug up, shipped to the museum, and assembled. Reinforces long *o* patterns. IL: 6–8.
Theme/subject: Dinosaurs

Barton, Byron. *The Wee Little Woman.* HarperCollins, 1995, 32 pp. After being put out of the house for drinking all the milk from the pail, the wee little cat comes back and is given a treat by the wee little woman. Reinforces short *o* patterns. IL: 5–8.
Theme/subject: Pets: cats; Forgiveness

Bennett, David. *One Cow Moo Moo!* Holt, 1990, 28 pp. A boy wonders why animals are rushing by. Repeated lines in this cumulative tale provide opportunities for choral or shared reading. Reinforces short vowel patterns. IL: 5–8.
Theme/subject: Cumulative tale; Animal sounds

Blackstone, Margaret. *This Is Baseball.* Holt, 1993, 30 pp. Pictures depict what baseball is and how it is played. Reinforces short *i* patterns. IL: 6–8.
Theme/subject: Sports: baseball

Boivin, Kelly. *Where Is Mittens?* Children's Press, 1990, 32 pp. Sad because she can't find her cat, a little girl finally discovers the missing cat taking care of four new baby kittens. Reinforces short vowel patterns. Available in paperback.
Theme/subject: Pets: cats; Cat having kittens

Brown, Margaret. *Where Have You Been?* Scholastic, 1952, 32 pp. A variety of animals tell where they have been in this rhyming tale. IL: 5–7. Available in paperback.
Theme/subject: Animals; Poetry

Brown, Margaret Wise. *Four Fur Feet.* Hyperion, 1961, 1994, 21 pp. Walking around the world, a creature with furry feet sees boats, a train, a stream, and tall grass, and feels the warmth of the sun. Repeated lines provide opportunities for choral or shared reading. Reinforces *r* pattern vowels. Available in paperback (Dell). IL: 5–8.
Theme/subject: Travel

Brown, Ruth. *A Dark Dark Tale*. Dial Press, 1981, 28 pp. At the end of a spooky journey into a deserted house and up dark stairways and into a mysterious box in a dark cupboard, the reader confronts a frightened mouse. Fosters making predictions about what will be found. IL: 6–8. Available in paperback.
Theme/subject: Scary tales

Bullock, Kathleen. *She'll Be Comin' Round the Mountain*. Simon & Schuster, 1993, 32 pp. This is a vividly illustrated version of an American folksong. Repeated lines provide opportunities for choral singing or reading. Reinforces short vowel patterns. IL: 6–10. Available in paperback.
Theme/subject: Traditional song

Carle, Eric. *Papa, Please Get the Moon for Me*. Picture Book Studio, 1986, 26 pp. When his daughter asks him to get the moon, Papa gets a very tall ladder and climbs to the moon. After waiting for the moon to shrink, he took it back down to his daughter. Foldout pages help convey the length of the ladder and the size of a full moon. IL: 5–7.
Theme/subject: Moon; Fantasy; Parents

Cebulash, Mel. *Willie's Wonderful Pet*. Scholastic, 1972, 28 pp. Although the other children don't think much of Willie's pet, it becomes the hit of the class's pet show. IL: 5–8.
Theme/subject: Pets; Pet show

Cohen, Caron Lee. *Where's the Fly?* Greenwillow, 1996, 28 pp. The reader is asked to guess where a fly is. Only a portion of the location is shown. The answer, which happens to be a dog's nose, is shown on the reverse page. The reader is then asked to guess where the dog is and so on. Repeated lines provide opportunities for choral or shared reading. IL: 5–8.
Theme/subject: Games/activities; Guessing the identity of items only partly shown

Coxe, Molly. *Cat Traps*. Random House, 1996, 32 pp. Wanting a snack, a cat sets traps of various kinds but fails to catch any creatures. Finally, it gets a snack by acting nice to a little girl. Reviews all short vowel patterns. IL: 5–8. Paperback.
Theme/subject: Pets: cats; Food: obtaining

Crews, Donald. *Flying*. Greenwillow, 1986, 32 pp. Shows the flight of a plane from boarding to landing. IL: 5–7.
Theme/subject: Transportation: flying; Airplanes

Dabcovich, Lydia. *Sleepy Bear*. Dutton, 1982, 22 pp. As winter approaches, a bear becomes sleepy and retreats to his cave until warm weather comes. Provides practice with sequence. IL: 6–8.
Theme/subject: Seasons; Hibernation

Damon, Laura. *Hide-and-Seek on the Farm*. Troll, 1988, 28 pp. In a game of hide-and-seek on the farm, mother animals try to find their babies. Readers are invited to help find the babies by using clues that have been provided. Fosters use of visual clues. Promotes active engagement. IL: 5–7.
Theme/subject: Games: visual clues; Animals: farm

DePaola, Tomie. *Andy, That's My Name*. Simon & Schuster, 1973, 30 pp. Big kids form a tower using Andy's name as a base, but the tower collapses when Andy takes his name home. Fosters knowledge of phonics. Shows how the name *Andy* can be used to build other words. IL: 5–7. Available in paperback.
Theme/subject: Playing with older kids; Word study: building words

DePaola, Tomie. *The Wind and the Sun*. Silver, 1995, 28 pp. The wind and the sun have a contest to see which one can get a traveler to remove his coat. Using its heat, the sun wins.
Theme/subject: Persuasion works better than force; Fable

Dodds, Ann Dayle. *Wheel Away*. HarperCollins, 1989, 28 pp. While a boy is fixing his bike, the front wheel rolls down a hill, through a mill, through a lake, over a cake, and on and on until it reaches the top of a hill and then rolls back again. Reinforces short vowels and clusters. IL: 5–8. Available in paperback.
Theme/subject: Accidents; Humor: exaggeration; Bicycles: fixing

Duffy, Dee Dee. *Forest Tracks*. Boyds Mill Press, 1996, 28 pp. Animal tracks are depicted and the sounds the animals make are presented. The reader is invited to guess who's there. Repeated lines provide opportunities for choral or shared reading. Fosters using clues to draw conclusions. IL: 5–8.
Theme/subject: Animals: wild; tracks, sounds

Economos, Chris. *Let's Take the Bus*. Raintree, 1989, 24 pp. Hot and tired, five animals take the bus but end up pushing it all the way home. Reinforces short vowel patterns. IL: 5–7. Available in paperback.
Theme/subject: Transportation: bus; Humor

Evans, Katie. *Hunky Dory Found It*. Dutton, 1994, 28 pp. Hunky Dory, the dog, picks up a ball, a baby's shoe, a tie, a toy boat, and other objects, and runs off with them. When she discovered Hunky Dory's hidden treasures, Julie made her return them. Repeated lines provide opportunities for choral or shared reading. Sequel to *Hunky Dory Ate It*. IL: 5–8.
Theme/subject: Pets: misbehavior; Humor

* Ford, Miela. *Little Elephant*. Greenwillow, 1994, 20 pp. Color photos and brief text depict a day in the life of a baby elephant. Highly recommended. IL: 5–7.
Theme/subject: Animals: elephants

* Ford, Miela. *Bear Play*. Greenwillow, 1995, 20 pp. Polar bear calls to a friend and the two of them play catch in the water with a large brown ball. Uses actual photos. Highly recommended. IL: 5–8.
Theme/subject: Polar bears; Friends having fun

Ford, Miela. *Sunflower*. Greenwillow, 1995, 19 pp. A young girl plants a sunflower seed and watches as it grows up to her knees, then up to her nose, and finally over her head. Fosters comprehending sequence. IL: 5–8.
Theme/subject: Plants

Giganti, Paul, Jr. *How Many Snails?* Greenwillow, 1988, 22 pp. The reader is invited to count plain snails, snails with striped shells, snails with striped shells that have their heads stuck out, and other items. Repeated lines provide opportunities for choral or shared reading. Fosters counting, noting details in illustrations, and following directions. IL: 5–7. Available in paperback (Mulberry).
Theme/subject: Games/activities; Counting

Ginsburg, Mirra. *Across the Stream*. Greenwillow, 1982, 21 pp. A duck family ferries a hen and her chicks across a stream so they can leave a bad dream behind. Reinforces short *u* patterns and clusters. IL: 5–7. Available in paperback (Mulberry).
Theme/subject: Dreams; Helping others

Gomi, Taro. *Coco Can't Wait*. Morrow, 1984, 30 pp. Grandma and Coco, who live far apart, hurry to see each other but miss one another because each has gone to the other's home. They agree that in the future they will meet

under an apple tree that is midway between their homes. IL: 5–7. Available in paperback (Puffin).
Theme/subject: Grandparents

Goode, Diane. *I Hear a Noise.* Dutton, 1988, 29 pp. A litttle boy and his mother are carried off by a young flying monster. When the monster's mother sees what her child has done, she yells "Take them back where you found them... and don't ever touch them again." IL: 6–8. Available in paperback (Puffin).
Theme/subject: Monsters; Parents

Gordon, Sharon. *What a Dog.* Troll, 1980, 32 pp. Because Bernie, the dog, runs wild when Billy takes him for a walk, he gets help from the rest of his family. Reinforces long *e* patterns. IL: 5–7.
Theme/subject: Pets: dog; Family

Gordon, Sharon. *The Jolly Monsters.* Troll, 1988, 28 pp. Holly, a jolly monster, after many tries, finally gets Wally to laugh, so that he becomes a jolly monster, too. Provides a possible writing topic: things that make me laugh. IL: 5–8.
Theme/subject: Laughter; Friendship

Greeley, Valerie. *Where's My Share?* Simon & Schuster, 1990, 32 pp. A bird seeks her share of bread and finds that a mouse has taken it. Through a series of questions, it is established that the bread became part of a field where wheat was grown, milled into flower, and made into bread for the birds to eat. Provides practice with a question-and-answer format and sequence. IL: 6–8.
Theme/subject: Plants: cycle of plants growing; How bread is made

Gregorich, Barbara. *Nine Men Chase a Hen.* School Zone, 1984, 16 pp. Men and hens find themselves in comic situations. Reinforces short *e* patterns. IL: 5–7. Paperback.
Theme/subject: Humor; Farm

Grejniec, Michael. *Albert's Nap.* North-South Books, 1995, 30 pp. Albert can't finish his nap until he gets rid of a pesky mosquito. Reinforces short vowel patterns. IL: 6–8.
Theme/subject: Insects: pests

Greydanus, Rose. *Let's Get a Pet.* Troll, 1988, 32 pp. A boy and a girl select a pet. Reinforces short *e* patterns. IL: 5–7. Paperback.
Theme/subject: Pet: selecting

Hale, Irina. *How I Found a Friend.* Viking, 1992, 27 pp. With some help from their teddy bears who mysteriously exchange hats while left on a wall, two small boys become friends. Neither boy can figure out how the hat exchange came about, but the reader knows. IL: 5–7.
Theme/subject: Friends: making new; Toys: teddy bears

Hamm, Diane Johnston. *How Many Feet in the Bed?* Simon & Schuster, 1991, 27 pp. On a family morning, the number of feet in the parents' bed change as people get in and get up. At one time there are 10, but the number changes when the phone rings, and cartoons come on, and it's time for breakfast. IL: 5–7.
Theme/subject: Counting; Family life

Hamm, Diane Johnston. *Rockabye Farm.* Simon & Schuster, 1992, 24 pp. A farmer rocks his baby and then all the farm animals to sleep before rocking himself to sleep. Repeated lines provide opportunities for choral or shared reading. IL: 5–7.
Theme/subject: Sleep: rocking to sleep

Hamsa, Bobbie. *Animal Babies.* Children's Press, 1985, 30 pp. Shows baby animals and tells what they are called. IL: 5–7. Available in paperback.
Theme/subject: Animals: babies

Herman, Gail. *My Dog Talks.* Scholastic, 1995, 29 pp. A little boy explains how he talks to his dog and how his dog "talks" to him with different kinds of woofs. The boy also explains how they have fun together. IL: 5–9.
Theme/subject: Pets: dogs; Communicating with animals

Herman, Gail. *Teddy Bear for Sale.* Scholastic, 1995, 29 pp. Distressed because no one will buy him, a teddy bear runs away. After traveling around the store by car and boat and then bouncing on a trampoline and flying over everyone's heads, the teddy bear lands on the store's counter, at which point a little boy decides to buy him. IL: 5–7. Available in paperback.
Theme/subject: Toys: teddy bears; Being wanted

Hill, Eric. *Spot's First Walk.* Putnam, 1981, 22 pp. Spot finds surprises behind lift-the-flap illustrations as he investigates his surroundings. Reinforces short *o* words. Provides opportunity for predicting. Part of Spot series. IL: 5–7.
Theme/subject: Exploring one's environment

Hill, Eric. *Where's Spot?* Putnam, 1980, 22 pp. Using lift the flaps, the reader searches for Spot. Part of Spot series. IL: 5–7
Theme/subject: Lost dog

Hindley, Judy. *The Big Red Bus.* Candlewick Press, 1995, 24 pp. When the wheel of the bus gets stuck in a hole, a van, a car, and a motorcycle are stuck behind it until a tractor pulls it out and the hole is filled in. Reinforces short *u* patterns. Repeated lines provide opportunities for choral or shared reading. IL: 5–7.
Theme/subject: Roads: repair; Transportation: bus

Hughes, Shirley. *Chatting.* Candlewick, 1994, 16 pp. A little girl likes chatting in the car, with friends in the park, with the lady in the supermarket, with her grandparents and toy dog, and mostly with her dad before she goes to sleep. Provides a possible writing topic: with whom do you like to chat? IL: 5–7.
Theme/subject: Talking with others; Friendliness

Hulbert, Jay, & Kantor, Sid. *Armando Asked, "Why?"* Raintree, 1990, 23 pp. Armando asks a lot of questions, but everyone seems too busy to answer them until finally his mother thinks of a solution to the problem. The family goes to the library and checks out a number of books so they will have answers to Armando's questions. Repeated lines provide opportunities for choral or shared reading. IL: 6–8. Available in paperback.
Theme/subject: Library: getting information from

Hutchins, Pat. *Little Pink Pig.* Greenwillow, 1994, 28 pp. Although Little Pink Pig is nearby, his mother can't see or hear him, so she enlists the help of the barnyard animals to help find him, even though he isn't really lost. Repeated lines provide opportunities for choral or shared reading. Provides possible writing topic: being lost. IL: 5–7.
Theme/subject: Lost children: looking for

Imai, Miko. *Sebastian's Trumpet.* Candlewick, 1995, 24 pp. Trying to soothe Sebastian, who is frustrated because he can't play his new trumpet, Mama Bear suggests that he rest and try later. Sure enough, after a good night's sleep, Sebastian is able to play his trumpet after just a few tries. IL: 5–7.
Theme/subject: Overcoming difficulties

Jakob, Donna. *My New Sandbox.* Hyperion, 1996, 30 pp. A little boy chases a bug, a bird, a dog, and another little boy out of his new sandbox. Realizing that it is no fun to play alone, he invites them all back. Repeated text lends itself to choral or shared reading. IL: 5–7.
Theme/subject: Sharing; Toys

Jonas, Ann. *Splash.* Greenwillow, 1995, 22 pp. A little girl counts the animals in her pond. The number changes because creatures are jumping or falling in and climbing out. Reinforces counting. IL: 5–7.
Theme/subject: Counting

Jones, Carol. *This Old Man.* Houghton Mifflin, 1990, 48 pp. Cutouts and colorful illustrations make this version of a traditonal counting song particulary easy to read. Refrain provides opportunities for choral singing or reading. IL: 5–9.
Theme/subject: Counting; Song

Kalan, Robert. *Jump, Frog, Jump.* Greenwillow, 1981, 1995, 30 pp. In this cumulative tale, frog escapes his enemies by jumping. Repeated lines provide opportunities for choral or shared reading. IL: 5–8.
Theme/subject: Animals: escaping from enemies

Kalan, Robert. *Stop, Thief.* Greenwillow, 1993, 22 pp. Animals take a nut from each other until it ends up with the squirrel who first found it and is the one who claims to have dropped it. Repeated lines provide opportunities for choral or shared reading. Reinforces short vowel patterns. IL: 6–7.
Theme/subject: Disagreements

Krauss, Ruth. *The Carrot Seed.* HarperCollins, 1945, 24 pp. A little boy has faith that the carrot seed he planted will grow. Reinforces long *e* patterns. IL: 5–7. Available in paperback.
Theme/subject: Having belief in oneself; Plants

Krauss, Ruth. *The Happy Day.* HarperCollins, 1949, 28 pp. The day that the first flower blooms is a happy one for the forest animals who have been hibernating. IL: 5–7. Available in paperback.
Theme/subject: Seasons: spring; Hibernation

Langstaff, John. *Oh, A-Hunting We Will Go.* Atheneum, 1974, 26 pp. Humorous verses in this traditional song tell of a fun-filled hunt in which children sing of such exploits as catching a fox and putting him in a box and catching a pig and putting him in a wig. Lends itself to choral or shared reading. Provides practice with vowel patterns. IL: 5–8. Available in paperback.
Theme/subject: Traditional song; Hunting; Humor

Leemis, Ralph. *Mister Momboo's Hat.* Dutton, 1991, 18 pp. After been blown off its original owner's head, a hat ends up with a variety of owners, including birds who use it for a nest. IL: 5–8.
Theme/subject: Hats; Animal homes

Lewison, Wendy Cheyette. *"Buzz" Said the Bee.* Scholastic, 1992, 30 pp. In this cumulative tale, a bee sits on a duck and starts a chain of events in which a series of animals sit on top of each other until the tower of animals becomes too heavy for the bottom animal and the tower collapses. Repeated lines provide opportunities for choral or shared reading. IL: 5–7. Paperback.
Theme/subject: Humor; Animal sounds

Lillegard, Dee. *Sitting in My Box.* Dutton, 1989, 28 pp. Sitting alone in a cardboard box, a little boy is joined by a number of large animals. Even though the box has

become too crowded, the animals refuse to leave until a flea appears on the scene. Reinforces short *u* patterns. Repeated lines provide opportunities for choral or shared reading. IL: 5–7. Available in paperback (Puffin).
Theme/subject: Play: imaginary visitors; Humor

Lionni, Leo. *On My Beach There Are Many Pebbles*. Mulberry, 1961, 1995, 25 pp. Both ordinary and unusual pebbles are depicted, including pebbles that look like letters and those that look like fish or people. IL: 6–8.
Theme/subject: Nature: pebbles; Observing our surroundings

Maccarone, Grace. *Cars, Cars, Cars*. Scholastic, 1995, 24 pp. Dogs are depicted riding in a variety of cars, including a limousine and a police car. IL: 5–8.
Theme/subject: Transportation: cars

Maris, Ron. *Are You There, Bear?* Greenwillow, 1984, 32 pp. Child searches for a teddy bear. Reinforces short *o* patterns. IL: 5–7.
Theme/subject: Toys: teddy bears

Martin, Bill, Jr., & Archambault, John. *Here Are My Hands*. Holt, 1987, 24 pp. Children show how they use their body parts: "Here are my hands for catching and throwing. Here are my feet for stopping and going." Could be a model for a pattern of writing. IL: 5–7. Available in paperback.
Theme/subject: Body parts

Matthias, Catherine. *I Love Cats*. Children's Press, 1983, 32 pp. A boy likes all kinds of insects and animals but loves cats. Reinforces long vowel patterns. IL: 6–7. Available in paperback.
Theme/subject: Pets: cats

McDaniel, Becky Bring. *Katie Did It*. Children's Press, 1983, 30 pp. Being the youngest in the family, Katie gets blamed for everything that goes wrong. Repeated lines provide opportunities for choral or shared reading. Available in paperback. IL: 5–7.
Theme/subject: Family: younger siblings

McKissack, Patricia, & McKissack, Frederick. *Cinderella*. Children's Press, 1985, 31 pp. Retells the story of Cinderella in simplified form. IL: 6–8. Available in paperback.
Theme/subject: Fairy tale; Prince and poor girl; Romance

McKissack, Patricia, & McKissack, Frederick. *King Midas and His Gold*. Children's Press, 1986, 30 pp. King Midas discovers that the golden touch does not bring him personal happiness. Reinforces long *e* patterns. IL: 6–8. Available in paperback.
Theme/subject: Fairy tale; Greed

McMillan, Bruce. *Super Super Superwords*. Lothrop, Lee & Shepard, 1989, 27 pp. Color photos and captions depict common adjectives and their comparative and superlative forms: *loud, louder, loudest*. Reinforces inflectional suffixes: *er, est*. IL: 6–7.
Theme/subject: Language study: adjectives

Milgrim, David. *Why Benny Barks*. Random House, 1994, 30 pp. Benny barks in the car, he barks in the house, and he barks outside. He barks in the morning and at night. His young owner can't help wondering why Benny barks. IL: 6–8. Available in paperback.
Theme/subject: Pets: dogs; Communication: animals

Milios, Rita. *Bears, Bears, Everywhere.* Children's Press, 1988, 32 pp. A house is full of teddy bears. IL: 5–7.
Theme/subject: Toys: teddy bears
Miller, Virginia. *Eat Your Dinner.* Candlewick, 1992, 24 pp. Despite getting a scolding, Bartholomew Bear refuses to eat his dinner but changes his mind when he finds out that he won't get a slice of honey cake with a cherry on top until his bowl is empty. IL: 5–7. Available in paperback.
Theme/subject: Family life; Dinnertime: eating one's dinner
Minarik, Else Holmelund. *It's Spring.* Greenwillow, 1989, 18 pp. Because it is spring, Pit and Pat are as happy as can be. They show their exuberance by bragging about their jumping ability. IL: 5–7.
Theme/subject: Seasons: coming of spring
Modesitt, Jeanne. *Mama, If You Had a Wish.* Green Tiger Press, 1993, 26 pp. Little Bunny asks Mama if she wishes that he would change in some way. Mama replies that she just wants him to be himself because "I love you just the way you are." IL: 5–7.
Theme/subject: Being oneself; Family: mother and child
Mora, Pat. *Listen to the Desert.* Clarion, 1994, 22 pp. The reader is invited to listen to the sounds of the desert: the call of the coyote, the plip of the rain, the zoom of the wind, the coo of the dove, the plop of the toad. Repeated lines provide opportunities for choral or shared reading. Reinforces phonics: making sounds of animals. Has text in Spanish and English. IL: 6–9.
Theme/subject: Nature: desert life; Multilingual
Morris, Ann. *Shoes Shoes Shoes.* Lothrop, Lee & Shepard, 1995, 29 pp. Shoes come in many styles and are used for a variety of activities: working, playing, dancing, riding horses, walking on ice, and walking on snow. IL: 5–8.
Theme/subject: Clothing: shoes around the world
Moss, Sally. *Peter's Painting.* Mondo, 1995, 24 pp. The more Peter paints, the more his paintings take on lives of their own. The bird he is painting flies; the snake slithers; the fish swim. Finally, Peter leaps into the world he has painted and becomes a part of it. IL: 7–8.
Theme/subject: Art: painting; Supernatural
Mueller, Virginia. *Monster Can't Sleep.* Whitman, 1986, 22 pp. Despite being given warm milk, a kiss good night, and having a story read to him, Monster isn't sleepy. However, after reading to his stuffed spider, giving him warm milk, and a kiss good night, Monster falls asleep. IL: 5–7.
Theme/subject: Bedtime: falling asleep
Neasi, Barbara J. *Just Like Me.* Children's Press, 1984, 30 pp. Twins find that they are alike but different. Reinforces long *e* patterns and comparing and contrasting. IL: 5–7. Available in paperback and big book.
Theme/subject: Peers: twins
Nichol, B. P. *Once: A Lullaby.* Greenwillow, 1986, 22 pp. Illustrated lullaby depicts animals sleeping. Repeated verses provide opportunities for choral singing or reading. IL: 5–7. Available in paperback (Mulberry).
Theme/subject: Song: lullaby; Sleep
Nodset, Joan L. *Who Took the Farmer's Hat?* HarperCollins, 1963, 28 pp. After his favorite hat blows away, the farmer asks the animals if they have seen it. They report seeing a round, brown bird with no wings but didn't realize it was the

farmer's hat. The farmer decides to get a new hat when he finally finds his old hat and discovers that it is being used as a nest. Repeated lines provide opportunities for choral or shared reading. IL: 5–7. Available in paperback.
Theme/subject: Animal homes: bird's nest

Ogburn, Jacqueline K. *The Noise Lullaby.* Lothrop, Lee & Shepard, 1995, 22 pp. A little girl hears all sorts of noises just before she falls to sleep. Fosters phonemic awareness and using phonics to decode nonspeech sounds. IL: 5–7.
Theme/subject: Sleep; Noise

Paxton, Tom. *Going to the Zoo.* Morrow, 1996, 29 pp. A song celebrates a family's visit to the zoo. The father took the children to the zoo and is exhausted at the end of the day. The mother plans to take the children back to the zoo the next day. Repeated lines provide opportunities for choral singing or reading. IL: 6–8.
Theme/subject: Zoo; Song

Raffi. *Down by the Bay.* Crown, 1987, 32 pp. A song celebrates silly rhymes: "Did you ever see a whale with a polka-dot tail, Down by the bay?" Lends itself to choral singing or reading. Reinforces rhyme and long *a* and long *o* patterns. Part of Raffi Songs to Read series. IL: 5–8. Available in paperback.
Theme/subject: Song; Silly rhymes

Raffi. *Shake My Sillies Out.* Crown, 1987, 32 pp. Forest animals, children, and grown-ups sing a song. Repeated lines provide opportunities for choral singing or reading about shaking their sillies out and wiggling their waggles away. Part of Raffi Songs to Read series. IL: 5–8. Available in paperback.
Theme/subject: Song

Raffi. *One Light, One Sun.* Crown, 1988, 32 pp. In this traditional song, the sun gives light and warmth to everyone. Lends itself to choral singing or reading. Part of Raffi Songs to Read series. IL: 5–8. Available in paperback.
Theme/subject: Song; Sun

Rockwell, Anne. *Sweet Potato Pie.* Random House, 1996, 32 pp. When Grandma bakes a sweet potato pie, all activity comes to a halt. Sis stops swinging, Tom stops swimming. Gramps stops chopping. They all head for the pie. Repeated lines provide opportunities for choral or shared reading. Reinforces short vowel patterns. IL: 5–8. Available in paperback.
Theme/subject: Family life; Food: pie

Serfozo, Mary. *Who Said Red?* Simon & Schuster, 1988, 28 pp. In response to the question, "Who said red?" two children explore the primary colors. Reinforces color words. Repeated lines provide opportunities for choral or shared reading. IL: 5–7. Available in paperback (Aladdin).
Theme/subject: Colors

Dr. Seuss. *The Foot Book.* Random House, 1968, 28 pp. Humorously depicts feet. Reinforces short *i* patterns. IL: 5–9.
Theme/subject: Word play; Feet; Humor

Shiefman, Vicky. *Sunday Potatoes, Monday Potatoes.* Simon & Schuster, 1994, 20 pp. Day after day a family eats potatoes. They grow tired of potatoes until they are served potato pudding. Can be used with older students. IL: 6–9.
Theme/subject: Eating; Humor; Poverty

Smith, Mavis. *Look Out.* Puffin, 1991, 16 pp. In this lift-the-flap book, a young boy gives a soccer ball such a powerful kick that it smashes through the window, knocks over a clothes tree, knocks over a can of paint, crashes into a vase, and

bounces into his brother's bowl of cereal before landing in the toy box. IL: 6–8.
Paperback.

Theme/subject: Parents and children; Soccer

Snow, Pegeen. *Eat Your Peas, Louise.* Children's Press, 1993, 30 pp. Parent pleads with
a reluctant Louise to eat her peas. Nothing works—neither threats nor bribery—
until he says "Please." Reinforces long *e* patterns. IL: 5–7. Available in paperback.

Theme/subject: Family life: dinnertime; Eating one's dinner

Sweet, Melissa. *Fiddle-I-Fee, A Farmyard Song for the Very Young.* Little, Brown, 1992,
25 pp. In this traditional song, barnyard animals are celebrated. Repeated lines
provide opportunities for choral singing or reading. IL: 5–8. Available in paperback.

Theme/subject: Traditional song; Farm animals

Tafuri, Nancy. *The Brass Ring.* Greenwillow, 1996, 30 pp. Now that she is no longer little, a young girl can have more fun on family vacations. She can float on her
back, ride her bike, and reach for the brass ring on the carousel. Writing topic:
Things I can do now that I am bigger. IL: 5–7.

Theme/subject: Growing up; Vacation; Beach

Tolstoy, Alexei. *The Great Big Enormous Turnip.* Franklin Watts, 1968, 28 pp. A farmer
grows a turnip so enormous that he needs the help of his family, pets, and a little
mouse to pull it up. Because of repeated sentences, this book lends itself to
shared or choral reading. IL: 5–8.

Theme/subject: Folktale; Cooperation

Vaughn, Marcia. *Hands Hands Hands.* Mondo, 1986, 1995, 16 pp. Children show what
they can do with their hands: tug, hug, feel eels, tickle tiny toes, plant, pick.
Reinforces long *e* and short vowel patterns. IL: 5–7.

Theme/subject: Hands

Waddell, Martin. *Squeak-A-Lot.* Greenwillow, 1991, 29 pp. Seeking a friend, a mouse
met a bee, who wanted to play buzz-a-lot, a dog who wanted to play woof-a-lot,
a chicken who wanted to play cluck-a-lot. Not wanting to play any of those, the
mouse finally met mice who wanted to play all of the games plus squeak-a-lot.
Reinforces short *u* patterns. Repeated lines provide opportunities for choral or
shared reading. IL: 5–7.

Theme/subject: Play; Establishing one's identity

Walsh, Ellen Stoll. *Hop Jump.* Harcourt, 1993, 26 pp. Frogs, who spend much of their
time hopping and jumping, are introduced to dancing by Betsy Frog. Reinforces
long *e* patterns. IL: 5–7.

Theme/subject: Individuality; Tolerance of others; Dancing

Walsh, Ellen Stoll. *Pip's Magic.* Harcourt, 1994, 29 pp. Afraid of the dark, Pip the lizard seeks help from Araba, the wizard. To find Araba, Pip must travel through
the dark forest, a tunnel, and over the hills at night. By the time he finds Araba,
Pip has conquered his fear by venturing into a number of dark places. Because it
has a significant amount of conversation, lends itself to a readers' theater presentation. IL: 6–8.

Theme/subject: Conquering fears: fear of darkness

West, Colin. *One Day in the Jungle.* Candlewick, 1995, 16 pp. A butterfly in the jungle
sneezes and starts a chain of sneeezes by a lizard, a parrot, a monkey, a tiger, a
hippo, and, finally, an elephant. Each sneeze is bigger than the preceding one,

until the elephant's is so gigantic that it blows away the jungle. Includes adjectives of increasing intensity: *big, enormous, gigantic.* IL: 6–8.
Theme/subject: Sneezes; Tall tale; Chain tale

West, Colin. *"I Don't Care!" Said the Bear.* Candlewick, 1996, 27 pp. A mouse warns a bear that some animals are following him. These include a moose on the loose, a bad-tempered goose, and a pig who is big. At first, the bear says that he doen't care, but he changes his mind. Repeated lines provide opportunities for choral or shared reading. IL: 5–8.
Theme/subject: Listening to others; Humor

Wheeler, Cindy. *Marmalade's Nap.* Knopf, 1983, 21 pp. Marmalade, the cat, finds a quiet place to take a nap. Part of Marmalade series. IL: 5–7.
Theme/subject: Nap; Quiet

Wildsmith, Brian. *Brian Wildsmith's Puzzles.* Franklin Watts, 1971, 28 pp. The reader is asked a series of questions that are answered by a careful examination of the illustrations: What is this donkey carrying in his basket? How many animals can you see in this picture? Fosters answering question and carefully examining illustrations. IL: 5–8.
Theme/subject: Puzzles: picture

Yoshi. *The Butterfly Hunt.* Picturebook Studio, 1990, 24 pp. A young boy goes to great lengths to capture a butterfly but then sets it free. Having freed the butterfly, it became forever and ever "his very own." IL: 6–9. Available in paperback.
Theme/subject: Freedom; Capturing creatures

BEGINNING A PLUS

Anholt, Catherine. *Good Days Bad Days.* Putnam, 1991, 24 pp. Pictures and text show the kinds of days on which a family might have: fun days, snowy days, sick days, school days, and so on. Reinforces short *i* patterns. IL: 5–7. Out of print.
Theme/subject: Family life

Asch, Frank. *Water.* Harcourt, 1995, 25 pp. Depicts what water is : "Water is rain. Water is dew. Water is salty tears." Could provide a model for writing. IL: 6–8.
Theme/subject: Water

Austin, Virginia. *Say Please.* Candlewick, 1994, 26 pp. *Please* and *thank you* are magical words, which, according to the author, even animals use. When they say "Woof, woof" or "Oink, oink," they are really saying "please" or "thank you." IL: 5–7.
Theme/subject: Communication: animals; Manners

Baker, Alan. *White Rabbit's Color Book.* Kingfisher Books, 1994, 22 pp. A white rabbit demonstrates how primary colors are mixed to produce secondary hues by dipping himself in tubs of red, yellow, and blue paint. In the end, he mixes red, yellow, and blue paint and ends up brown, which is just the color he wanted to be. IL: 5–7.
Theme/subject: Colors

Brown, Craig. *City Sounds.* Greenwillow, 1992, 24 pp. This book depicts the sounds that Farmer Brown hears as he comes into the city to pick up some baby chicks. Reinforces long *e* patterns. Promotes use of phonics skills to decode city sounds. IL: 5–7.
Theme/subject: City: sounds of

Brown, Craig. *In the Spring*. Greenwillow, 1994, 24 pp. In the spring, the farm animals have babies, and the farmer's wife has twins. Reinforces short *i* patterns. IL: 5–7.
Theme/subject: Birth; Babies: animal and people

Browne, Anthony. *I Like Books*. Knopf, 1989, 18 pp. A young monkey talks about and shows the kinds of books he likes: fairy tales, nursery rhymes, comic books, coloring books, song books, books about space, and so on. Provides a model writing format and a topic: composing a similar booklet. IL: 6–7. Out of print.
Theme/subject: Interests; Books

Browne, Anthony. *Things I Like*. Knopf, 1989, 18 pp. A young monkey talks about all the things he likes: painting, riding his bike, playing, hiding, dressing up, building sandcastles, and so on. Provides writing format and topic: composing a similar booklet. IL: 5–7. Out of print.
Theme/subject: Personal preferences

Butterworth, Nick, & Inkpen, Mick. *Just Like Jasper*. Little, Brown, 1989, 28 pp. At the toy store, Jasper decides to buy a stuffed cat that looks just like him. Reinforces short vowel patterns. Part of Jasper the Cat series. IL: 5–7. Out of print.
Theme/subject: Toys: stuffed animals

Butterworth, Nick, & Inkpen, Mick. *Jasper's Beanstalk*. Bradbury. Little, Brown, 1993, 24 pp. Jasper's beanstalk finally grows. Now he is waiting for a giant to appear. Introduces names of days of the week. Part of Jasper the Cat series. IL: 5–7.
Theme/subject: Humor; Gardening

Calhoun, Mary. *While I Sleep*. Morrow, 1992, 30 pp. Answering the questions of a child who is getting ready for bed, a mother and a father tell where a squirrel, a bird, a bear, a horse, a fish, a fox, a cat, boats, a train, a plane, and the sun sleep. Repeated lines provide opportunities for choral or shared reading. IL: 5–7.
Theme/subject: Sleep: animals and people; Bedtime

Cobb, Annie. *Wheels*. Random House, 1996, 32 pp. Many kinds of wheels and some of the uses of wheels are depicted: wheels on bikes, cars, and trucks, and wheels on shopping carts and skates. Gear wheels, a steering wheel, and a paddle wheel are also shown. IL: 6–7.
Theme/subject: Wheels

Crews, Donald. *Freight Train*. Greenwillow, 1978, 22 pp. A freight train moves across the land through a tunnel, over a trestle, and past a city. The reader may need help identifying the following words: *freight, gondola, hopper, tank, trestle*. IL: 5–7.
Available in paperback and big book.
Theme/subject: Transportation: trains

Dodds, Dayle Ann. *Shape of Things to Come*. Candlewick, 1994, 16 pp. Shows how basic shapes can be made into various items. A square, for instance, becomes a house when a roof, two windows, and a door are added. Lends itself to choral, shared, or partner reading. IL: 5–7.
Theme/subject: Shapes

Donnelly, Liza. *Dinosaur Days*. Scholastic, 1987, 30 pp. While pretending that mounds of snow are dinosaurs, a boy and his dog find a monster dinosaur. Contains a glossary of dinosaur names phonetically respelled. IL: 6–9. Available in paperback.
Theme/subject: Dinosaurs; Fantasy

Emberley, Ed. *Go Away, Big Green Monster*. Little, Brown, 1992, 30 pp. By turning pages that have cutouts, the reader assembles a big green monster and then dis-

assembles it. Reinforces *s* clusters: *scraggly, squiggley.* IL: 5–7.
Theme/subject: Monsters
Fleming, Denise. *Count.* Holt, 1992, 30 pp. In this counting book, zebras jump, kanga-
roos bounce, worms wiggle, fish swim, and lizards line up. The reader may need
help identifying the following words: *gnu, toucans.* IL: 5–7. Available in paperback.
Theme/subject: Counting; Animals
Florian, Douglas. *A Beach Day.* Greenwillow, 1990, 32 pp. Captioned text shows and
tells how a family spends a day at the beach.
Theme/subject: Family life; Beach
Gomi, Taro. *Who Ate It?* Millbrook Press, 1991, 22 pp. The reader is asked who ate the
cherries, strawberries, eggs, donuts, and other foods. The answer is provided by
a visual clue. The food can be seen in the creature that ate it. Repeated lines provide opportunities for choral or shared reading. Fosters using picture clues.
IL: 5–7. Available in paperback.
Theme/subject: Games/activities; Using visual clues; Visual riddles
Janina, Domanska. *Busy Monday Morning.* Greenwillow, 1985, 30 pp. In this Polish
folk song, a boy and his father mow, rake, dry, pitch, stack, and haul hay during
the week but rest on Sunday. Long repeated verses provide opportunities for
choral singing or reading. IL: 5–9.
Theme/subject: Folk song; Farming; Parent and child working together
Janovitz, Marilyn. *Is It Time?* North-South Books, 1994, 24 pp. A young wolf ask a
series of rhyming questions that lead up to going to sleep: Is it time to run the
tub? Is it time to brush my fangs? Is it time to go to sleep? Reinforces short vowel
patterns. Repeated lines provide opportunities for choral or shared reading. Provides practice with sequence. IL: 5–7.
Theme/subject: Getting ready for bed
Koch, Michelle. *Hoot Howl Hiss.* Greenwillow, 1991, 22 pp. Words and illustrations
depict sounds that animals make. The reader may need help identifying the following words: *bleat, marmots.* Decoding skills are needed to help decipher captions that go with the illustrations. IL: 6–8.
Theme/subject: Animals: where they live, sounds they make
Kulman, Andrew. *Red Light Stop, Green Light Go.* Simon & Schuster, 1993, 24 pp.
Except for police cars and fire engines, which sometimes hurry through, everyone waits at stop lights: all kinds of cars, trucks, and even skate boards. But
when the light turns green, no one waits. IL: 5–7.
Theme/subject: Traffic: stop lights
Leman, Jill, & Leman, Martin. *Sleepy Kittens.* Tambourne, 1993, 24 pp. The kittens nap
on the table, in the sock drawer, on Granny's hat, and just about anywhere else,
except in their special box. The reader may need help identifying the following
words: *hearth, snuggling.* IL: 5–7.
Theme/subject: Pets: kittens
Maccarone, Grace. *Oink! Moo! How Do You Do?* Scholastic, 1994, 20 pp. Various
animals gather for a feast when a truckload of produce overturns. IL: 6–8.
Paperback.
Theme/subject: Animals; Animal sounds
Maris, Ron. *I Wish I Could Fly.* Greenwillow, 1986, 30 pp. After trying to fly, run, dive,
and climb, Turtle learns to appreciate his own abilities. Repeated lines provide

opportunities for choral or shared reading. IL: 5–7. Available in paperback (Mulberry).
Theme/subject: Being oneself

McDonnell, Flora. *I Love Animals.* Candlewick, 1994, 24 pp. Drawing and words show why a little girl loves all animals. The reader may need help identifying the following words: *strutting, bleating, braying.* Repeated lines provide opportunities for choral or shared reading. Provides a model for writing. IL: 6–7.
Theme/subject: Animals

McMillan, Bruce. *Kitten Can.* Lothrop, Lee & Shepard, 1984, 24 pp. Text and full-color photos show the things a kitten can do: stare, sniff, hide, stalk. Provides practice with initial *s* clusters. IL: 5–7.
Theme/subject: Cats: kittens

McMillan, Bruce. *Puffins Climb, Penguins Rhyme.* Harcourt, 1995, 30 pp. Vivid color photos and rhyming captions describe puffins and penguins. The reader may need help identifying the following words: *preen, peer, brawl.* Provides model for writing. IL: 6–7.
Theme/subject: Animals: puffins, penguins

Miller, Margaret. *Guess Who.* Greenwillow, 1994, 36 pp. Asks a series of questions about who does what: Who cuts your hair? Who makes your bread? After showing silly possibilities (a giraffe, a juggler, an artist, a potter), the correct answer is revealed by showing a captioned photo. The reader may need help identifying the following words: *mechanic, photographer.* IL: 5–7.
Theme/subject: Community helpers

Miller, Margaret. *My Five Senses.* Simon & Schuster, 1994, 22 pp. Children show how they use their five senses: "With my nose I smell popcorn, a horse, flowers, and garbage." IL: 5–7.
Theme/subject: Senses

Morris, Neil. *I'm Big, A Fun Book of Opposites.* Carolrhoda, 1990, 26 pp. Opposites are portrayed in the context of pairs of sentences: "I'm tall!" cries the giraffe. "I'm short," says the boy. IL: 5–7. Available in paperback.
Theme/subject: Word study; Opposites

Noll, Sally. *Watch Where You Go.* Greenwillow, 1990, 30 pp. Although ignoring the warnings of a dragonfly, a field mouse dashes over a series of dangerous animals to safety. Repeated lines provide opportunities for choral or shared reading. IL: 5–7.
Theme/subject: Animals: escape from enemies

Norworth, Jack. *Take Me Out to the Ballgame.* Four Winds, 1993, 32 pp. This book illustrates the lyrics to a popular baseball song. Some knowledge of baseball is required. Repeated lines provide opportunities for choral singing or reading. IL: 6–12.
Theme/subject: Sports: baseball; Song

Novak, Matt. *Elmer Blunt's Open House.* Orchard, 1992, 22 pp. Having overslept, Elmer Blunt rushes to work, leaving his door open. Wild animals walk into his home and are having a good time until a thief walks in. The thief runs out of the house when he discovers the animals. IL: 6–9.
Theme/subject: Helping others; Humor

Parnall, Peter. *Feet!* Simon & Schuster, 1988, 26 pp. Words and drawings depict the feet of 18 animals and a human child. This book fosters interpreting drawings and

drawing conclusions based on visual clues. Promotes active engagement. IL: 6–9.
Theme/subject: Animals: feet

Paschkis, Julie. *So Sleepy, So Wide Awake.* Holt, 1994, 32 pp. Printed in opposite directions, one portion of the book depicts animals who are sleeping; turn the book over, and it depicts animals who are wide awake. The reader may need help identifying the following words: *slithers, prances, raven.* IL: 5–7.
Theme/subject: Animals: sleep

* Peek, Merle. *Mary Wore Her Red Dress and Henry Wore His Green Sneakers.* Clarion, 1985, 22 pp. In this traditional song, Mary Squirrel and a series of other characters wear a distinctively colored article of clothing to Katy Bear's birthday party. Repeats the refrain: "Mary wore her red dress, red dress, red dress, Mary wore her red dress all day long." Lends itself to shared reading or singing. Students can also add verses. Highly recommended. IL: 5–10. Available in paperback.
Theme/subject: Traditional song; Birthday party

Phillips, Joan. *Tiger Is a Scaredy Cat.* Random House, 1986, 32 pp. Although afraid of mice, dogs, trucks, and vacuum cleaners, Tiger overcomes his fear by rescuing a baby mouse. IL: 5–7. Available in paperback.
Theme/subject: Overcoming fears

Pirotta, Saviour. *Little Bird.* Tambourine, 1992, 32 pp. When she asks her friends what she should do, Little Bird is told to jump, gallop, roll, and do other unbirdlike tasks, until, finally, her mother suggests that she fly. IL: 5–7.
Theme/subject: Using one's abilities; Being oneself

Pomerantz, Charlotte. *Flap Your Wings and Try.* Greenwillow, 1989, 22 pp. Wondering when he'll be able to fly, a baby bird is advised to flap his wings and try. Because of repeated lines, the book lends itself to choral or shared reading. IL: 5–7.
Theme/subject: Learning new skills; Birds; Growing up

Raffi. *Everything Grows.* Crown, 1989, 28 pp. This song celebrates the growth of babies, animals, sisters, brothers, plants, mamas, and papas, too. Words are illustrated with Bruce McMillan's color photos. Could be used as a model for a writing activity: assembling a photo album showing child's growth and writing captions to go with the photos. IL: 5–8. Available in paperback.
Theme/subject: Growing up

Raffi. *Tingalayo.* Crown, 1989, 30 pp. In this traditional Calypso song, the donkey Tingaylo, after working all day, is persuaded by a little girl to have some fun. Tingalayo dances, sings, and goes swimming. Lends itself to shared, partner, or choral reading or singing. IL: 5–9.
Theme/subject: Traditional song; Balancing work and play

Raffi. *Spider on the Floor.* Crown, 1993, 28 pp. This song tells about a spider that is on the floor and then crawls up the singer's leg, stomach, neck, face, and head. Reinforces short *e* patterns. Lends itself to choral reading or singing. IL: 6–9.
Theme/subject: Song; Spiders; Humor

Rehm, Karl, & Koike, Kay. *Left or Right?* Clarion, 1991, 24 pp. Readers are asked to look at pairs of photos and tell whether a green leaf, spotted cow, or other items can be found in the photo on the left or the one on the right. Fosters noting visual details. IL: 5–7.
Theme/subject: Left and right

* Reiser, Lynn. *Any Kind of Dog.* Greenwillow, 1992, 20 pp. Saying that a dog was too much trouble, Richard's mother gets him a variety of other pets, including an

alligator, a pony, and a bear, until she finally changes her mind. Because of repeated phrases, the book lends itself to shared or choral reading. Highly recommended. IL: 5–9. Available in paperback (Mulberry).
Theme/subject: Pets; Parents; Humor

Rockwell, Anne. *Boats.* Dutton, 1982, 22 pp. Drawings and brief captions depict a variety of boats and some of the ways in which boats are used. Reinforces long vowel patterns. IL: 6–8. Available in paperback (Puffin).
Theme/subject: Transportation: boats

Rockwell, Anne. *Cars.* Dutton, 1984, 22 pp. Drawings and brief captions depict a variety of cars and some of the ways in which cars are used. IL: 5–8. Available in paperback (Puffin).
Theme/subject: Transportation: cars

Rockwell, Anne. *Willy Can Count.* Arcade, 1989, 24 pp. While on a walk with his mom, Willy counts the animals that he sees. IL: 5–7.
Theme/subject: Counting; Animals

Roe, Eileen. *All I Am.* Bradbury Press, 1990, 22 pp. A little boy tells about his unique qualities and interests: "I am a friend. I am an artist. I am a dancer." Provides a writing model: I am ___. Reinforces er suffix. IL: 6–7.
Theme/subject: Individuality; Knowledge of self

Roffey, Maureen. *Here, Kitty Kitty.* Random House, 1991, 22 pp. In this peep-through-the-hole book, a little girl tries to find kitty. Every time she thinks she sees kitty's striped body, it turns out to be a sock, a hat, or some other object. Uses conversation balloons. Fosters responding to question: "Have you seen kitty?" IL: 5–7.
Theme/subject: Pet: cat, finding

Rotner, Shelley, & Kreisler, Ken. *Citybook.* Orchard, 1994, 29 pp. Kevin takes a trip to the city where there is much to see: people on the go, window shopping, mimes, music, museums, neon signs, fountains, statue, and much more, all in color photos. The reader may need help identifying the following words: *neon signs, photos.* IL: 5–8.
Theme/subject: City life

Runcie, Jill. *Cock-a-Doodle-Doo.* Simon & Schuster, 1991, 30 pp. Although the farmer gives the rooster credit for awakening him each morning, it is actually a chain of events involving a number of farm animals that are responsible for rousing the farmer. The farmer's snoring awakens the owl, who wakes up the woodpecker, and on and on until the dog wakes the rooster who begins crowing. Reinforces sequence. IL: 5–8. Out of print.
Theme/subject: Sleep: waking up; Animal noises; Humor

Russo, Marisabina. *Time to Wake Up.* Greenwillow, 1994, 22 pp. Mother wakes up her son and, with tenderness and good humor, persuades him to get ready for school. Fosters comprehension of sequence of getting ready. Provides possible writing topic: getting ready for school. IL: 5–8.
Theme/subject: School: getting ready for

Sheppard, Jeff. *Splash, Splash.* Simon & Schuster, 1994, 40 pp. Different animals react in different ways when they fall into the water. Has repeated lines. Good for shared reading. IL: 5–7.
Theme/subject: Animals

Sill, Cathryn. *About Birds: A Guide for Children.* Peachtree, 1991, 30 pp. In brief text and illustrations, some major characteristics and behaviors of birds are depicted. IL: 6–9.
Theme/subject: Animals: birds

Stickland, Paul. *All about Trucks*. Gareth Stevens, 1988, 16 pp. Brief text and color illustrations depict a variety of trucks and the jobs they do. IL: 5–8.
Theme/subject: Transportation: trucks

Stobbs, William. *There's a Hole in My Bucket*. Oxford University Press, 1982, 24 pp. A song tells about a young man who can't fix the hole in his bucket because he can't get water needed to wet the straw that will plug up the hole. Good for choral or shared singing or reading. IL: 5–9.
Theme/subject: Song; Solving problems; Humor

Testa, Fulvio. *If You Take a Paintbrush: A Book of Colors*. Dial, 1982, 24 pp. Colors are described in illustrations and statements: "Blue is the color of the sea." Provides a writing model and topic idea. IL: 5–7. Available in paperback.
Theme/subject: Colors

Truus, Jan. *What Kouka Knows*. Lothrop, Lee & Shepard, 1992, 24 pp. Kouka is afraid that if he goes to the donkey's tea party, he won't have time to teach the cat to fly. If he helps the cat, he won't have time to play hide-and-seek with the frog. The list of conflicts goes on and on. At last, Kouka thinks of a good solution to the problem. Fosters problem solving. IL: 5–7.
Theme/subject: Friends: finding time for

Walter, Virginia. *"Hi, Pizza Man!"* Orchard, 1995, 30 pp. A little girl imagines who, beside the pizza man, might deliver the pizza. She imagines a pizza duck, a pizza cat, and other unlikely delivery creatures. Fosters predicting who might deliver pizza. IL: 6–8.
Theme/subject: Delivery; Humor

Wang, Mary Lewis. *The Ant and the Dove*. Children's Press, 1989, 32 pp. After being saved by a dove, a grateful ant comes to the dove's rescue. IL: 5–8. Available in paperback.
Theme/subject: Fable

West, Colin. *"Pardon?" Said the Giraffe*. HarperCollins, 1986, 16 pp. Getting higher and higher by hopping up on animals of increasing size, Frog asks the giraffe, "What's it like up there?" Giraffe's response is as funny as it is unexpected. Because it has two speaking parts, this book fosters shared, partner, or choral reading. IL: 6–7. Available in paperback.
Theme/subject: Giraffes; Manners: asking rude questions; Humor

Wildsmith, Brian, & Wildsmith, Rebecca. *Wake Up, Wake Up*. Harcourt, 1993, 16 pp. Rooster starts a chain reaction by waking one animal who wakes up another animal and so on until the last animal wakes up the farmer, who feeds them all. Provides practice with cause-effect relationships. IL: 6–7. Available in paperback.
Theme/subject: Farm; Cumulative tale

Wolff, Ashley. *A Year of Beasts*. Dutton, 1986, 26 pp. Illustrations and brief captions depict animals and a human family for each month of the year. IL: 6–7.
Theme/subject: Animals; Months of the year

Ziefert, Harriet. *Sleepy Dog*. Random House, 1984, 32 pp. Sleepy puppy goes to bed, falls asleep, dreams, and awakens in the morning. IL: 5–7. Available in paperback.
Theme/subject: Bedtime; Parents

Ziefert, Harriet. *Say Good Night*. Viking Kestrel, 1987, 30 pp. Hearing her mom and dad, say "Good night" and "Good morning," a little girl wonders what is good about night and morning. Provides possible writing topic: writing about what's good about night or morning. IL: 6–7. Available in paperback (Puffin).

Theme/subject: Sleep; Night and morning

Zinnemann-Hope, Pam. *Let's Go Shopping, Ned.* Margaret K. McElderry Books, 1986, 24 pp. Ned and his dog Fred create chaos when they go shopping with Ned's dad. Part of Ned series. IL: 6–7. Out of print.

Theme/subject: Shopping; Humor

Zinnemann-Hope, Pam. *Let's Play Ball, Ned.* Margaret K. McElderry Books, 1987, 24 pp. Ned and his dog Fred have fun playing ball but wreck the house. Part of Ned series. IL: 6–7. Out of print.

Theme/subject: Playing; Humor

BEGINNING B

Aldis, Dorothy. *Hiding.* Viking, 1993, 30 pp. Benny's parents search for him, but Benny has made himself so small that they can't find him until he becomes his regular size. IL: 6–8.

Theme/subject: Parents; Fantasy

Alexander, Martha. *You're a Genius, Blackboard Bear.* Candlewick, 1995, 22 pp. After a boy's father reads him a book about the moon, the boy and Blackboard Bear build a spaceship to take them to the moon. Part of Blackboard Bear series. IL: 6–7.

Theme/subject: Moon; Fantasy: imaginary friends

Aliki. *Hush Little Baby.* Simon & Schuster, no date, 30 pp. In this illustrated version of a traditional lullaby, papa promises to buy a series of items. Repeated lines provide opportunities for choral singing or reading. IL: 6–9.

Theme/subject: Song: lullaby

Aliki. *My Five Senses.* Crowell, 1962, 1989, 32 pp. A small boy explains how he uses each of his senses individually and how he uses two or more at a time. As he explains, his senses "make me aware." IL: 6–7. Available in paperback.

Theme/subject: Senses

Anholt, Catherine, & Anholt, Laurence. *All about You.* Viking, 1991, 26 pp. A series of questions ask the students to tell about themselves. Possible illustrated answers are included. The reader may need help identifying the following words: *curry, melon, pasta.* Provides preparation for writing an autobiographical piece. Promotes active engagement. IL: 6–7.

Theme/subject: Knowledge of self; Individuality

Arnold, Kataya. *Knock, Knock, Teremok.* North-South, 1994, 24 pp. One after another, beginning with a fly, a series of creatures knocks on the door of the teremok, a hut, and asks to be allowed to live there. By the time bear knocks on the door, there is no room left. When bear attempts to sit on the roof, the house collapses. Students might enjoy acting out the part of each animal. IL: 6–8.

Theme/subject: Russian cumulative folktale

Arnosky, Jim. *Deer at the Brook.* Lothrop, Lee & Shepard, 1986, 24 pp. A family of deer come to a sparkling brook to drink, eat, play, and nap. Brief prose is complemented by Jim Arnosky's realsitic drawings. Part of Nature series. IL: 6–8. Available in paperback (Mulberry).

Theme/subject: Nature: deer

Asch, Frank. *The Last Puppy.* Simon & Schuster, 1980, 24 pp. Overly anxious to be chosen, the runt of the litter is the last to be selected for a home. Reinforces long *o* patterns. IL: 6–9. Available in paperback.
Theme/subject: Pets: selecting

Asch, Frank. *Moongame.* Simon & Schuster, 1984, 28 pp. While playing hide and seek with the moon, Bear is unable to find the moon because it slipped behind the clouds while he was hiding his eyes. Bear is greatly relieved when the moon reappears. Can be used to reinforce cause and effect relationships: why Bear couldn't find the moon. Part of Bear series. IL: 6–7. Available in paperback and big-book format (Scholastic).
Theme/subject: Games: hide and seek; Moon

Averill, Esther. *Fire Cat.* HarperCollins, 1960, 64 pp. Although given a home by Mrs. Goodkind, Pickles, a mischievous cat, runs away and becomes the mascot at a nearby fire house. IL: 6–9. Available in paperback.
Theme/subject: Mascots; Firefighters

Bang, Molly. *Delphine.* Morrow, 1988, 24 pp. Delphine worries about her ability to handle a two-wheel bike. Reinforces long *o* patterns. IL: 6–7.
Theme/subject: Bicycles: learning to ride

Barton, Byron. *Dinosaurs, Dinosaurs.* Crowell, 1989, 36 pp. This book shows some of the dinosaurs that inhabited the earth. IL: 6–8. Available in paperback.
Theme/subject: Dinosaurs

Barton, Byron. *The Little Red Hen.* HarperCollins, 1993, 28 pp. In this version of the classic tale, the other animals refuse to help Hen grow wheat and bake bread, so she and her three little chicks eat the bread all by themselves. Reinforces long *e* patterns. Repeated lines provide opportunities for choral or shared reading. Can be compared/contrasted with other versions. IL: 6–8.
Theme/subject: Work: sharing work leads to sharing rewards

Bender, Robert. *The Preposterous Rhinoceeros or Alvin's Beastly Birthday.* Holt, 1994, 24 pp. Upset because no one remembered his birthday, Alvin pays no attention when his mother urges him to look outside because she sees a toad driving down the road and a rhinocerous that looks preposterous. He does perk up when his mom describes a cake-eating snake. Looking out the door, he sees a birthday cake and his friends. Provides opportunities for predicting what will happen. IL: 6–8.
Theme/subject: Birthday; Birthday party

Berends, Polly Berrien. *"I Heard," Said the Bird.* Dial, 1995, 29 pp. Hearing that a new one was coming, the animals wondered what it was. Could it be a duckling or a piglet? Finally, they learn from the boy that the new one is a baby. Repeated lines provide opportunities for choral or shared reading. Offers opportunities for predicting what the new one is. IL: 6–8.
Theme/subject: New baby

* Bonsall, Crosby. *And I Mean It, Stanley.* HarperCollins, 1974, 32 pp. A young girl prepares a surprise for Stanley, whose identity remains a mystery until the end of the story. IL: 6–7. Highly recommended. Available in paperback and audiotape.
Theme/subject: Pets: dogs

Bonsall, Crosby. *Who's Afraid of the Dark?* HarperCollins, 1980, 32 pp. A little girl tells a little boy how to help his dog overcome its fear of the dark. In fact, both the dog and the boy help each other cope with darkness and fear. Readers' theater might be used to dramatize conversations. Provides possible writing topic: fears. IL: 6–7. Available in paperback.

Theme/subject: Pets; Fears: fear of darkness

Bornstein, Ruth. *Little Gorilla*. Clarion, 1976, 28 pp. All the creatures in the jungle love Little Gorilla, but then Little Gorilla grows and grows until he is big, so the creatures throw a birthday party for him. IL: 6–7. Available in paperback.

Theme/subject: Growing up; Birthdays

Bornstein, Ruth Lercher. *Rabbit's Good News*. Clarion Books, 1995, 28 pp. A baby rabbit discovers that spring has arrived. Reinforces *r* vowel patterns. IL: 6–7.

Theme/subject: Seasons: spring

Brenner, Barbara. *Annie's Pet*. Bantam, 1989, 32 pp. While searching for a suitable pet to buy, Annie spends all her money but still manages to obtain a pet puppy. IL: 6–8. Available in paperback.

Theme/subject: Pets: obtaining a pet

Brenner, Barbara. *Too Many Mice*. Bantam, 1992, 32 pp. When their house is overrun by mice, Nita calls in neighborhood cats to help out, but then their house is overrun by dogs and then alligators. Finally, an elephant scares off the alligators but is wrecking the home. The story comes full circle as Nita suggests getting a mouse to scare off the elephant. Reinforces sequence, cause-effect, and solving problems. Provides possible writing topic: solving problems. IL: 6–8. Available in paperback.

Theme/subject: Solving problems with solutions that are worse than the problems; Humor

Brisson, Pat. *Benny's Pennies*. Doubleday, 1993, 28 pp. Spending his five pennies wisely, Benny is able to buy his mother something beautiful, his brother something good to eat, and his sister something to wear. He is even able to buy a treat for his dog and one for his cat. Reinforces comprehending sequence and main idea/details. Could also be dramatized through readers' theater. IL: 6–8.

Theme/subject: Cumulative tale; Gifts: buying; Thoughtfulness

Brown, Rick. *Who Built the Ark?* Viking, 1994, 15 pp. A song describes the building of Noah's ark and how the animals came aboard: "Now in come the animals two by two, Hippopotamus and kangaroo." The reader may need help identifying the following words: *hickory, hew*. Repeated lines provide opportunities for choral singing or reading. IL: 6–10.

Theme/subject: Biblical selection: Noah's Ark; Song

Buckley, Helen E. *Grandfather and I*. Lothrop, Lee & Shepard, 1994, 22 pp. A young boy enjoys being with his grandfather because they never have to hurry. There is time to stop and look just as long as you like. Repeated lines provide opportunities for choral or shared reading. IL: 5–7.

Theme/subject: Grandparents

Bucknall, Caroline. *One Bear All Alone: A Counting Book*. Bucknall, 1985, 20 pp. This counting rhyme depicts the activities of a group of bears from morning until bedtime: "Ten tired bears have gone to bed. Can you count each sleepy head?" IL: 6–7. Available in paperback.

Theme/subject: Counting; Daily activities

Burningham, John. *Aldo*. Crown, 1991, 30 pp. When lonely or feeling sad, a little girl spends time with Aldo, an imaginary rabbit. IL: 6–7.

Theme/subject: Imaginary friend; Loneliness

Calemenson, Stephanie. *It Begins with an A.* Hyperion, 1993, 28 pp. Readers use picture and verbal clues and the beginning letter to guess the identity of a series of 26 items, each of which starts with a different letter of the alphabet: "You travel in this. It begins with an A. It starts on the ground, then flies up, up, and away." Reinforces using context and initial letters. IL: 5–7. Available in paperback.
Theme/subject: Riddles; Using clues to solve riddles

Carle, Eric. *The Secret Birthday Message.* HarperCollins, 1971, 22 pp. With the help of cutouts, the reader follows Tim as he follows directions in a secret message. Reinforces predicting and following directions. IL: 6–8. Available in paperback.
Theme/subject: Birthdays; Secret messages

Carle, Eric. *Today Is Monday.* Philomel, 1993, 18 pp. Touting a different food for each day, a song urges hungry children to come and eat up: "Today is Monday, today is Monday, Monday, string beans, All you hungry children, Come and eat it up." Repeated lines provide opportunities for choral singing or reading. IL: 5–7.
Theme/subject: Food; Song

Carle, Eric. *Little Cloud.* Philomel, 1996, 24 pp. Little Cloud drifts away from the other clouds and takes various shapes: a sheep, airplane, two trees, and even a cloud. Rejoining the other clouds, Little Cloud helps create rain. IL: 6–8.
Theme/subject: Clouds

Carlson, Judy. *Here Comes Kate!* Raintree, 1989, 31 pp. A reckless wheelchair driver, Kate is forever knocking over things, ruining flower gardens, and even smashing into the birdhouse that her brother just put up. With her mom's help, Kate learns when to go fast and when to go slow. She also becomes interested in wheelchair racing. IL: 6–9. Available in paperback.
Theme/subject: Disabilities: wheelchairs

Carter, Penny. *A New House for the Morrisons.* Viking, 1993, 32 pp. After looking at new homes that are too old, too small, or too big, the Morrisons, a family of alligators, decide that they like their old home best of all. IL: 6–9.
Theme/subject: Home; Appreciating what one has

Coffelt, Nancy. *Good Night, Sigmund.* Harcourt, 1992, 26 pp. Accompanied by Sigmund the cat, a little boy tells about his day, from getting out of bed through going to bed. Sigmund is humorously depicted in every illustration of the boy's activities. Reinforces sequencing. Repeated lines provide opportunities for choral or shared reading. IL: 6–8.
Theme/subject: Pet: cat; Daily activities

Coulter, Hope Norman. *Uncle Chuck's Truck.* Bradbury, 1993, 24 pp. Uncle Chuck takes his young nephew along as he drives around the farm feeding the cows. IL: 6–7.
Theme/subject: Farm: feeding animals

Cousins, Lucy. *Za-Za's Baby Brother.* Candlewick, 1995. After her little brother is born, Za-Za, the zebra, doesn't get as much attention. But Za-Za discovers that it's fun to play with the baby, and there is time for a hug and a story after the baby is put to bed. IL: 6–7.
Theme/subject: New baby

Dale, Nora. *The Best Trick of All.* Raintree, 1989, 22 pp. Circus clowns show their tricks. Each clown claims that his or hers is best. Repeated lines provide opportunities for choral or shared reading. Clowns tricks can be compared/contrasted. IL: 6–7. Available in paperback.
Theme/subject: Circus: clowns; Clown tricks

de Brunhoff, Laurent. *Babar's Little Circus Story.* Random House, 1988, 32 pp. Although too little to do most of the things that bigger children do, Isabelle the elephant is just the right size to be a circus star. Available in paperback. IL: 6–8. Theme/subject: Circus; Appreciating and using one's talents

Demi. *Find Demi's Sea Creatures.* Putnam & Grosset, 1991, 36 pp. The reader is invited to find drawings of a variety of sea creatures. Fosters careful analysis of illustrations. IL: 6–9.
Theme/subject: Sea creatures; Endangered animals

Dobkin, Bonnie. *Just a Little Different.* Children's Press, 1993, 30 pp. Although Josh is confined to a wheelchair, he and his friend have much in common. They both like computers, Frisbee, monster movies, music, and swimming. Offers opportunities for comparison/contrast of two boys. IL: 6–9. Available in paperback.
Theme/subject: Friendship; Disabilities: wheelchair

Donnelly, Liza. *Dinosaur Beach.* Scholastic, 1989, 30 pp. While at the beach, Rex and his dog Bones hop a ride on a prehistoric marine reptile who takes them to dinosaur beach where the two meet a variety of prehistoric creatures. Has glossary of dinosaur names phonetically respelled. Part of Dinosaur series. IL: 6–9. Paperback.
Theme/subject: Dinosaurs; Return to past; Humor

Donnelly, Liza. *Dinosaur Garden.* Scholastic, 1990, 28 pp. Rex and his dog are transported into the land of the dinosaurs when they attempt to plant a dinosaur garden. Chased by an angry tyranosaurus, the two are carried back to their garden by a flying reptile. Has glossary of dinosaur names phonetically respelled. Part of Dinosaur series. IL: 6–9. Paperback.
Theme/subject: Dinosaurs; Return to past; Humor

Dorros, Arthur. *Alligator Shoes.* Puffin, 1982, 22 pp. Locked in a shoe store overnight, Alvin Alligator tries on many different kinds of shoes but eventually decides that alligator feet are better than alligator shoes. IL: 6–9. Available in paperback.
Theme/subject: Clothes: shoes; Humor

Dunbar, Joyce. *A Cake for Barney.* Orchard, 1987, 30 pp. Each time Barney starts to eat his cake, someone demands a piece of it. Repeated lines provide opportunities for choral or shared reading. IL: 5–7.
Theme/subject: Being tricked or bullied out of one's possessions

Dunbar, Joyce. *Seven Sillies.* Western, 1993, 30 pp. Six animals jump in the pond at the urging of Frog so as to free the animals they see there. When they realize that there was nothing in the pond, they feel silly. IL: 6–7.
Theme/subject: Being tricked; Vanity

* Eastman, P. D. *Are You My Mother?* Random House, 1960, 64 pp. A baby bird who falls out of its nest searches for his mother. A series of animals and objects— including a kitten, a cow, dog, a junk car, a tractor, and an airplane—are asked: "Are you my mother?" Repeated lines provide opportunities for choral or shared reading. Highly recommended. IL: 5–7.
Theme/subject: Searching for parent; Humor

* Eastman, P. D. *Go, Dog, Go.* Random House, 1961, 64 pp. Dogs of various sizes and colors are on the go. They are climbing in trees, driving in cars, swimming, flying, working, and playing. At the end, they have a wonderful dog party. Highly recommended. IL: 6–9. Theme/subject: Having fun; Humor

Economos, Chris. *The New Kid.* Raintree, 1989, 30 pp. Short a player, a Little League team allows a chimp to play. IL: 6–9. Available in paperback.
Theme/subject: Baseball: Little League; Animals: chimp

Ehlert, Lois. *Growing Vegetable Soup.* Harcourt, 1987, 30 pp. A vegetable garden is planted, and when the vegtables ripen, they are used to make a delicious soup. IL: 6–8. Available in paperback.
Theme/subject: Gardening: vegetables

Ehlert, Lois. *Fish Eyes: A Book You Can Count On.* Harcourt, 1990, 32 pp. The reader counts a variety of fish: one green fish, two jumping fish, three smiling fish, four striped fish, and so on. Reinforces clusters. Available in paperback. IL: 5–7.
Theme/subject: Counting; Fish

Elting, Mary, & Folsom, Michael. *Q Is for Duck.* Houghton Mifflin, 1980, 60 pp. Readers are invited to guess why A is for Zoo, B is for Dog (Animals live in the zoo, Dog barks), and so forth. The reader may need help identifying the following words: *chamelon, extinct, vanish, coyote.* Fosters making predictions and using initial consonants. IL: 6–8. Available in paperback.
Theme/subject: Language play

Flack, Marjorie. *Ask Mr. Bear.* Simon & Schuster, 1932, 32 pp. Wondering what he should get his mother for her birthday, Danny seeks suggestions from his animal friends. Repeated lines provide opportunities for choral or shared reading. IL: 6–7. Available in paperback and audio (Live Oak).
Theme/subject: Birthday: gifts

Florian, Douglas. *Nature Walk.* Greenwillow, 1989, 28 pp. A family takes a nature walk through a forest. They see a hidden lake and spot a bull frog, an ant mound, and a swallowtail. IL: 6–8.
Theme/subject: Nature walk

Fowler, Alan. *Seeing Things.* Children's Press, 1995, 31 pp. Color photos and brief text describe how we use our eyes and how we should take care of them. Some of the parts of the eye are depicted as well. Part of Rookie Read-About Science series. IL: 6–9. Available in paperback and big-book format.
Theme/subject: Senses: vision; Eyes

Fox, Mem. *Hattie and the Fox.* Bradbury Press, 1987, 30 pp. Hattie the hen spots danger, but the other animals don't seem to care until a fox jumps out. Repeated lines provide opportunities for choral or shared reading. IL: 5–8. Available in paperback.
Theme/subject: Escaping from danger

Fox, Mem. *Time for Bed.* Harcourt, 1993, 28 pp. Mother animals and a human mother lull their babies to sleep. Rhyme. IL: 5–7.
Theme/subject: Sleep; Bedtime

Fox, Mem. *Sophie.* Harcourt, 1994, 27 pp. Sophie's close relationship with her grandfather is traced from the time of her birth until his death, when she is a grown woman. Sweetness returns when Sophie feels the hand of a newborn child in hers. IL: 7–11.
Theme/subject: Grandparents: death

Fox, Mem. *Zoo Looking.* Mondo, 1996, 27 pp. Flora takes a trip to the zoo with her dad. Although she has come to look at the animals, she finds that the animals are looking back at her. Repeated lines provide opportunities for choral or shared reading. IL: 6–8.

Theme/subject: Zoo; Humor

Galdone, Paul. *Henny Penny.* Clarion, 1968, 30 pp. Hit on the head by an acorn, Henny Penny sets out to warn the king. Accompanied by other barnyard creatures, the animals disappear when Foxy Loxy tricks them into going into his cave. Repeated lines provide opportunities for choral or shared reading. IL: 5–8. Available in paperback.

Theme/subject: Drawing hasty or false conclusions; Fables

Galdone, Paul. *The Teeny Tiny Woman.* Clarion, 1984, 30 pp. After she takes a bone from atop a grave in order to make soup, a teeny tiny woman hears a voice calling out, "Give me my bone!" This is slightly more difficult than the O'Connor version. IL: 8–10. Available in paperback and audio.

Theme/subject: Ghost story

* Gelman, Rita Golden. *More Spaghetti, I Say!* Scholastic, 1977, 30 pp. Monkey has fun playing with and eating spaghetti. Reinforces long *e* patterns. Highly recommended. IL: 6–8. Available in paperback.

Theme/subject: Food; Humor

Geraghty, Paul. *Slobcat.* Simon & Schuster, 1991, 30 pp. Judged to be a lazy cat that does nothing but lie around and sleep, Slobcat is actually very active. Unseen by his owners, he saves kittens from big dogs, chases away snakes, hawks, and other intruders, and even keeps burglars away. Provides opportunity for comparison/contrast between what owners think and what cat actually does. IL: 6–8.

Theme/subject: Pets: cats; Irony

Gerstein, Mordicai. *Follow Me!* Morrow, 1983, 30 pp. In a hurry because they are hungry, a flock of ducks and geese are in disagreement about which way to go. Reinforces color words. IL: 6–7.

Theme/subject: Lost; Color words

Giganti, Jr., Paul. *Each Orange Had 8 Slices: A Counting Book.* Greenwillow, 1992, 22 pp. The narrator tells how many objects or people he saw and asks the reader a series of questions that could be answered by counting, adding, or multiplying. Colorful illustrations accompany the word problems. Promotes active engagement. IL: 6–8. Available as big book.

Theme/subject: Math: counting, adding, multiplying

Ginsburg, Mirra. *Good Morning, Chick.* Greenwillow, 1980, 32 pp. A newly hatched chick has a series of misadventures but is comforted by his mother. IL: 5–7.

Theme/subject: Mother caring for young; Misadventures

Goennel, Heidi. *I Pretend.* Tambourine, 1995, 29 pp. While engaged in everyday activities, a little girl pretends that she is doing something unusual or adventurous. While tobogganing, she pretends that she is on a magic carpet. Playing in the sand, she pictures herself as a beautiful mermaid. Provides possible writing topic and model: an I Pretend booklet. IL: 6–8.

Theme/subject: Daydreaming; Pretend

Gomi, Taro. *Santa through the Window.* Millbrook Press, 1983, 1995, 35 pp. Looking through windows that are cutouts in the book, Santa gets a partial but misleading view of who lives in each home and thus Santa leaves inappropriate gifts. Mistaking rabbit ears for crocodile teeth, he leaves a gift for a crocodile. Focusing on the pig's face on a bear's pajama top, he leaves a gift for a pig. Although

the animals are given the wrong gifts, they still enjoy them. IL: 6–8.
Theme/subject: Christmas; Gifts; Santa Claus

Greenfield, Eloise. *Honey, I Love.* HarperCollins, 1978, 1995, 16 pp. A young girl talks about some of the things she loves: the way her cousin talks, getting squirted on a hot day, laughing, going to the country, her mother's touch. And she loves herself too. Provides possible writing topic: Things I love. IL: 6–9. Available in paperback.
Theme/subject: Favorite things; Personal preferences

Gretz, Susanna. *Duck Takes Off.* Four Winds, 1991, 24 pp. A show-off, Duck loses her friends until she learns not to be so bossy. Repeated lines provide opportunities for choral or shared reading. IL: 6–7.
Theme/subject: Friendship; Getting along with others: being bossy

Gretz, Susanna. *Rabbit Rambles On.* Four Winds, 1992, 24 pp. Because Rabbit is always boasting about things that he can do, the other animals persuade him to stop. However, they take him up on his boast of being able to make chocolate sandwiches. IL: 6–7.
Theme/subject: Getting along with others; Bragging

Hale, Sara Joseph. *Mary Had a Little Lamb.* Holiday House, 1984, 26 pp. Tomie dePaola illustrates this classic nursery rhyme about a lamb who followed Mary to school. IL: 5–7.
Theme/subject: Traditional rhyme/song; Pet: lamb

Hale, Sara Joseph. *Mary Had a Little Lamb.* Scholastic, 1990, 26 pp. Using color photos, Bruce McMillan illustrates this classic nursery rhyme about a lamb who followed Mary to school. Full-color photos and easy-to-follow design make this one of the easiest-to-read versions. Repeated lines provide opportunities for choral reading. Available in paperback. IL: 5–7.
Theme/subject: Traditional rhyme/song; Pet: lamb

Harrison, David L. *Wake Up, Sun.* Random House, 1986, 32 pp. Awakened by the bite of a flea, a dog believes it is morning and wakes up the other animals, telling them that the sun has failed to come up. Reinforces long *i* patterns. IL: 6–8. Available in paperback.
Theme/subject: Drawing hasty or false conclusions; Sleep

Hawkins, Colin, & Hawkins, Jacqui. *I Know an Old Lady Who Swallowed a Fly.* Putnam, 1987, 22 pp. In this lift-the-flap version of a folksong, an old lady swallows a fly and then swallows a succession of increasing larger creatures until she swallows a horse, at which point she sneezes and all the creatures escape. Repeated lines provide opportunities for choral singing or reading. IL: 6–9.
Theme/subject: Folksong; Cumulative tale; Humor

Hawkins, Colin, & Hawkins, Jacqui. *Jen the Hen.* Putnam, 1988, 19 pp. In a text written to provide practice with *-en* words, Jen the Hen celebrates her birthday. A flip-the-page feature allows readers to form words by adding consonants to *-en*. Part of a series on short vowel patterns. IL: 6–7. Out of print.
Theme/subject: Word study: short *e* words; Birthday

Hawkins, Colin, & Hawkins, Jacqui. *Zug the Bug.* Putnam, 1988, 19 pp. In a text written to provide practice with *-ug* words, Zug the Bug captures a slug. A flip-the-page feature allows readers to form words by adding consonants to *-ug*. Part of a series on short vowels. IL: 6–7. Out of print.
Theme/subject: Word study: short *u* words

Hayes, Sarah. *This Is the Bear.* HarperCollins, 1986, 24 pp. A little boy spends a day at the trash dump looking for his teddy bear. The dog who pushed the teddy bear into the trash also helped find him. Reinforces short *u* patterns and sequence. IL: 5–7.
Theme/subject: Lost toy; Making amends; Humor

Hayes, Sarah. *Nine Ducks Nine.* Lothrop, Lee & Shepard, 1990, 24 pp. Nine ducks waddling in a line manage to elude a hungry fox. Each duck uses a different method for tricking the fox. IL: 5–7. Out of print.
Theme/subject: Escaping from enemies; Outwitting enemies

Hayes, Sarah. *This Is the Bear and the Scary Night.* Walker, 1992, 24 pp. Left in the park by his owner, bear has a very scary night that includes being picked up by an owl and dropped in a pond. He is finally rescued by a trombone player. Reinforces sequence. IL: 6–8.
Theme/subject: Toys: teddy bear; Rescue from danger; Humor

Hayward, Linda. *Hello, House!* Random House, 1988, 29 pp. Brer Rabbit outsmarts Brer Wolf, who is hiding in Brer Rabbit's home. IL: 6–8.
Theme/subject: Outwitting enemies

Herman, Gail. *What a Hungry Puppy!* Grosset & Dunlap, 1993, 32 pp. Lucky, a hungry puppy, finds a bone, but then encounters the owner of the bone, a large dog. Afraid that the dog is angry with him, Lucky runs away, but the big dog catches up with him and licks Lucky as a way of thanking him for finding the lost bone. Reinforces short *i* patterns. Offers opportunities for predicting what Lucky will find and what will happen to Lucky. IL: 5–7.
Theme/subject: Pets: dogs. Friendship

Hill, Eric. *Spot Goes to the Circus.* Putnam, 1986, 22 pp. Spot has a series of humorous encounters in this lift-the-flap book as he chases his ball. Part of Spot series. IL: 5–7.
Theme/subject: Finding lost object; Circus

Hines, Anna Grossnickle. *What Joe Saw.* Greenwillow, 1994, 30 pp. Last in line for the class walk to the park and sometimes called "Slowpoke, Pokey Joe," Joe lingers and sees things, such as a trail of ants or a turtle in the grass, that the others miss. Repeated lines provide opportunities for choral or shared reading. IL: 6–7.
Theme/subject: Nature: careful observation; Individual differences

Hughes, Shirley. *Hiding.* Candlewick, 1994, 16 pp. A little girl talks about good places to hide and how animals hide when they are afraid, are going to sleep, or don't want to be given a bath. She also notices that the moon hides behind the clouds and the sun behind trees. IL: 5–7.
Theme/subject: Hiding; Talking with others; Friendliness

Hutchins, Pat. *Clocks and More Clocks.* Simon & Schuster, 1970, 30 pp. In this recently reissued humorous tale, Mr. Higgins, erroneously believing that his many clocks are inaccurate, gets some practical help from a clockmaker. Good reinforcement for children who have just learned to tell time. Comprehending the story would require being able to tell time to the minute. IL: 6–8.
Theme/subject: Telling time; Humor; Problem solving

Hutchins, Pat. *The Doorbell Rang.* Greenwillow, 1986, 24 pp. When Ma gives her two children a dozen cookies to share, visitors keep popping in and so there are fewer cookies for each until Grandma comes to the rescue. Repeated lines provide opportunities for choral or shared reading. Reinforces math skill of divid-

ing. IL: 6–8. Available in paperback (Mulberry) and big-book format.
Theme/subject: Family life; Sharing

Hutchins, Pat. *Shrinking Mouse.* Greenwillow, 1997, 28 pp. Fox, Rabbit, Squirrel, and Mouse are worried. As Owl flies off to the nearby forest, he seems to be shrinking, and his friends are afraid that he might disappear entirely. IL: 5–8.
Theme/subject: Humor

Jackson, Ellen. *Brown Cow, Green Grass, Yellow Melon Sun.* Hyperion, 1995, 27 pp. Using white milk from the brown cow who has eaten green grass that grew with the help of the yellow sun, Granny makes yellow mellow butter. Provides practice with sequence. IL: 6–7.
Theme/subject: Food: making butter; Colors

Jacobs, Daniel. *What Does It Do? Inventions Then and Now.* Raintree, 1990, 23 pp. This book shows what cameras, telephones, bikes, and clocks look like today and what they looked like when first invented and what their limitations were. It also shows early planes, trains, and cars. Provides comparison/contrast between today's and yesterday's inventions. IL: 6–9.
Theme/subject: Inventions: now and long ago

* Johnson, Crockett. *A Picture for Harold's Room.* HarperCollins, 1960, 64 pp. While drawing a picture for his room, Harold steps into the picture and becomes a part of it as he draws ships, mountains, and animals, and, finally, a door that he uses to get back into his room. Highly recommended. IL: 6–7. Available in paperback.
Theme/subject: Art: drawing; Fanatasy: creating places

Jones, Maurice. *I'm Going on a Dragon Hunt.* Simon & Schuster, 1987, 30 pp. To get to the cave where the dragon lives, a small boy has to charge through tall grass, plow through mud, and swing over a ravine. Once he locates the dragon, he hurries back to the safety of his home. Repeated lines provide opportunities for choral or shared reading. Reinforces sequence. IL: 6–9.
Theme/subject: Adventure: dragons; Humor; Fantasy

Joyce, William. *George Shrinks.* HarperCollins, 1985, 28 pp. Having shrunk to the size of a toy soldier, George finds that ordinary activities such as taking a bath and feeding the fish are adventures. However, the family's cat becomes downright dangerous. IL: 6–9. Theme/subject: Adventure; Fantasy

Kandoian, Ellen. *Maybe She Forgot.* Dutton, 1990, 28 pp. A little girl fears her mother forgot her when the mother is delayed and is late picking her up. IL: 6–7.
Theme/subject: Parents; Trust

Kasza, Keiko. *The Pigs' Picnic.* Putnam, 1988, 28 pp. Wanting to make a good impression on Miss Pig, Mr. Pig takes the advice of his friends and borrows the fox's tail, the lion's mane, and the zebra's stripes. Far from from being impressed, Miss Pig thinks Mr. Pig is a monster. Repeated lines provide opportunities for choral or shared reading. IL: 6–8.
Theme/subject: Be yourself

Kasza, Keiko. *When the Elephant Walks.* Putnam's, 1990, 26 pp. The elephant scares the bear who scares the crocodile who scares the hog until finally a little mouse scares the elephant. The reader may need help identifying the following words: *scurrries, flees, terror.* IL: 6–7.
Theme/subject: Fear: animals frightening each other; Humor

Kennedy, Jimmy. *Teddy Bears' Picnic.* Holt, 1992, 28 pp. Drawings and song lyrics tell about the teddy bears' picnic. Repeated lines provide opportunities for choral singing or reading. IL: 5–7.

Theme/subject: Toys: teddy bears; Song

Koch, Michelle. *By the Sea*. Greenwillow, 1991, 22 pp. This book depicts seaside related opposites. IL: 5–8.

Theme/subject: Word study; Opposites; Sea: words

Kraus, Robert. *Leo the Late Bloomer*. Simon & Schuster, 1971, 28 pp. Leo's father was concerned because Leo couldn't read, write, draw, or say a word and was a sloppy eater. When Leo's father stops watching, Leo became a capable young person. IL: 6–8. Available in paperback.

Theme/subject: Growing; Learning skills

Kraus, Robert. *Come Out and Play, Little Mouse*. Greenwillow, 1987, 28 pp. Tricked into coming out to play by a hungry cat, the little mouse is saved by his big brother. Repeated lines provide opportunities for choral or shared reading. Part of Little Mouse series. IL: 6–8. Available in paperback (Mulberry).

Theme/subject: Protection from enemies; Families: siblings helping each other

Landstrom, Olaf, & Landstrom, Lena. *Will Gets a Haircut*. R&S Books, 1993, 24 pp. Unhappy because he has to get a haircut, Will brightens up when he gets an idea for a special kind of cut. His classmates are fascinated by the haircut, which resembles the twist atop a soft ice cream cone. Offers possibility of predicting what type of haircut Will is choosing. Part of Will series. IL: 6–9.

Theme/subject: Growing up: haircuts; Humor

Lewison, Wendy Cheyette. *Going to Sleep on the Farm*. Dial, 1992, 22 pp. A father explains to his young son how farm animals sleep. Repeated lines provide opportunities for choral or shared reading. IL: 5–7.

Theme/subject: Farm animals: sleep; Bedtime

Lionni, Leo. *Little Blue and Little Yellow*. Astor-Honor, 1959, 36 pp. Two children, Little Yellow and Little Blue, become green when they merge, but manage to regain their original hues. Reinforces concept of colors and cause and effect. IL: 5–7. Available in paperback (Mulberry).

Theme/subject: Friendship; Colors

Lionni, Leo. *Color of His Own*. Knopf, 1975, 28 pp. Wanting to have a color of his own, a chameleon decided to live on a green leaf so he would always be green. However, as the leaf changed colors, so did he. A friend wisely suggested that the two stay together so that they would always be the same color even though that color might change. Not accurate science. Would need to compare story with actual facts about chameleons. IL: 6–8.

Theme/subject: Identity; Friendship

Lipniacka, Ewa. *Asleep at Last*. Crocodile Books, 1993, 12 pp. When Dad puts his two active boys to bed, it takes a long time. When Mom investigates, it turns out that Dad has fallen asleep but one of the boys is still awake. IL: 6–7.

Theme/subject: Bedtime

Lopshire, Robert. *Put Me in the Zoo*. Random, 1960, 61 pp. The zoo rejects the four-legged spotted creature that can change its spots and even put spots on people and objects. Two children who witness the creature's unique talents persuade it to join the circus. Reinforces long *i* patterns. Part of Spotted Creature series. IL: 6–9.

Theme/subject: Imaginary creatures; Finding one's place in the world; Humor

Lunn, Carolyn. *Bobby's Zoo.* Children's Press, 1989, 31 pp. Wondering what to do with his house full of animals, including a bedroomful of bears and a hippo in the hall, Bobby decides to turn his home into a zoo. IL: 6–8. Available in paperback and big-book format.
Theme/subject: Animals: too many animals in house; Exaggeration

Maccarone, Grace. *Monster Math.* Scholastic, 1995, 23 pp. In this integration of math and reading, the reader subtracts one monster from scenes that depict from 12 mosters to 1 monster: "Twelve little monsters wake up at seven. One jogs away. Now there are.... " Part of Hello Math Reader series. IL: 6–7. Paperback.
Theme/subject: Math: subtracting; Counting

MacDonald, Elizabeth. *John's Picture.* Viking, 1991, 24 pp. The picture of the little man that John drew took on a life of its own. The man picked up a pencil and drew a wife, who picked up a pencil and drew two children, and the whole family drew a backyard. Reinforces sequence. Provides possible writing topic: What would you draw? IL: 6–8. Out of print.
Theme/subject: Family life; Drawing; Fantasy

Maestro, Betsy, & Maestro, Giulio. *Harriet Reads Signs and More Signs.* Crown, 1981, 30 pp. Harriet, the elephant, reads common signs as she travels across town to her grandmother's house. Part of Harriet Elephant series. IL: 6–7. Out of print.
Theme/subject: Reading signs; Grandparents: visiting

Marquardt, Max. *Working Dogs.* Raintree, 1989, 24 pp. Color photos and text shows some of the ways in which dogs help people. Mature format. IL: 6–9. Available in paperback.
Theme/subject: Dogs: working

Martin, Jr., Bill. *Polar Bear, Polar Bear, What Do You Hear?* Holt, 1991, 24 pp. Each animal hears another animal making a noise: "Polar Bear, Polar Bear, what do you hear? I hear a lion roaring in my ear." The reader may need help identifying the following words: *bellowing, fluting, braying, yelping, snarling.* Repeated lines provide opportunities for choral or shared reading. IL: 5–7.
Theme/subject: Animal sounds

Mayer, Mercer. *There's a Nightmare in My Closet.* Dial, 1968, 28 pp. Determined to get rid of the nightmare in his closet, a little boy shot him with his popgun. The nighmare was so upset that the little boy had to let him sleep in his bed with him. Provides opportunity for predicting what boy will do about the nightmare. IL: 6–8.
Theme/subject: Sleep: nightmares

McGuire, Richard. *Night Becomes Day.* Viking, 1994, 32 pp. In this journey from night to day and back again, there are many changes. Night becomes day. Day becomes bright. Oceans become waves and a beach becomes a hill. The changes continue until "dream becomes good and good becomes night." IL: 6–8.
Theme/subject: Time: changes

McLenighan, Valjean. *You Can Go Jump.* Modern Curriculum Press, 1991, 32 pp. A selfish princess treats a frog badly after it retrieves her ball from a well. Later, when the frog turns into a handsome prince, he spurns the princess. IL: 6–10.
Theme/subject: Selfishness; Lack of gratitude; Humor

McNaughton, Colin. *Suddenly.* Harcourt, 1995, 24 pp. Every time the wicked wolf is about to capture Preston the pig, something happens that saves Preston. Reinforces making predictions. IL: 6–8.

Theme/subject: Escaping from enemies; Luck

McPhail, David. *Lost!* Little, Brown, 1990, 28 pp. David helps a bear lost in the city find his way back to the woods. IL: 6–8. Available in paperback.

Theme/subject: Helping others; Being lost; Humor

Medearis, Angela Shelf. *Here Comes the Snow.* Scholastic, 1996, 29 pp. In this rhyming story, children enjoy slipping and sliding in the snow and making a snowman. They also enjoy the hot cocoa when they go inside. IL: 5–7. Available in paperback.

Theme/subject: Snow; Playing

Merriam, Eve. *The Hole Story.* Simon & Schuster, 1995, 32 pp. A poem explains a variety of holes displayed in color photos: holes for keys, holes for cheese, and so on. IL: 5–8.

Theme/subject: Holes

Minarik, Else Holemelund. *The Little Girl and the Dragon.* Greenwillow, 1991, 20 pp. A little girl outsmarts a dragon who has swallowed all her toys. Reinforces problem solving. IL: 6–7.

Theme/subject: Monsters: dragons

Moore, Inga. *A Big Day for Little Jack.* Candlewick, 1994, 24 pp. Little Jack Rabbit is unsure of himself as he attends a birthday party for the first time. But Grandpa has a suggestion that helps Little Jack feel more confident, and he has a good time. IL: 5–7.

Theme/subject: Parties: getting along with others

Morley, Carol. *Farmyard Song.* Simon & Schuster, 1994, 24 pp. In this farmyard song, animals and their sounds are portrayed: "I had a sheep and the sheep pleased me, I fed my sheep by yonder tree; Sheep goes baa baa...." Reinforces phonics through requiring decoding of animal sounds: *swish-swadshu, chimmy-chuck, griffy, gruffy.* Repeated lines provide opportunities for choral or shared reading. IL: 5–7.

Theme/subject: Song; Animal sounds

Most, Bernard. *Hippopotamus Fun.* Harcourt, 1994, 31 pp. As children travel through the jungle with a hippopotamus, they hunt for words that are formed with the letters used to spell *hippopotamus.* IL: 6–8.

Theme/subject: Word game; Spelling

Noll, Sally. *That Bothered Kate.* Greenwillow, 1991, 30 pp. Having her little sister imitate her and follow her around bothers Kate, but she also is upset when her little sister stops following her around. IL: 6–8. Available in paperback (Puffin).

Theme/subject: Family: younger peers

O'Connor, Jane. *The Teeny Tiny Woman.* Random, 1986, 32 pp. After she takes a bone from atop a grave in order to make soup, a teeny tiny woman hears a voice calling out, "Give me my bone!" IL: 8–10. Available in paperback.

Theme/subject: Ghost story

Oppenheim, Joanne. *Wake Up, Baby.* Bantam, 1990, 32 pp. When an imagined herd of elephants, five-alarm fire, and giant fail to wake up Kate's sleeping baby brother so that the family can go to the beach, Kate falls asleep. Reinforces long *a* patterns. IL: 5–7. Available in paperback.

Theme/subject: Family life; Younger peers; Humor

Oppenheim, Joanne. *The Show and Tell Frog.* Bantam, 1992, 32 pp. Allie's frog slips into her backpack when she isn't looking and surprises everyone during show and tell. Reinforces long *o* patterns. IL: 6–8. Available in paperback.
Theme/subject: School: show and tell; Pets: frogs

Oram, Hiawyn. *In the Attic.* Holt, 1984, 26 pp. Climbing up the ladder on his toy fire truck, a small boy has a series of adventures in the attic, including taking a trip in a flying machine. When he tells his mother where he's been, she replies, "But we don't have an attic." Provides possible writing topic: imaginary trip. IL: 6–8. Available in paperback.
Theme/subject: Playing: imaginary trip

Phillips, Joan. *My New Boy.* Random House, 1986, 32 pp. A puppy teaches his new boy tricks and finds him when he is lost. IL: 6–8. Available in paperback.
Theme/subject: Pets: dogs

Philpot, Lorna, & Philpot, Graham. *Amazing Anthony Ant.* Random House, 1993, 22 pp. A song portrays Anthony Ant traveling through a maze and stopping for various reasons, which are revealed when the reader lifts a series of flaps. Repeated lines provide opportunities for choral singing or reading. IL: 6–9. Available in paperback.
Theme/subject: Song; Marching

Raschka, Chris. *Can't Sleep.* Orchard, 1995, 32 pp. A puppy has difficulty falling asleep and is still awake after his brother, mother, and father have gone to bed. He feels frightened and lonely but is comforted by the moon. IL: 6–7.
Theme/subject: Sleep: difficulty falling asleep; Fears: nighttime

Rathmann, Peggy. *Ruby the Copycat.* Scholastic, 1991, 27 pp. A new girl in school, Ruby copies Angela's way of dressing and even claims that she has done the same things that Angela has done, such as being the flower girl in a wedding. When she begins copying the teacher, the teacher leads Ruby to tell about one thing that she really did on her own. Ruby shows the class her special hop and the class begins copying her. IL: 6–9. Available in paperback.
Theme/subject: Being oneself

Reiser, Lynn. *Bedtime Cat.* Greenwillow, 1991, 20 pp. A little girl gets ready for bed but can't find her cat. After searching everywhere, she spies a pair of ears sticking out from under the covers of her bed. Offers opportunity to predict where cat might be. IL: 5–7.
Theme/subject: Pets: cats; Bedtime

Robart, Rose. *The Cake that Mack Ate.* Kids Can Press, 24 pp. This is a cumulative tale about dog that ate a cake. Reinforces long *a* patterns. IL: 5–7. Available in paperback (Little, Brown).
Theme/subject: Cumulative tale; Food: cake; Humor

Roe, Eileen. *With My Brother.* Simon & Schuster, 1991, 29 pp. A little boy loves his big brother. Sometimes they wrestle or go to the park together or do puzzles. He looks forward to the day when he can help him with his newspapers and ride on the school bus with his brother. Text is in English and Spanish. IL: 6–9. Available in paperback.
Theme/subject: Family life: siblings; Bilingual

Sage, James. *To Sleep.* Simon & Schuster, 1990, 22 pp. A mother explains to her young son what the end of the day is. She tells him that it is beyond his room and beyond

the garden and beyond the town and the sea, and even beyond the stars. IL: 5–7.
Theme/subject: Bedtime; End of day

Samton, Shiela White. *Frogs in Clogs*. Crown, 1995. Emphasizing short vowels, this book uses word play to tell the silly story of frogs in clogs from a bog who rescued pigs in wigs who were lugged to a rug by bugs during a fog. The bugs wanted all the clogs, figs, and wigs. Reinforces short vowel patterns. IL: 6–8.
Theme/subject: Word play; Rhyming words

Schade, Susan. *Toad on the Road*. Random House, 1992, 32 pp. Toad takes Cat and other friends for a long ride, showing them the many places one can go in a car. Toad also shows that he is a careful driver and doesn't go too fast or too slow. Reinforces long *o* patterns. Part of Toad series. IL: 6–8. Available in paperback.
Theme/subject: Traveling: cars; Humor

Schenk De Regniers, Beatrice. *How Joe the Bear and Sam the Mouse Got Together.* Lothrop, Lee & Shepard, 1990, 28 pp. Because their interests are so different, a mouse and a bear despair of being able to live together until they discover that they both like ice cream. Repeated lines provide opportunities for choral or shared reading. Offers opportunity to compare/contrast Joe and Sam. Provides possible writing topic: writing about one's interests. IL: 6–9.
Theme/subject: Friendship; Personal interests

Schindel, John, & O'Malley, Kevin. *What's for Lunch?* Lothrop, Lee & Shepard, 1994, 21 pp. In this cumulative tale, Sidney the mouse isn't worried when a cat threatens to eat him because behind the cat is a dog who threatens to chase the cat and behind the dog is a goose who threatens to bite the dog. The threats go on until Sidney's friend Shirley puts an end to them. Lends itself to choral, partner, or shared reading and readers' theater. IL: 6–8.
Theme/subject: Cumulative tale; Small animal scaring larger animal; Humor

Schneider, Richard M. *Add It, Dip It, Fix It*. Houghton Mifflin, 1995, 28 pp. This book depicts a series of verbs: *grab, fix, sew, tie, kick, add, dip*. IL: 6–9.
Theme/subject: Word study: verbs

Serfozo, Mary. *There's a Square, A Book about Shapes*. Scholastic, 1996, 32 pp. The reader is introduced to and asked to find the major shapes: circle, square, rectangle, oval, and diamond. IL: 6–7.
Theme/subject: Shapes

* Dr. Seuss. *Green Eggs and Ham*. Random House, 1960, 62 pp. Finally persuaded by Sam-I-Am to try a plate of green eggs and ham, the creature agrees to try them and finds them to be delicious in this easy-to-read but zany tale. Highly recommended. IL: 6–9.
Theme/subject: Food: fantasy; Language: word play

* Dr. Seuss. *Ten Apples up on Top*. Random House, 1961, 62 pp. Creatures balance apples on their heads while performing a variety of antics until their act comes crashing down on them. Reinforces short vowel patterns. Features much repetition. Highly recommended. IL: 6–9.
Theme/subject: Circus-type tricks; Word play

* Dr. Seuss. *Hop on Pop*. Random House, 1963, 64 pp. Features humorously illustrated rhymes that incorporate common vowel patterns. Highly recommended. IL: 5–8.
Theme/subject: Language: word play

Shulevitz, Uri. *One Monday Morning*. Simon & Schuster, 1967, 36 pp. On Monday, the king, the queen, and the little prince came to visit a little boy, but he wasn't

home. For each visit, they were accompanied by an additional person or animal. They continued to visit each day, even though the little boy wasn't there, until Sunday, at which point the number of visitors had grown considerably. Repeated lines in this cumulative tale provide opportunities for choral or shared reading. IL: 6–9.
Theme/subject: Visitors; Humor

Sis, Peter. *Going Up*. Greenwillow, 1989, 19 pp. A little girl meets all kinds of strange creatures on an elevator, including a witch, a man dressed as a banana, a chef, a clown, and Little Red Riding Hood. As it turns out, they are all going to a surprise birthday party for the little girl's mother. Reinforces predicting: Where are the people going? Why are they wearing costumes? Also reinforces counting. IL: 6–7. Available in paperback.
Theme/subject: Birthday party; Counting

Sis, Peter. *An Ocean World*. Greenwillow, 1992, 21 pp. Peter sends a postcard explaining that a whale is being released into the ocean. He wonders what it will be like for the whale who has seen people but never another whale. Illustrations show what happens to the released whale. Provides model for writing a postcard. IL: 6–10.
Theme/subject: Animals: whales; Postcards

Slate, Joseph. *Who Is Coming to Our House?* Putnam, 1988, 26 pp. The animals are excited. Someone is coming. They clean the barn and prepare a crib. Finally, Mary and Joseph arrive. The reader would need background knowledge of nativity. IL: 6–8. Out of print.
Theme/subject: Christmas; Coming of Joseph & Mary

Soman, David. *One of Three*. Orchard, 1991, 28 pp. Three sisters spend a lot of time together, but sometimes the youngest gets left behind. IL: 6–8. Available in paperback.
Theme/subject: Family: siblings; Growing up

Stadler, John. *Cat at Bat*. Dutton, 1979, 32 pp. This book features 14 funny rhymes. Reinforces short and long vowel patterns. IL: 6–8. Available in paperback (Puffin).
Theme/subject: Word play: humorous rhymes

Stadler, John. *Cat Is Back at Bat*. Dutton, 1991, 32 pp. This book, a sequel to *Cat at Bat*, features 14 funny rhymes. Reinforces short and long vowel patterns. IL: 6–8. Available in paperback (Puffin).
Theme/subject: Word play: humorous rhymes

Stadler, John. *Hooray for Snail!* HarperCollins, 1984, 32 pp. Despite hitting the ball to the moon, Snail barely makes it to home plate in time to score. Reinforces long *a* patterns. Part of Snail series. IL: 6–8. Available in paperback.
Theme/subject: Sports: baseball; Humor

Stadler, John. *Snail Saves the Day*. Crowell, 1985, 32 pp. Asleep when the game begins, Snail makes it to the stadium just in time to catch the winning touchdown pass. Reinforces long *o* patterns. Part of Snail series. IL: 6–10. Out of print.
Theme/subject: Sports: football; Humor

Stevenson, James. *If I Owned a Candy Factory*. Greenwillow, 1968, 1989, 28 pp. A little boy tells what he would do if he owned a candy factory. Provides a model and topic for writing. IL: 6–9.
Theme/subject: Sharing with others; Food: candy

Stoeke, Janet Morgan. *A Hat for Minerva Louise.* Dutton, 1994, 22 pp. Taking a stroll on a snowy morning, Minerva Louise, a hen, searches for a hat to keep her warm. Not sure what a hat looks like, she tries on a flower pot and a boot. Finally, she spies a pair of mittens and puts one mitten on her head and the second on her tail feathers. IL: 6–7.
Theme/subject: Clothing: hats; Snow
Strickland, Paul, & Strickland, Henrietta. *Dinosaur Roar.* Dutton, 1994, 24 pp. Dinosaurs are used to portray opposites: dinosaur fierce–dinosaur meek, dinosaur short–dinosaur very long, dinosasur fast–dinosaur slow. The reader may need help identifying the following words: *meek, fierce, spiky, lumpy.* IL: 6–7.
Theme/subject: Word study: opposites
Strub, Susanne. *My Cat and I.* Morrow, 1993, 26 pp. A little girl compares her life with that of her cat's and discovers that both have their good times and bad times. Reinforces making comparisons and contrasts. IL: 6–9.
Theme/subject: Pets: cats
Tibo, Gilles. *Simon and the Boxes.* Tundra Books, 1992, 22 pp. Simon builds homes out of boxes for the animals, but they don't use them. Jack-in-the-box suggests another use for the boxes. Part of the Simon series. IL: 6–7.
Theme/subject: Ecology: cleaning up trash
Titus, Eve. *Kitten Who Couldn't Purr.* Morrow, 1991, 22 pp. Unable to purr, a kitten seeks help from a duck who suggests quacking, a cow who suggests mooing, and a donkey who says braying might be the solution. At last, a dog shows the kitten how to wag its tail. Karen, the kitten's owner, is pleased because now the kitten can show it's happy. Repeated lines provide opportunities for choral or shared reading. IL: 5–7.
Theme/subject: Animals: communication
Tripp, Valerie. *Baby Koala Finds a Home.* Children's Press, 1987, 24 pp. After a long search during which time they are chased away by a number of animals, a baby koala and her mother find a tree branch of their own. Reinforces long *e* patterns. IL: 6–7. Available in paperback and big-book format.
Theme/subject: Home: finding
Waddell, Martin. *When the Teddy Bears Came.* Candlewick, 1994, 24 pp. When Tom's mother brings the new baby home, the teddy bears start coming, brought by a variety of visitors and Tom himself. Tom, his mom, and his dad take turns taking care of the baby and the teddy bears. IL: 6–7.
Theme/subject: New baby; Teddy bears
Walsh, Ellen Stoll. *Mouse Paint.* Harcourt, 1989, 30 pp. Two mice change colors as they experiment with paint. Reinforces concept of colors and color words. IL: 5–7. Available in paperback.
Theme/subject: Colors; Creation of colors
Walsh, Ellen Stoll. *Mouse Count.* Harcourt, 1991, 28 pp. In this counting book, mice outwit a snake who plans to eat them. IL: 5–7. Available in paperback.
Theme/subject: Outwitting enemies; Counting
Watson, John. *We're the Noisy Dinosaurs.* Candlewick, 1992, 26 pp. Behaving more like lively children than prehistoric creatures, dinosaurs show how they act when they are noisy, hungry, happy, thirsty, angry, sleepy, and quiet. Repeated lines provide opportunities for choral or shared reading. IL: 6–8.
Theme/subject: Dinosaurs; Humor

Waverly, Barney. *How Big? How Fast? How Hungry? A Book about Cats.* Raintree, 1990, 23 pp. Tigers, cheetahs, and lions are compared with house cats. Although all are cats, a tiger is bigger, a cheetah is faster, and a lion is hungrier. Both photos and drawings are used as illustrations. Offers an opportunity for comparison/contrast of wild and domestic cats. IL: 6–10.
Theme/subject: Animals: cat family; Wild and domestic cats
Weiss, Nicki. *Where Does the Brown Bear Go?* Greenwillow, 1989, 22 pp. When nighttime falls, animals around the world head for home. Repeated lines provide opportunities for choral or shared reading. IL: 5–8. Available in paperback (Puffin).
Theme/subject: Nighttime; Animal homes
Westcott, Nadine Bernard. *I Know an Old Lady Who Swallowed a Fly.* Little, Brown, 1980, 28 pp. In this folksong, an old lady swallows a fly and then swallows a succession of increasing larger creatures until she swallows a horse, at which point she dies. Repeated lines provide opportunities for choral or shared reading. IL: 6–9. Available in paperback.
Theme/subject: Folksong; Cumulative tale; Humor
Wikler, Linda. *Alfonse, Where Are You?* Crown, 1996, 28 pp. Alfonse, the goose, hides so well that Little Bird can't find him. Then Alfonse can't find Little Bird. Not noticing that Little Bird is nearby, Alfonse and the other geese begin a worried search. Reinforces sequence. IL: 6–7.
Theme/subject: Playing: hide-and-seek
Wilson, Sarah. *Muskrat, Muskrat, Eat Your Peas.* Simon & Schuster, 1989, 27 pp. Muskrat's relatives explain to him how they planted peas, weeded and watched over them, and cooked them for him. When Muskrat exclaims that he doesn't like peas, the relatives have a conference and decide to give him spaghetti instead. Reinforces sequence: growing and cooking peas. Repeated lines provide opportunities for choral or shared reading. IL: 6–9. Available in paperback.
Theme/subject: Vegetables: peas; Picky eaters; Humor
Wood, Jakki. *Dads Are Such Fun.* Simon & Schuster, 1992, 24 pp. Gorilla dads swing their children, koala dads carry their children piggyback, and turtle dads play peek-a-boo. Human dads do all of these and more. IL: 6–7.
Theme/subject: Family: fathers
Yolen, Jane. *Mouse's Birthday.* Putnam's, 1993, 26 pp. Mouse's small house collapses around the guests when he blows out the candles on his birthday cake. Lends itself to partner, shared, or choral reading. IL: 6–7.
Theme/subject: Birthday party; Friendship
Young, Ruth. *Who Says Moo?* Viking, 1994, 28 pp. Readers are asked to identify animals on the basis of verbal and visual clues. IL: 5–7.
Theme/subject: Animals: major characteristics; Riddles
Ziefert, Harriet. *Jason's Bus Ride.* Puffin, 1987, 32 pp. Jason saves the day when he persuades a dog to move out of the way of a bus. Reinforces long *i* patterns and problem solving. IL: 6–8. Available in paperback.
Theme/subject: Animals: understanding
* Ziefert, Harriet. *Dark Night, Sleepy Night.* Penguin, 1988, 32 pp. This book shows how animals and people sleep. Reinforces long *e* patterns. Highly recommended. IL: 6–8. Available in paperback.
Theme/subject: Animals: sleep

Ziefert, Harriet. *Strike Four.* Viking, 1989, 30 pp. Urged to play ball outside because she is in everyone's way, Debbie hits a home run that breaks a window. Repeated lines provide opportunities for choral or shared reading. IL: 6–8.
Theme/subject: Sports: baseball; Accident

* Ziefert, Harriet. *The Little Red Hen.* Puffin, 1995, 32 pp. In this classic tale that is simply told, the other animals refuse to help Hen grow wheat and bake bread, so Hen refuses to share the bread with them. Repeated lines provide opportunities for choral or shared reading. Reinforces long *i* patterns. Compare/contrast with other versions. Highly recommended. IL: 5–8. Available in paperback.
Theme/subject: Work: sharing work leads to sharing rewards

Ziefert, Harriet. *Oh, What a Noisy Farm!* Tambourine, 1995, 27 pp. In this cumulative tale, the farmer's wife shouts when the bull chases a cow. The farmer, smacking a pan, joins in, as do most of the farm animals, each one making its characteristic sound. The chase and the noise stop when the cow quits running and the bull asks, "Will you be my friend?" IL: 6–8.
Theme/subject: Cumulative tale; Drawing hasty or false conclusions; Understanding others

Zimmermann, H. Werner. *Henny Penny.* Scholastic, 1989, 28 pp. Hit on the head by an acorn, Henny Penny sets out to warn the king. Accompanied by other barnyard creatures, the animals disappear when Foxy Loxy tricks them into going into his cave. Repeated lines provide opportunities for choral or shared reading. IL: 6–9. Available in paperback.
Theme/subject: Fables; Drawing hasty or false conclusions

Zolotow, Charlotte. *Do You Know What I'll Do?* HarperCollins, 1958, 26 pp. A little girl tells her little brother what she will do to make life better for him. Repeated lines provide opportunities for choral or shared reading. Opportunity for making predictions: What will little girl do for her brother? IL: 6–8.
Theme/subject: Family: younger sibling

Zolotow, Charlotte. *Sleepy Book.* HarperCollins, 1958, 26 pp. This book explains how animals sleep. IL: 5–8. Available in paperback.
Theme/subject: Animals: sleep

Zolotow, Charlotte. *The Old Dog.* HarperCollins, 1972, 1995, 29 pp. Waking up one morning, a young boy discovers the lifeless body of his dog. Although he spends much of the day mourning the loss of his pet, he welcomes the black-and-white puppy that his father brings home. IL: 6–8.
Theme/subject: Pet: death of

BEGINNING B PLUS

Aker, Suzanne. *What Comes in 2's, 3's, and 4's?* Simon & Schuster, 1990, 29 pp. Items that come in 2's, 3's, and 4's are depicted: 2 eyes and ears, 2 pieces of bread, 3 meals a day, 3 sizes, 4 wheels on a car, 4 seasons, and 4 corners on a book. IL: 6–7. Available in paperback.
Theme/subject: Counting

Brown, Margaret Wise. *Big Red Barn.* HarperCollins, 1956, 1989, 30 pp. In rhythmic, rhyming text and vivid illustrations, this book depicts the lives of animals on a farm during the day and at night. Their lives are centered around a big red barn

and a nearby cornfield. IL: 6–7. Available in paperback and big-book format.
Theme/subject: Farm: lives of animals on a farm

Bunting, Eve. *Flower Garden*. Harcourt, 1994, 29 pp. With the help of her father, a litle girl buys plants and puts them in a window box. The window box is a surprise birthday gift for her mom, but it delights the people on the street, too. The reader might need help with the following words: *potting soil, trowel, jamboree,* and the names of common flowers. IL: 6–8.
Theme/subject: Birthday gifts; Flowers

Costeau Society, The. *Turtles*. Simon & Schuster, 1992, 16 pp. The birth of sea turtles and their venture to the sea are depicted. IL: 6–8.
Theme/subject: Turtles

Crebbin, June. *The Train Ride*. Candlewick, 1995, 24 pp. A mother and a daughter take a train ride. They roll past meadows, farms, a market square, and a seaside town until they reach the station where grandma awaits them. The reader may need help with the following words: *market square, lighthouse, gaggle of geese*. Because of repeated sentences, this book lends itself to partner, shared, or choral reading.
Theme/subject: Transportation: trains; Visiting grandparents

Dobkin, Bonnie. *Go-With Words*. Children's Press, 1993, 30 pp. Some words go together: "You clap with you hands. You wink with your eye. Square goes with box and round goes with ball." IL: 6–7. Available in paperback.
Theme/subject: Word study: words that go together; Opposites

Drescher, Henrik. *Whose Scaly Tail? African Animals You'd Like to Meet.* Lippincott, 1987, 28 pp. As a young boy walks through the African grasslands, the reader is asked to identify a partially depicted animal. The animal is fully shown and named on the reverse page. Readers may need help with the following words: *aardvark, pangolin, scaly*. Reinforces clusters and using clues to draw conclusions about identity of animals. IL: 6–8. Out of print.
Theme/subject: African animals: characteristics; Guessing from visual and verbal clues

Dubowski, Cathy East, & Dubowski, Mark. *Snug Bug*. Grossett & Dunlap, 1995, 32 pp. A mother bug helps her baby bug get ready for bed, which includes assuring him that the human child sleeping nearby will not harm him. Reinforces short *u* patterns. IL: 6–7. Available in paperback.
Theme/subject: Parenting; Bedtime

Ehlert, Lois. *Planting a Rainbow*. Harcourt, 1988, 28 pp. With brilliant drawings and brief text, readers are taken through the steps of growing a colorful flower garden, with emphasis on the many colors of the flowers. Readers may need help with *bulbs, sprouts, seedlings,* and the names of flowers. IL: 6–7. Available in paperback.
Theme/subject: Gardening; Flowers

Ehlert, Lois. *Color Zoo*. Lippincott, 1989, 28 pp. Colors and shapes form animals' faces when placed on top of each other. Readers may need help with *hexagon, octagon,* and *oval*. IL: 6–7.
Theme/subject: Drawing; Animals; Shapes

Ehlert, Lois. *Feathers for Lunch*. Harcourt, 1990, 26 pp. A cat is on the prowl looking for birds to eat. However, the cat is wearing a bell, so the birds are warned of its presence. As students read the story, they can try to identify the 12 species of birds that the cat sees. Fosters predicting whether cat will get a bird. IL: 6–7.

Available in paperback.

Theme/subject: Escaping from enemies; Cats

Emberley, Rebecca. *Let's Go: A Book in Two Languages.* Little, Brown, 1993, 23 pp. Using illustrations and print, words are introduced in both English and Spanish. IL: 6–8.

Theme/subject: Words; Language: Spanish & English

Fleming, Denise. *In the Tall, Tall Grass.* Holt, 1991, 30 pp. A caterpillar explores life in the tall, tall grass. Provides practice in using short vowel patterns and, to a lesser degree, long vowel patterns, and clusters. IL: 6–8. Available in paperback and big-book format.

Theme/subject: Nature; Animals

Fleming, Denise. *Lunch.* Holt, 1992, 28 pp. A very hungry mouse eats a turnip, an orange, carrots, corn, peas, grapes, an apple, and other food, and then takes a nap until dinnertime. Provides a possible writing topic: foods I like.

Theme/subject: Food

Florian, Douglas. *A Carpenter.* Greenwillow, 1991, 22 pp. This book shows the tools a carpenter uses and the kinds of things that he or she makes. IL: 6–7.

Theme/subject: Tools

Goennel, Heidi. *My Day.* Little, Brown, 1988, 28 pp. A day in the life of a young girl is depicted. Provides a model for creating a similar book. IL: 6–7. Out of print.

Theme/subject: Everyday activities

Goennel, Heidi. *My Dog.* Orchard, 1989, 26 pp. Children tell what kinds of dogs they like: "I like a dog who has a silky coat like a collie. I like a dog who is as big as a pony, like a Saint Bernard." IL: 6–8. Out of print.

Theme/subject: Pets; Dogs: kinds of

Kline, Suzy. *Don't Touch.* Whitman, 1985, 30 pp. A little boy is told by adults and older peers not to touch cooking food, a rose, a toy in a store, a freshly painted wall, and so on. Reinforces *fl* clusters. IL: 6–7.

Theme/subject: Family life: rights of others

Konigsburg, E. L. *Samuel Todd's Book of Great Colors.* Atheneum, 1990, 24 pp. Sam, a young boy, depicts what he thinks are the great colors and objects that have those colors: "egg yolks are yellow, and so are bananas, except for the speckles, which are brown like freckles and chocolate." Provides possible writing topic: favorite colors. IL: 6–7.

Theme/subject: Colors; Personal preferences; About me

Rockwell, Anne. *On Our Vacation.* Dutton, 1989, 30 pp. Illustrations and captions depict what Bear Child and his family saw and did on their vacation. IL: 6–8. Available in paperback.

Theme/subject: Vacation

Rockwell, Anne. *What We Like.* Simon & Schuster, 1992, 24 pp. Animals in book tell all about themselves, what they like to do and make, and invite readers to do the same. Provides a model for writing. IL: 6–7. Available in paperback (Puffin).

Theme/subject: Personal interests

Rogers, Paul. *What Will the Weather Be Like Today?* Greenwillow, 28 pp. Captions and pictures depict various kinds of weather in different parts of the world and show how weather affects a number of creatures. Lizards, for example, like it dry but ducks like it wet. IL: 6–8.

Theme/subject: Weather

Shaw, Nancy. *Sheep in a Jeep.* Houghton Mifflin, 1986, 32 pp. Sheep have misadventures in a jeep. Reinforces long *e* patterns. Part of sheep series. IL: 6–9. Available in paperback.
Theme/subject: Humorous misadventures

Ward, Leila. *I Am Eyes—Ni Macho.* Greenwillow, 1978, 1991, 28 pp. A small girl in Kenya tells of the wonders that she sees: "I see pineapples and pelicans." IL: 6–9. Available in paperback (Scholastic).
Theme/subject: Senses: eyes; Being aware of one's surroundings; Africa

Westcott, Nadine Bernard. *The Lady with the Alligator Purse.* Little, Brown, 1988, 22 pp. In this adaptation of a jump-rope rhyme, Tiny Tim becomes ill when he drinks all the bath water and eats the soap. Both the doctor and the nurse prescribe medicine, but the lady with the alligator purse calls for pizza, which makes everyone happy. Repeated lines make this a natural for choral or shared reading. IL: 6–9. Available in paperback.
Theme/subject: Word play; Jump-rope rhyme

BEGINNING C

Alborough, Jez. *Where's My Teddy?* Candlewick, 1992, 24 pp. Searching for his lost teddy bear in the woods, a little boy discovers that his teddy has apparently grown and is almost as big as a house. Meanwhile, a giant bear discovers that his teddy bear has shrunk and is now very tiny. It's a case of mistaken identity. The two are soon reunited with their own teddy bears. Part of Eddie and Big Bear series. IL: 6–7. Available in paperback.
Theme/subject: Toys: teddy bears; Humor

Aliki. *We Are Best Friends.* Greenwillow, 1982, 28 pp. Sad and lonely after his best friend Peter moves away, Robert feels better after he gets to know Will, a new boy at school. Robert begins to have fun again but doesn't forget about Peter. Reinforces letter writing. IL: 6–7.
Theme/subject: Friendship; Moving

Allen, Johnathan. *My Dog.* Gareth Stevens, 1987, 30 pp. A girl describes her dog's habits and how she cares for it. Provides model for writing about pets. IL: 6–10.
Theme/subject: Pets: caring for

Allen, Pamela. *Who Sank the Boat?* Coward-McCann, 1982, 28 pp. Who sank the boat? Was it the cow who tilted the boat, the donkey who balanced her weight, the pig as fat as butter, the sheep who knew where to sit, or the mouse who jumped in last? Reinforces concept of cause and effect. IL: 6–7. Available in paperback.
Theme/subject: Boat: balance; Humor

Anholt, Catherine, & Anholt, Laurence. *Twins, Two by Two.* Candlewick, 1992, 24 pp. After hearing the story of Noah's ark, the twins pretend to be tigers, crocodiles, elephants, monkeys, bats, bears, kangaroos, and finally two nice mice, as they drift off to sleep. IL: 6–7.
Theme/subject: Bedtime; Play: pretend

Anholt, Catherine, & Anholt, Laurence. *What I Like.* Putnam, 1991, 24 pp. Text and drawings show what kinds of things boys and girls like and what types of things they don't like. Provides a model for creating a book of personal likes and dislikes. IL: 6–8.
Theme/subject: Personal preferences

Arnold, Tedd. *Green Wilma.* Dial, 1993, 30 pp. Having turned into a frog, Martha starts acting strangely, with some very humorous consequences. IL: 6–9.
Theme/subject: Turning into animal; Fantasy; Humor

Arnosky, Jim. *Come Out, Muskrats.* Lothrop, Lee & Shepard, 1989, 22 pp. In late afternoon, when the cove is calm, the muskrats come out. They dive, swim, and eat green water weeds. Brief prose is complemented by Jim Arnosky's realistic drawings. Part of Nature series. Can be used to reinforce imaging. IL: 6–8. Available in paperback.
Theme/subject: Animals: muskrats; Animal habitat

Asch, Frank. *Bear Shadow.* Simon & Schuster, 1985, 28 pp. Noting that his shadow is scaring the fish, Bear tries to get rid of it. Running away and hiding doesn't work; neither does trying to nail the shadow to the ground. Finally, Bear learns to live with his shadow. Can be used to reinforce cause-effect: Why is shadow around? IL: 6–7. Available in paperback.
Theme/subject: Shadows

Asch, Frank. *Goodbye House.* Simon & Schuster, 1986, 28 pp. After the van is packed and the house is empty, Baby Bear feels that he has forgotten something. His dad explains that the house is full of memories, and he and Baby Bear say goodbye to each room. IL: 6–7. Available in paperback.
Theme/subject: Moving; Memories

Ashforth, Camilla. *Horatio's Bed.* Candlewick, 1992, 24 pp. Because Horatio, the stuffed rabbit, has no bed, he can't sleep. James, the stuffed bear, draws him a bed but that doesn't work. Part of James series. IL: 6–7. Available in paperback.
Theme/subject: Sleep: bed

Axworthy, Anni. *Along Came Toto.* Candlewick, 1993, 22 pp. After being followed around all day by Toto, the kitten, Percy, the dog, is feeling very grumpy and chases Toto away so that he can sleep in peace. However, after having a nightmare, Percy is more than happy to have Toto's company. Reinforces *gr* clusters. IL: 6–8.
Theme/subject: Friendship: appreciating; Sleep: nighmares

Ayers, Beryl. *Lucky Duck.* ERA Publications, 1995, 29 pp. A duckling doesn't like to swim and wanders in the woods, but changes his mind when chased by a fox. The duckling escapes by diving into a pond and swimming away. IL: 6–8.
Theme/subject: Learning important skills; Escape from enemies

Baker, Alan. *Gray Rabbit's Odd One Out.* Kingfisher, 1995, 23 pp. Unable to find his favorite book among his toys, Gray Rabbit begins sorting his toys. As he sorts each pile, there is something amiss. The reader is told: "But one thing did not belong. What was it?" Reinforces categorizing. Promotes involvement of reader. IL: 6–7.
Theme/subject: Cleaning up: putting things away; Categorizing

Baker, Barbara. *One Saturday Morning.* Dutton, 1994, 48 pp. Mama bear, papa bear, and the four little bears have a special Saturday. Each of the six chapters features one of the bears as the main character. IL: 6–8.
Theme/subject: Family life

Barton, Byron. *Airport.* HarperCollins, 1982, 32 pp. The journey of air travelers is traced from arrival to take-off. The story includes showing the cockpit, ground crew, and contol tower. IL: 6–7. Available in paperback.
Theme/subject: Transportation: airplanes; Air travel

Barton, Jill. *The Happy Hedgehog Band*. Candlewick, 1991, 28 pp. Harry, the hedgehog, and his friends form a band composed mainly of drummers. Other animals join in by humming, hooting, buzzing, whistling, clapping, clicking, and popping. Opportunity is provided for students to apply phonics skills by reading many regularly spelled nonwords: *tum-tum-te-tum, ratta-tat-tat*. Repeated lines provide opportunities for choral or shared reading. IL: 6–8. Available in paperback.
Theme/subject: Music: band; Cooperation

Blocksma, Mary. *Yoo Hoo, Moon!* Bantam, 1992, 32 pp. Unable to sleep because the moon is not out, Bear sings to the moon and awakens her friends, who call to the moon until the moon finally appears from behind a cloud. Reinforces *oo* pattern as in *moon*. Repeated lines provide opportunities for choral or shared reading. IL: 6–7. Available in paperback.
Theme/subject: Moon; Sleep: difficulty with

Bonsall, Crosby. *The Case of the Cat's Meow*. HarperCollins, 1965, 64 pp. Four young private eyes take on the case of the lost cat. After trying several elaborate schemes, the boys use a simple plan to locate the cat, who, as they soon discover, has just had kittens. Offers opportunity to predict what happened to Mildred. Part of Case of ___ series. IL: 6–9. Available in paperback.
Theme/subject: Detective mystery; Pets: cats having kittens

Borden, Louise. *Caps, Hats, Socks, and Mittens*. Scholastic, 1992. The sights, sounds, and activities of each of the four seasons are discussed. Fall, for instance, is soccer, frost, and black cats. Provides possible writing topic and format: Fall is ___. IL: 6–8. Available in paperback.
Theme/subject: Seasons

Brandenberg, Franz. *Otto Is Different*. Greenwillow, 1985, 21 pp. Disturbed because he is different, Otto Octopus learns to appreciate having four times as many arms as the other kids. He can get his work done faster and he is an outstanding hockey goalie. IL: 6–9.
Theme/subject: Being oneself; Appreciating one's talents; Sports: hockey

Brenner, Barbara. *The Plant that Kept on Growing*. Bantam, 1996, 29 pp. Hoping to win a prize at the 4-H fair, the twins planted a vegetable garden. All of their plants, except one, were destroyed by animals or insects. As they watched, their last plant sprouted into a tomato tree that grew giant tomatoes. They won the prize, and the town was treated to raw and cooked tomatoes and 200 pizza pies. IL: 6–8. Available in paperback.
Theme/subject: Gardens; Fantasy

Breslow, Susan, & Blakemore, Sally. *I Really Want a Dog*. Dutton, 1990, 37 pp. A Boy gives all the reasons why he wants a dog. Talking to an imaginary dog in the sky, he promises to take care of the dog, and then goes through the process of deciding what kind of a dog he would like. Reinforces grasping main idea/details. IL: 6–9. Available in paperback (Puffin).
Theme/subject: Pets: dogs, choosing, taking care of

* Bridwell, Norman. *Clifford the Small Red Puppy*. Scholastic, 1972, 28 pp. The runt of the litter and a sickly puppy, Clifford grows into a giant dog. Part of Clifford series. IL: 6–8. Highly recommended. Available in paperback.
Theme/subject: Pets: dogs; Fantasy; Humor

Brown, Marc. *Pickle Things*. Gareth Stevens, 1980, 1994, 44 pp. Pickles are seen in unusual places: pickle toes, pickle pie, pickle kites, and pickle candies. And, of course, there are pickle shoes and pickle trains and boats. IL: 6–9. Available in paperback (Parents).

Theme/subject: Food: pickles; Humor

Brown, Margaret Wise. *Little Donkey, Close Your Eyes.* HarperCollins, 1957, 1985, 1995, 26 pp. As night falls, various creatures, including a child, put a halt to their activities and close their eyes. Provides possible writing topic: prebedtime activities. IL: 6–7.

Theme/subject: Sleep; Bedtime; Poetry

Burningham, John. *Mr. Gumpy's Outing.* Henry Holt, 1970, 32 pp. Taken for a ride on Mr. Gumpy's boat, two children and a variety of animals misbehaved and turned over the boat but shared hot tea later on. IL: 6–8. Available in paperback and big-book format.

Theme/subject: Humorous misadventure; Travel

Byars, Betsy. *My Brother Ant.* Viking, 1996, 32 pp. Ant's big brother gets rid of a monster that is hiding under Ant's bed and also helps him write a letter to Santa Claus in July. Ant repays his big brother's kindness by illustrating his homework. Reinforces letter writing. IL: 6–8.

Theme/subject: Sibling relationships; Humor

Capucilli, Alyssa Satin. *Inside a Barn in the Country.* Scholastic, 1995, 27 pp. In this cumulative tale, the squeak of a mouse started a chain of events that woke up all the animals in the barn who woke up the farmer who ordered everyone back to bed because it was not morning yet. Repeated lines provide opportunities for choral or shared reading. IL: 6–8.

Theme/subject: Cumulative tale; Waking up others

Carle, Eric. *The Very Hungry Caterpillar.* Philomel, 1969, 22 pp. A tiny but very hungry caterpillar eats an enormous amount of food, including a strawberry, plum, cheese, cake, and salami, and turns into a very big caterpillar. The hungry caterpillar then builds a cocoon and emerges two weeks later as a beautiful butterfly. Contains cutouts to show food eaten. Reinforces concept of caterpillar turning into butterfly. Part of "Very" series. IL: 6–7. Available in paperback.

Theme/subject: Growing up; Changing

Carle, Eric. *The Very Lonely Firefly.* Philomel, 1995, 26 pp. The last of the four-part "Very" series, this text follows a firefly as it searches for companions but is fooled by lightbulbs, car headlights, and a fireworks display. In the end, it discovers a group of fireflies. The fireflies on the last page light up when that page is turned. IL: 6–7.

Theme/subject: Loneliness; Belonging

Carlstom, Nancy White. *I'm Not Moving, Mama.* Simon & Schuster, 1990, 28 pp. Little mouse doesn't want to move and leave favorite places and memories behind. Repeated lines provide opportunities for choral or shared reading. IL: 6–7.

Theme/subject: Moving; Memories

Cazet, Denys. *"I'm Not Sleepy."* Orchard, 1992, 29 pp. To help his son fall asleep, a father tells his son about a little boy who walked into a boily jungle, was pursued by a thingamajig, but was rescued by a shooting star that lifted him over the clouds and brought him home. IL: 6–8.

Theme/subject: Bedtime: falling asleep; Adventure: flying, fantasy

Cerf, Bennett. *Bennett Cerf's Book of Animal Riddles.* Random House, 1964, 64 pp. This is a collection of timeless, easy-to-read riddles. IL: 6–9.
Theme/subject: Word play: riddles

Chapman, Cheryl. *Snow on Snow on Snow.* Dial, 1994, 29 pp. While playing in the snow, a small boy loses his dog Clancy. After a long search, the boy hears a woof from one of the snow drifts. IL: 6–8.
Theme/subject: Pets: lost

Child, Lydia Maria. *Over the River and Through the Woods: A Song for Thanksgiving.* HarperCollins, 1993, 28 pp. This traditional song tells about a family's trip to the grandparents' house for Thanksgiving dinner. Repeated lines provide opportunities for choral singing or reading. IL: 6–10. Available in paperback.
Theme/subject: Traditional song; Thanksgiving; Grandparents

Cole, Joanna. *It's Too Noisy.* Crowell, 1989, 28 pp. Feeling that his home with his wife, a grandmother, and lots of children was too noisy, a farmer sought advice from a wise man, who suggested that he let the animals in. The animals made so much noise that after the farmer put them out of his home, he no longer minded the noise that his family made. IL: 6–10.
Theme/subject: Folktale; Family life: noise

Collins, Pat Lowery. *Don't Tease the Guppies.* Putnam, 1994, 30 pp. While on a trip to the aquarium with his older brother, Tim misreads many of the signs but gives himself a scare when he opens a door marked "Keep Out" that he thinks says "Come In." Reinforces reading signs. IL: 6–9.
Theme/subject: Siblings; Aquarium; Reading signs; Humor

Cowen-Fletcher, Jane. *Mama Zooms.* Scholastic, 1993, 30 pp. As he travels about sitting in his mother's lap in her wheelchair, a little boy imagines the wheelchair to be a racehorse, a ship at sea, a race car, a spaceship, and other speedy conveyances. Lends itself to partner, shared, or choral reading. IL: 6–7.
Theme/subject: Family: mother-child; Disabilities: wheelchair

de Regniers, Beatrice Schenk. *May I Bring a Friend?* Simon & Schuster, 1964, 42 pp. A little boy brings friends from the zoo when he goes to visit the king and the queen. Repeated lines provide opportunities for choral or shared reading. IL: 6–8. Available in paperback.
Theme/subject: Animals: friends

Denton, Kady MacDonald. *Would They Love a Lion?* Kingfisher, 1995, 24 pp. After wondering whether she should be a bird, a rabbit, a bear, or a dinoasur, Anna decides to be a lion. Lions stalk, pounce, eat fast, and run fast. She's sure her family would like her if she were a lion. Provides possible writing topic: What kind of animal would I like to be? IL: 6–7.
Theme/subject: Play: pretending to be animals

Dodds, Dayle Ann. *Color Box.* Little, Brown, 1992, 26 pp. Entering a magical box, Alexander Monkey encounters a series of worlds, each in a different color. A question and a cutout circle ask the reader to predict what Alexander found. Reinforces predictions based on visual and verbal clues. IL: 6–8.
Theme/subject: Colors.

Dubowski, Cathy East, & Dubowski, Mark. *Cave Boy.* Random, 1988, 32 pp. Harry, the cave boy, creates a wheel for Chief Grump's birthday. When Chief Grump kicks it down a hill because he doesn't know what to do with it, Harry notices that it rolls, and so he makes a tricycle for the chief. IL: 6–9. Available in paperback.

Theme/subject: Gift: birthday; Inventions: wheel; Humor

Dunbar, Joyce. *The Spring Rabbit.* Lothrop, Lee & Shepard, 1994, 24 pp. Wanting a brother or sister rabbit, Smudge is told to wait until spring. During fall and winter, Smudge searches for brothers and sisters, but to no avail. Finally, spring comes and Smudge finds himself with two baby brothers and a baby sister. Repeated lines provide opportunities for choral or shared reading. IL: 6–7.

Theme/subject: Birth; Younger peers; Spring

Durant, Alan. *Snake Supper.* Western, 1995, 30 pp. A hungry snake slithers through the forest swallowing every animal he sees. When he attempts to swallow an elephant, the elephant wedges a log in snake's jaws and pulls the other animals out. IL: 6–9.

Theme/subject: Outwitting enemies

Dussling, Jennifer. *Stars.* Grosset & Dunlap, 1996, 32 pp. This book tells what stars are and how big they are, and explains why the sun seems bigger than the other stars. It also describes the Big Dipper and an eclipse and tells what people once thought stars were. IL: 6–9. Available in paperback.

Theme/subject: Stars

Edwards, Richard. *Something's Coming.* Candlewick, 1995, 24 pp. Sensing in the middle of the night that something is coming, Elephant warns his friends. That something turns out to be two powerful sneezes. Offers students the opportunity to predict what's coming. IL: 6–7.

Theme/subject: Sneezing; Humor

Ehlert, Lois. *Snowballs.* Harcourt, 1995, 32 pp. When it snowed, the children made a snow dad, a snow mom, a snow boy, a snow girl, a snow baby, a snow cat, and a snow dog. And then the sun came out. IL: 6–7.

Theme/subject: Snow: snowman; Playing in snow

Falwell, Cathryn. *Feast for Ten.* Clarion, 1993, 29 pp. Members of the family prepare a feast for 10: five kinds of beans, six bunches of greens, seven dill pickles stuffed in a jar, eight ripe tomatoes, nine plump potatoes. Reinforces counting. IL: 6–7.

Theme/subject: Family: special meal; Counting

Fanelli, Sara. *My Map Book.* HarperCollins, 1995, 24 pp. A map book shows a map of the artist's room, her family, her day, her tummy and favorite foods, her favorite colors, and her neighborhood. A map of her heart, face, and dog are also shown. The map of her heart shows the things that mean the most to her. Provides possible writing topic and format: creating personal maps. IL: 6–10.

Theme/subject: Autobiography; Likes and dislikes

Fowler, Allan. *Hearing Things.* Children's Press, 1991, 31 pp. Text and full-color photos describe how we use our sense of hearing and how we should care for our ears. Part of Rookie Read-About Science series. IL: 6–9. Available in paperback.

Theme/subject: Senses: hearing

French, Vivian. *Oliver's Vegetables.* Orchard, 1995, 22 pp. When Oliver visits Grandpa, he confesses that the only vegetable he eats is french fries. Grandpa promises to fix french fries if Oliver is able to pick potatoes from the garden, but if he mistakenly picks another vegetable, then he will have to eat it. Oliver ends up picking and enjoying a variety of vegetables. IL: 6–9.

Theme/subject: Eating habits: picky eaters; Vegetables

Frith, Michael. *I'll Teach My Dog 100 Words.* Random, 1973, 26 pp. A dog owner explains how he plans to teach his dog to respond to 100 words. But when the owner thinks of the effort involved, he says that he'll wait for a year before starting. IL: 6–9.
Theme/subject: Pets; Dogs: teaching; Humor

Gackenbach, Dick. *Claude Has a Picnic.* Clarion, 1993, 30 pp. Claude the dog solves neighborhood problems in his own special way. Because Mickey is bored with his ball and Buddy is tired of his Frisbee, Claude carries Mickey's ball to Buddy's yard and Buddy's Frisbee to Mickey's yard. Claude also helps prevent a neighborhood quarrel and brings happiness to lonely Mrs. Duncan. IL: 6–8.
Theme/subject: Community; Helping others

Galdone, Paul. *The Gingerbread Boy.* Clarion, 1975, 40 pp. Jumping out of the oven and running away, the Gingerbread Boy challenges the little old woman and others to catch him if they can. However, the fox tricks the Gingerbread Boy and eats him. Repeated lines provide opportunities for choral or shared reading. IL: 6–7. Available in paperback.
Theme/subject: Tricking creatures; Pride: bragging; Cumulative tale

Geisel, Theodor. *Great Day for Up.* Random House, 1974, 64 pp. This book uses the word *up* in a variety of humorous contexts. IL: 6–9.
Theme/subject: Word play

Gerstein, Mordicai. *The Sun's Day.* HarperCollins, 1989, 28 pp. As the sun moves across the sky, it looks down on various activities: the beginning of the day, chirping chicks, babies waking up, breakfast, buzzing bees, workers stopping for lunch, and on and on, until the sun goes down and night falls. IL: 6–7.
Theme/subject: Time; Concept of day; Daily activities

Goennel, Heidi. *The Circus.* Tambourine, 1992, 26 pp. The circus comes to town. A boy and girl watch as the circus is set up. They also attend a performance. IL: 6–8.
Theme/subject: Circus

Goldish, Meish. *Does the Moon Change Shape?* Raintree, 1989, 32 pp. Text and illustrations explain why the moon seems to change shape. Provides clear coverage of concept. IL: 7–10. Available in paperback.
Theme/subject: Moon: changing shape

Goldish, Meish. *How Do Plants Get Food?* Steck-Vaughn, 1992, 24 pp. This book explains what makes plants grow and how to take care of them. IL: 6–10. Available in paperback.
Theme/subject: Plants

Greeley, Valerie. *White Is the Moon.* Simon & Schuster, 1990, 18 pp. Each of the colors is portrayed in a verse: "White is the moon shining bright, Sees an owl in the night." IL: 6–8.
Theme/subject: Colors; Poetry

Green, Norma. *The Hole in the Dike.* HarperCollins, 1974, 26 pp. Coming home from a friend's house, Peter notices a leak in the dike. Unable to stop the flow in any other way, he plugs up the hole with his finger and stays there all night until help is summoned. He is praised as a hero for preventing a flood and saving Holland. IL: 6–9.
Theme/subject: Heroes; Courage; Legends

Gretz, Susanna, & Sage, Alison. *Teddy Bears at the Seaside.* Simon & Schuster, 1972, 1989, 30 pp. The teddy bears and Robert the dog take a trip to the beach. They eat, fish, swim, build sand castles, and doze in the sun just as people do. Part of Teddy Bears series. IL: 6–8.
Theme/subject: Beach fun; Humor

Guarino, Deborah. *Is Your Mama a LLama?* Scholastic, 1989, 27 pp. In this rhyming tale, a young llama asks a variety of creatures: "Is your mama a llama?" The animals explain why their mothers are not llamas. The baby bat says, "She hangs by her feet, and she lives in a cave. I do not believe that's how llamas behave." IL: 6–8. Available in paperback.
Theme/subject: Animals; Animal mothers

Harrison, Joanna. *Dear Bear.* Carolrhoda, 1994, 29 pp. Frightened by the imaginary bear that lives under the stairs, a little girl seeks help from her mother, who suggests that the girl write a letter to the bear. After exchanging several letters, the bear invites the little girl to a tea party. Reinforces writing letters. IL: 6–8. Available in paperback.
Theme/subject: Fears: overcoming; Fantasy

Hazen, Barbara Shook. *Stay, Fang.* Atheneum, 1990, 28 pp. Young owner tries to make his large dog understand that there are times when he must be left behind, but Fang doesn't seem to comprehend that he can't go to school or baseball practice. Sequel to *Fang.* Contains possible writing topic: leaving pets behind. IL: 6–10.
Theme/subject: Pets; Dogs: leaving behind

Heller, Nicholas. *Happy Birthday, Moe Dog.* Greenwillow, 1988, 21 pp. On his birthday, Moe is greeted by a series of letters of the alphabet who fix him a special breakfast and give him presents. At his party, the letters spell out "Happy Birthday." IL: 6–8.
Theme/subject: Birthday; Word games: spelling

Hendrick, Mary Jean. *If Anything Ever Goes Wrong with the Zoo.* Harcourt, 1993, 27 pp. A little girl who lives in a house on a hill near the zoo tells several keepers to send their animals to her if anything ever goes wrong at the zoo. When the zoo is flooded, the keepers take the little girl up on her offer. Zebras, monkeys, crocodlies, ostriches, elephants, and a lion become house and yard guests. IL: 6–10. Available in paperback.
Theme/subject: Zoo animals; Helping others; Humor

Himmelman, John. *The Day-off Machine.* Silver Press, 1990, 22 pp. Because his family is too busy working to have fun, Graham devises a machine that piles up snow in front of the fix-it shop so that his dad can't get to work and therefore decides to take the day off. The other members of the family also take the day off. IL: 6–8.
Theme/subject: Family life: taking time to have fun; Balancing work and play

Himmelman, John. *A Guest Is a Guest.* Dutton, 1991, 28 pp. Believing that a guest is a guest, whether it be a person or an animal, the Beanbucket family treat their animals like people. The animals take over the house and put the people out; however, in the end, the Beanbuckets outsmart the animals. IL: 6–9.
Theme/subject: Guests; Animals acting like people; Humor

* Hoff, Syd. *Danny and the Dinosaur.* HarperCollins, 1958, 64 pp. The dinosaur from the museum enjoys his day off as he and his young friend Danny play games

and take a tour of the town. Highly recommended. IL: 6–9. Available in paperback and audiotape.
Theme/subject: Dinosaurs; Appreciating one's home

Hoff, Syd. *Oliver.* HarperCollins, 1960, 64 pp. Unable to get a job with the circus, Oliver Elephant seeks a job elsewhere but is unsuccessful. While dancing to entertain some children, Oliver is spotted by the circus owner and given a job. IL: 6–9.
Theme/subject: Using one's talents; Humor; Fantasy

Hoff, Syd. *Grizzwold.* HarperCollins, 1963, 64 pp. When the forest that he lives in is cut down, Grizzwold, the giant bear, has a difficult time finding a new home. IL: 6–9. Available in paperback.
Theme/subject: Finding a new home

* Hoff, Syd. *The Horse in Harry's Room.* HarperCollins, 1970, 32 pp. Harry's imaginary horse is fun to ride, especially since Harry can ride him in his room, but the horse also provides a sense of security and friendship. Highly recommended. IL: 6–9. Available in paperback.
Theme/subject: Pets: horses; Imaginary playmates

Hoff, Syd. *Barkley.* HarperCollins, 1975, 32 pp. Replaced by a younger dog because he is growing old, Barkley, the circus dog, tries to find a useful job. The circus owner arranges for him to teach young dogs how to perform. IL: 6–8.
Theme/subject: Growing old; Finding new talents; Humor

Hoff, Syd. *Albert the Albatross.* HarperCollins, 1988, 32 pp. After a fierce storm, an albatross finds himself over land. Unable to find the ocean or get directions from other birds, he is escorted back to the ocean in a very imaginative but humorous way. Can be used to reinforce predicting. IL: 6–9.
Theme/subject: Ocean; Birds; Humor

Hoff, Syd. *Mrs. Brice's Mice.* HarperCollins, 1988, 32 pp. Mrs. Brice's 24 mice dance, exercise, go shopping, and run away from a cat. IL: 6–9. Available in paperback.
Theme/subject: Humor; Pets: mice

* Howe, James. *The Day the Teacher Went Bananas.* Dutton, 1984, 28 pp. Because of a mix-up, a gorilla is sent to teach a class. Learning to count on their toes, swing from trees, and paint with their fingers, the children are delighted with their teacher, even though he doesn't speak but only grunts. IL: 6–9. Available in paperback.
Theme/subject: School: learning; Teachers: substitute; Humor

Hutchins, Pat. *Don't Forget the Bacon.* Greenwillow, 1976, 28 pp. Distracted as he heads toward the grocery store, the boy distorts his memorized grocery list with humorous results. Can be read aloud to illustrate rhyme and substitution of sounds. IL: 6–8. Available in paperback, big book, and audiotape.
Theme/subject: Shopping list; Word play

Hutchins, Pat. *Tidy Titch.* Greenwillow, 1986, 24 pp. When Titch's older brother and sister tidy up their rooms, they give Titch many of their discarded possessions so that Tidy Titch's room becomes messy. Repeated lines provide opportunities for choral or shared reading. IL: 6–8.
Theme/subject: Family; Cleaning up

Hutchins, Pat. *Silly Billy.* Greenwillow, 1992, 26 pp. When Silly Billy wrecks her games, Hazel outsmarts him. Repeated lines provide opportunities for choral or shared reading. IL: 6–8. Available in paperback.

Theme/subject: Younger siblings

Hutchins, Pat. *Three-Star Billy.* Greenwillow, 1994, 27 pp. In monster school, children get stars for being bad. Billy gets a star for his terrible painting, his dreadful singing, and his monstrous dancing. Sequel to *Silly Billy.* IL: 6–8.

Theme/subject: School: behavior; Monsters; Humor

Inkpen, Mick. *Kipper's Toybox.* Harcourt Brace Jovanovich, 1992, 24 pp. Kipper is surprised when one of his toys begins to crawl away. Students can make predictions about why this is happening. IL: 6–7.

Theme/subject: Toys; Getting along with others

Jakob, Donna. *My Bike.* Hyperion, 1994, 30 pp. A boy learns to ride a bike. IL: 6–7.

Theme/subject: Bicycles: learning to ride; Growing up

Janovitz, Marilyn. *Look Out, Bird!* North-South, 1994, 30 pp. Snail slips and hits bird, starting a chain of events in which one animal after another splashes, bumps, hits, or in some other way bothers another animal. Reinforces clusters: *fl, sp, sl, sc, fr.* IL: 6–8.

Theme/subject: Cumulative tale; Humor

Johnson, Angela. *Do Like Kyla.* Orchard Books, 1990, 27 pp. From morning to night, Kyla's little sister imitates her as she greets the birds, braids her hair, eats breakfast, goes to the store in the snow, and reads a book. But at bedtime, Kyla says good night to the birds just like her little sister did. Can be used to reinforce sequence: events of the day. IL: 6–8. Available in paperback.

Theme/subject: Peers; Imitating older peer

Johnson, Angela. *Shoes Like Miss Alice's.* Orchard Books, 1995, 26 pp. While taking care of Sara, Miss Alice changes shoes everytime she changes activities. She puts on dancing shoes for dancing, walking shoes for walking, and soft slippers for napping. IL: 6–7.

Theme/subject: Shoes; Babysitters; Having fun

Jonas, Ann. *The Trek.* Greenwillow, 1985, 27 pp. For two young girls the walk to school is a dangerous trek through the jungle. Wild animals are hiding everywhere. What looks like a pond is really a watering hole with lots of jungle animals gathered around. The coffee shop is a trading post. The steps to school are a mountain to climb. Fosters interpreting illustrations: locating animals in pictures. IL: 6–9. Available in paperback (Mulberry).

Theme/subject: Adventure: imaginary

Kasza, Keiko. *A Mother for Choco.* Putnam, 1992, 30 pp. Unable to find his mother, Choco, a small bird, begins sobbing, until Mrs. Bear offers to become his mother. She shows that she would do all the things that a mother might do: hug and kiss him, dance and sing with him, and bake him an apple pie. IL: 6–7.

Theme/subject: Family: mother and child; Love is more important than appearance; Adoption

* Keats, Ezra Jack. *Whistle for Willie.* Puffin, 1964, 29 pp. Peter learns to call his dog Willie by whistling. Highly recommended. IL: 6–8. Available in paperback (Puffin).

Theme/subject: Pets: dog; Learning a new skill

Keller, Holly. *Goodbye, Max.* Greenwillow, 1987, 28 pp. Angry and hurt because his dog Max has died, Ben rejects the puppy his dad brought home. After having a good laugh with his friend Zach over the many funny things Max did and then having a good cry, Ben feels better and begins to accept the new puppy. IL: 6–10. Theme/subject: Pets: death of dog

Kessler, Leonard. *Old Turtle's Riddle and Joke Book.* Greenwillow, 1986, 48 pp. Old Turtle's friends tell him their favorite riddles, which include such gems as: "What fish chase mice? Cat fish. What happens when ducks fly upside down? They quack up." Reinforces awareness of multiple meanings of words. IL: 6–9. Theme/subject: Word play: riddles; Humor

Kimmel, Eric A. *The Gingerbread Man.* Holiday House, 1993, 28 pp. Jumping out of the oven and running away, the Gingerbread Man challenges the little old woman and others to catch him if they can. However, the fox tricks the Gingerbread Man and eats him. Lends itself to partner, shared, or choral reading. IL: 6–7. Available on audiotape (Live Oak). Theme/subject: Tricking creatures; Pride: bragging; Cumulative tale

Koontz, Robin Michal. *I See Something You Don't See.* Dutton, 1992, 32 pp. A brother and sister challenge each other with riddles, which the reader is invited to solve. IL: 6–9. Theme/subject: Word play: riddles

Kuskin, Karla. *Which Horse Is William?* Greenwillow, 1959, 1987, 21 pp. William asks his mother if she would still know him if he were a horse, a skunk, or some other animal. His mother replies yes because he'd be the only horse with a hat on or the only skunk wearing a scarf. Repeats basic 9 lines with the name of different animals filled in. Because there is a two-part conversation throughout, the text lends itself to buddy or shared reading. IL: 6–7. Theme/subject: Family: mother and child; Love

Landstrom, Olof, & Landstrom, Lena. *Will Goes to the Post Office.* R&S Books, 1994, 24 pp. Will and his friends pick up a very large package from the post office and struggle to get it to Will's home. At first, there seems to be nothing but paper inside the huge box, but then they find a gift from Uncle Ben. Students can predict what's inside the box. Part of Will series. IL: 6–8. Theme/subject: Gifts; Mail

Lenski, Lois. *Sing a Song of People.* Little, Brown, 1965, 1987, 28 pp. This book depicts the variety of people who might be seen in a city: people walking fast or slow, people on buses, people on subways, people walking alone, people in crowds. IL: 6–10. Theme/subject: People: in the city, variety of; Poetry

Lillie, Patricia. *Floppy Teddy Bear.* Greenwillow, 1995, 29 pp. Each time little sister damages big sister's teddy bear, Mama repairs it and finally buys little sister one of her own. IL: 6–7. Theme/subject: Sharing; Peers; Toys: teddy bears

Lionni, Leo. *Inch by Inch.* Astor-Honor, 1960, 27 pp. About to be eaten by a hungry robin, an inchworm shows how it can be useful by measuring the tail of the robin, the neck of the flamingo, a toucan's beak, and the leg of a heron. Challenged to measure the song of a nightingale, the inchworm pretends to be measuring but inches out of sight. Can be used to reinforce compound words. IL: 6–8. Available in paperback (Mulberry). Theme/subject: Outwitting enemies

Lobel, Arnold. *Grasshopper on the Road.* HarperCollins, 1978, 62 pp. On his journey, Grasshopper encounters a housefly who would like to sweep the whole world, butterflies who insist on following exactly the same routine each day, and other interesting creatures. IL: 6–9. Available in paperback.
Theme/subject: Traveling; Meeting varied people

MacDonald, Amy. *Little Beaver and the Echo.* Putnam's, 1990, 24 pp. Hearing an echo across the pond, a lonely little beaver sets off to find the voice that he heard. Instead, he finds a duck, a turtle, and an otter who are also searching for friends. IL: 6–7.
Theme/subject: Friendship: finding friends; Loneliness

Marquardt, Max. *Wilbur and Orville and the Flying Machine.* Raintree, 1989, 31 pp. From the time they were boys playing with kites, the Wright brothers became interested in flight. Opening up a bicycle shop and experimenting with gliders and then motorized flying machines, they invented the airplane. Can be used to reinforce sequence. IL: 6–10. Available in paperback.
Theme/subject: Inventions: airplane; Biography

Martino, Teresa. *Pizza.* Raintree, 1989, 30 pp. The creation of pizza is traced from its origins more than 1,000 years ago as a flat, round food to the addition of tomatoes soon after and then the addition of cheese about a 100 years ago and its appearance in the United States less than 50 years ago. Can be used to reinforce sequence and cause and effect. Provides possible writing topic: my favorite pizza. IL: 6–11. Available in paperback.
Theme/subject: Food: origins; Pizza

Mayer, Mercer. *There's Something in My Attic.* Dial, 1988, 29 pp. Hearing a noise in her attic, a little girl discovers a frightened nightmare who has been stealing her toys. Lassoing the nightmare, she hauls it down to her parents' room, but it slips away before they can see it. Compare with *Nightmare in my Closet.* IL: 6–8. Available in paperback (Puffin).
Theme/subject: Sleep: nightmares; Monsters

McGeorge, Constance W. *Boomer Goes to School.* Chronicle Books, 1996, 24 pp. Boomer the pet dog is confused when his young master takes him to school. But he begins to understand when his master talks about him during show-and-tell and gives him a big pat on the head. Fosters predicting why Boomer has been brought to school. IL: 6–8.
Theme/subject: Pets: dogs; Schools: show-and-tell

McGovern, Ann. *Too Much Noise.* Houghton Mifflin, 1967, 40 pp. Disturbed by ordinary household noises such as the creaking of the floor, an old man is advised to obtain a series of animals, each one noisier than the one previously acquired. Then the old man is advised to get rid of all the animals, who were creating bedlam. Having been exposed to the noisy animals, the old man is no longer bothered by household sounds. Repeated lines provide opportunities for choral or shared reading. Can be used to reinforce sequence and problem solving. Also lends itself to readers' theater presentation. IL: 6–9. Available in paperback.
Theme/subject: Noise; Solving problems; Cumulative tale

McGovern, Maureen. *I Want to Learn to Fly.* Scholastic, 1995, 31 pp. In this song, a little girl explains why she wants to learn to fly: to see the parrots in the jungle, to fly away from crocodiles, and to fly where parents don't yell and kids aren't

mean. Lends itself to choral or shared singing or reading. IL: 6–9.
Theme/subject: Flying: person; Song

Milios, Rita. *The Hungry Billy Goat*. Children's Press, 1989, 30 pp. A goat eats everything in sight, including items of clothing. IL: 6–8.
Theme/subject: Animals: goats

Milstein, Linda. *Coconut Mon*. Tambourine, 1995, 29 pp. Coconut man peddles his wares by proclaiming his coconuts are "luv-ly," "crrr-unchy," "crrr-isp," "tender." Reinforces clusters and multisyllabic words. IL: 6–9.
Theme/subject: Food: coconuts; Multicultural

Minarik, Else Holmelund. *Little Bear's Visit*. HarperCollins, 1961, 64 pp. Little Bear visits his grandparents, both of whom have interesting stories to tell. Grandmother Bear tells how Mother Bear once had a robin for a pet but finally let it go. Grandfather tells a story about a goblin who was followed by his own shoes. Part of Little Bear series. IL: 6–8. Available in paperback and on audiotape (Caedmon).
Theme/subject: Family: grandparents

Minarik, Else Holmelund. *A Kiss for Little Bear*. HarperCollins, 1968, 32 pp. Thankful for a picture that Little Bear sent her, Grandmother asks Hen to take a kiss to him. The kiss is passed along from animal to animal until it finally reaches Little Bear. Part of Little Bear series. IL: 6–7.
Theme/subject: Grandparents; Travel

Moncure, Jane Belk. *I Never Say I'm Thankful, But I Am*. The Child's World, 1979, 30 pp. A little boy reflects on the many things he is thankful for: family, friends, crickets, frogs, waves, and so on. Repeated lines provide opportunities for choral or shared reading. Provides possible writing topic: things for which I'm thankful. IL: 6–9.
Theme/subject: Being thankful

Morris, Neil. *What a Noise: A Fun Book of Sounds*. Carolrhoda, 1991, 28 pp. Trying to keep everything quiet so that his baby sister won't be awakened, Sam sets off a chain of events that causes him to sneeze loudly and awaken everyone. Chain story. Can be used to reinforce sequence. IL: 6–8.
Theme/subject: Family: babies; Sleeping; Younger siblings

Most, Bernard. *If the Dinosaurs Came Back*. Harcourt, 1978, 25 pp. If the dinosaurs came back, they could carry people to work, scare away robbers, take down trees, plow fields, and would make great pets for people who love dinosaurs. Provides possible writing topic: if dinosaurs or other animals came back. IL: 6–9. Available in paperback and audiotape.
Theme/subject: Dinosaurs

Most, Bernard. *Pets in Trumpets and Other Word-Play Riddles*. Harcourt. 1991, 32 pp. The answer to each riddle is a word that is the key word in the riddle and bold-faced in the text: "Why did the musician find a dog in his trumpet? Because he always finds a **pet** in his trumpet." Reinforces seeking pronounceable word parts in words. IL: 6–9.
Theme/subject: Word play: riddles

Munsch, Robert N. *The Dark*. Annick Press, 1989, 28 pp. When Jule Ann turned the cookie jar upside down, the dark (a small black lump) fell out. The dark made itself larger by eating shadows. Sittting on the roof, the dark threw the area outside Julie Ann's home into darkness. However, the light returned when Julie

Ann tricked the dark back into the cookie jar. IL: 6–10. Available in paperback.
Theme/subject: Adventure/Fantasy; Fighting darkness
Nerlove, Miriam. *I Meant to Clean My Room Today.* Macmillan, 1988, 26 pp. A young
girl has a host of imaginative excuses for not cleaning her room. After all, a yellow turtle standing on its head, a pink monkey dropping in to play, and other
strange creatures took her time. IL: 6–8.
Theme/subject: Chores: cleaning one's room; Fantasy
Nims, Bonnie Larkin. *Where Is the Bear?* Whitman, 1988, 20 pp. The reader searches
for a bear in a series of scenes. The text provides a description of each scene and
a request to help find the bear. Promotes active engagement. Repeated lines provide opportunities for choral or shared reading. Part of *Where Is the Bear?* series.
IL: 6–8.
Theme/subject: Games/Activities; Locating hidden items
Nims, Bonnie Larkin. *Where Is the Bear at School?* Whitman, 1989, 19 pp. Hidden in
among the scenes of a busy elementary school is a small bear. Readers are asked
to find the bear. Repeated lines provide opportunities for choral or shared read-
ing. Part of *Where Is the Bear?* series. IL: 6–8.
Theme/subject: Games/Activites; Locating hidden items
Nims, Bonnie Larkin. *Where Is the Bear in the City?* Whitman, 1992, 20 pp. The reader
searches for a bear in a series of city scenes. The text provides a description of
each scene and a request to help find the bear. Promotes active engagement.
Repeated lines provide opportunities for choral or shared reading. Part of *Where
Is the Bear?* series. IL: 6–8.
Theme/subject: Games/Activites; Locating hidden items
Noble, Trinka Hakes. *The Day Jimmy's Boa Ate the Wash.* Dial, 1980, 26 pp. Although
described as dull by one of the participants, the class field trip was anything but,
especially since Jimmy took his pet boa constrictor along. Part of Jimmy's Boa
series. IL: 6–9. Available in paperback (Puffin).
Theme/subject: School trip; Humor
Numeroff, Laura. *Dogs Don't Wear Sneakers.* Simon & Schuster, 1993, 27 pp. This book
portrays things that animals don't do: dogs don't wear sneakers, pigs don't wear
hats, dresses look silly on Siamese cats. Readers are invited to imagine animals
doing strange things, like ducks riding bikes or snails saving twine. Provides a
model for a writing topic and format. Readers might create a similar book. IL: 6–
10. Has a sequel: *Chimps Don't Wear Glasses.*
Theme/subject: Animal fantasy; Humor
O'Donnell, Elizabeth Lee. *I Can't Get My Turtle to Move.* Morrow, 1989, 26 pp. A little
girls gets the rabbits to hop, the hens to peck, and the crows to fly away, but she
can't get the turtle to move, until she says the magic word: *lunch.* Repeated lines
provide opportunities for choral or shared reading. IL: 6–8.
Theme/subject: Food: eating; Humor
O'Donnell, Peter. *Carnegie's Excuse.* Scholastic, 1992, 24 pp. As Carnegie explained,
she was late for school because she overslept after being out late with a tiger, a
shark, and a gorilla. Believing that Carnegie had a very big imagination, the
teacher kept her after school, but the teacher changed her mind when the three
animals said good morning to her the next day. IL: 6–9.
Theme/subject: Fantasy; Lateness; Humor

Oppenheim, Joanne. *"Not Now!" Said the Cow.* Bantam, 1989, 32 pp. When the other animals refuse to help, Crow grows corn and, later, makes popcorn, and then he eats it all by himself. Repeated lines provide opportunities for choral or shared reading. IL: 6–9. Available in paperback.
Theme/subject: Fable; Those who expect to share in the rewards should share in the work

Oppenheim, Joanne. *The Donkey's Tale.* Bantam, 1991, 32 pp. As they head to town to sell their donkey, the farmer and his son heed the advice of everyone they meet and learn that when you try to please everyone, you please no one. IL: 6–8. Out of print.
Theme/subject: Fable; Using one's own judgment; Not attempting to please everyone

* Parish, Peggy. *Dinosaur Time.* HarperCollins, 1974, 32 pp. This book depicts 11 major types of dinosaurs. Highly recommended. IL: 6–9. Available in paperback.
Theme/subject: Dinosaurs

Poland, Janice. *A Dog Named Sam.* Dial, 1995, 40 pp. Although beloved by the family, Sam has some strange habits. He loves to fetch, and once fetched all the newspapers in the neighborhood. He also loves water and will swim everywhere. And he likes to make all kinds of noises at night. IL: 6–9.
Theme/subject: Pets: dogs; Strange habits; Humor

Rayner, Shoo. *My First Picture Joke Book.* Viking, 1989, 30 pp. This book presents a variety of jokes and riddles: "How do you know if carrots are good for your eyesight? Have you ever seen a rabbit wearing glasses?" IL: 6–9. Available in paperback (Puffin).
Theme/subject: Jokes and riddles

Robins, Joan. *Addie's Bad Day.* HarperCollins, 1993, 32 pp. Upset because of an unbecoming haircut, Addie doesn't want to attend her friend's birthday party because she is afraid she will be laughed at, but her friend has a very imaginative solution to the problem. Provides a possible writing topic: an embarrassing time. Can be used to foster predicting Addie's problem and then problem solving. IL: 6–9. Available in paperback.
Theme/subject: Friendship; Personal appearance; Birthday parties

Rockwell, Anne. *Fire Engines.* Dutton, 1986, 22 pp. Fire engines and related equipment are shown and explained: ladder trucks, pumpers, fire-fighting boats, and firehouse ambulances. IL: 6–7. Available in paperback (Puffin).
Theme/subject: Fire fighting

Rogers, Paul, & Rogers, Emma. *Quacky Duck.* Little, Brown, 1995, 23 pp. Quacky Duck quacked so much that the other animals pleaded for a little quiet. But when they didn't hear any quacking for a month, they complained that it was too peaceful. Finally, Quacky reappears with her newly hatched ducklings. IL: 6–7.
Theme/subject: Understanding and tolerating others

Roth, Susan L. *Creak, Thonk, Bump: A Very Spooky Mystery.* Simon & Schuster, 1996, 30 pp. Investigating strange, middle-of-the-night noises that have awakened everyone, the family fears a dragon or giant is on the loose but discovers that it's only the baby. Reinforces clusters. IL: 6–8.
Theme/subject: Frightening noises

Rowe, John. *Rabbit Moon*. Picture Book Studio, 1992, 22 pp. Unable to sleep, Rabbit becomes nervous when he can't see the moon. He tried all kinds of devices to put up a picture of the moon in the sky, including a catapult, which tossed him through the air. Just then, the moon appeared from behind a cloud and Rabbit claimed credit for saving the moon. IL: 6–8.
Theme/subject: Sleep; Moon; Humor

Rylant, Cynthia. *Mr. Putter and Tabby Walk the Dog*. Harcourt, 1994, 38 pp. When Mr. Putter agreed to walk Zeke, a neighbor's dog, he didn't know what he was getting into. Zeke was a nightmare to walk. After three days of being tugged along as Zeke chased dogs and ran through yards and houses, Mr. Putter devised a plan. If Zeke behaved each day, he would get a surprise. Can be used to reinforce solving problems. Part of Mr. Putter series. IL: 6–8. Available in paperback.
Theme/subject: Pets; Dogs: walking; Humor

Samuels, Barbara. *Duncan and Dolores*. Bradbury, 1986, 28 pp. After frightening her new cat away, Dolores finally wins his affection. IL: 6–8. Available in paperback.
Theme/subject: Pets: cats; Humor

Schade, Susan, & Buller, Jon. *Snug House, Bug House!* Random House, 1994, 39 pp. A group of bugs find a tennis ball and decide to use it as a shell for building a home. Each bug has a room and there are also special rooms: rooms for games and music and just having fun. Reinforces clusters. IL: 6–8.
Theme/subject: Home: building

Schlein, Miriam. *Just Like Me*. Hyperion, 1993, 29 pp. Cottontail's mother tells the story of a young rabbit who jumps so high that he flies over a mountain. Unable to jump back over the mountain because the wind had changed, the little rabbit has to figure out how to get back home. IL: 6–7. Available in paperback.
Theme/subject: Parents and children; Growing up; Problem solving

Schulman, Janet. *The Big Hello*. Greenwillow, 1976, 32 pp. Soon after moving to California, a little girl loses her doll. But she and her new dog find the doll, and the little girl makes a new friend. A brief chapter book. IL: 6–7. Available in paperback (Mulberry).
Theme/subject: Moving; Making friends

Scott, Ann Herbert. *On Mother's Lap*. Clarion, 1972, 1992, 29 pp. Feeling snug and secure on his mother's lap, Michael brings his dolly, his blanket, his boat, and his puppy, but is reluctant to have his little brother join him. But in the end, it seems there is always enough room on mother's lap. IL: 6–7. Available in paperback.
Theme/subject: Parents; Younger sibling: jealousy

Dr. Seuss. *The Cat in the Hat*. Random House, 1957, 62 pp. Unable to play outside, Sally and her brother are entertained by the Cat in the Hat and his two companions, who perform some amazing tricks. Reinforces short vowel and long *a* vowel patterns. IL: 6–8. See *The Cat in the Hat Comes Back*.
Theme/subject: Word play; Tricks: entertaining; Humor

Dr. Seuss. *The Cat in the Hat Comes Back*. Random House, 1958, 62 pp. The Cat in the Hat returns to entertain Sally and her brother with his amazing tricks. Sequel to *The Cat in the Hat*. Reinforces major vowel patterns. IL: 6–8.
Theme/subject: Word play; Tricks: entertaining; Humor

Dr. Seuss. *One Fish, Two Fish, Red Fish, Blue Fish*. Random House, 1960, 62 pp. Portrays a number of strange creatures: the Yink that winks, Neds who are pets that have single hairs on their heads, and the seven-hump Wump owned by Mr.

Gump. Reinforces short and long vowel patterns. Forces use of phonics because of strange names of creatures. IL: 6–9.

Theme/subject: Strange creatures; Word play; Humor

Shapiro, Arnold L. *Who Says That?* Dutton, 1991, 30 pp. The noises that animals make are contrasted with those that boys and girls make. Mice squeak, pigs oink, and lions roar; but boys and girls whisper, giggle, talk, shout, sing, chuckle, holler, laugh, scream, and whistle. IL: 6–7.

Theme/subject: Communication: sounds made by animals and people

Sheppard, Jeff. *Full Moon Birthday.* Atheneum, 1995, 28 pp. Monkey and Dinosaur decide to get Owl the moon for his birthday. Unable to reach the moon, they cover a window of a hut with red paper, and when Owl appears on the night of his birthday, they tear it off, exposing a perfect view of a full moon. Can be used to reinforce problem solving. IL: 6–8.

Theme/subject: Birthday; Gifts

Simon, Norma. *Fire Fighters.* Simon & Schuster, 1995, 22 pp. Using dalmatians, this book shows how firefighters respond to an alarm, how they put out a fire and search for victims, how they investigate the cause of a fire, and how they take care of their equipment. IL: 6–8.

Theme/subject: Fire fighting

Siracusa, Catherine. *Bingo, the Best Dog in the World.* HarperCollins, 1991, 64 pp. Sleepy because she ate too many dog treats, the normally mischievous Bingo wins a blue ribbon for being well behaved. IL: 6–9.

Theme/subject: Pets: dogs

Sis, Peter. *Komodo!* Greenwillow, 1993, 28 pp. A young dragon lover's dream comes true when his parents take him to the island of Komodo and he meets a Komodo dragon (a monitor lizard). IL: 6–10.

Theme/subject: Dragons: interest in; Komodo dragon

Slavin, Bill. *The Cat Came Back.* Whitman, 1992, 26 pp. In this traditional song, Mr. Johnson sends his cat away by rail, ship, and hot air balloon, but the cat keeps returning. Lends itself to singing or choral or shared reading. IL: 6–10.

Theme/subject: Song; Pets: cats; Humor

* Slobodkina, Esphyr. *Caps for Sale.* HarperCollins, 1947, 42 pp. When a peddler's caps are stolen by a troop of monkeys, he gets his caps back in an unexpected way. Highly recommended. IL: 6–8. Available in paperback, audiotape (Live Oak), and big book (Scholastic).

Theme/subject: Outwitting others to right a wrong; Monkeys; Humor

Snyder, Carol. *One Up, One Down.* Atheneum, 1995, 26 pp. Katie helps out when her mom has twins. For a time, life in the household is hectic. When one twin sleeps, the other is up. Later, when one twin was sitting up in his highchair, the other was sliding down, and when one twin was creeping up the stairs, the other was scooting down. Can be used for comparison/contrast of twins' actions. IL: 6–9.

Theme/subject: Growing up; New babies: helping out with; Twins

Spurr, Elizabeth. *The Gumdrop Tree.* Hyperion, 1994, 28 pp. A little girl plants a gumdrop tree. IL: 6–8.

Theme/subject: Family life; Fantasy; Food: candy

Stevenson, James. *B, R, R, R, R!* Greenwillow, 1991, 30 pp. When his grandchildren complained about the cold, Grandpa told them about the winter of 1908. It snowed so hard that while grandpa and his little brother went sledding, the whole town was completely covered. The houses were uncovered when a giant snowball rolled over them. But then they were frozen solid until Grandpa came up with a clever plan for breaking up the ice. Uses conversation bubbles. Part of Grandpa series. IL: 6–9.

Theme/subject: Tall tale; Grandparents; Humor

Stevenson, Robert Louis. *The Moon*. HarperCollins, 1984, 27 pp. In this poem by Robert Louis Stevenson, the moon shines down on various noctural activities: thieves on a garden wall, a father and his daughter fishing, sleeping birds, and noisy animals. IL: 6–8. Available in paperback.

Theme/subject: Moon; Poetry

Sullivan, Charles. *Numbers at Play: A Counting Book*. Rizzoli, 1992, 40 pp. In paintings, photos, and other works of art, students count items from one through ten—for example, "How many girls can you see dancing in France? The answer is three." IL: 6–7.

Theme/subject: Counting; Works of art

Taylor, Livingston, & Taylor, Maggie. *Can I Be Good?* Harcourt, 1993, 30 pp. Despite good intentions, a golden retriever just can't seem to behave. Repeated lines provide opportunities for choral or shared reading. IL: 6–8.

Theme/subject: Pets; Dogs: behavior

Titherington, Jeanne. *A Child's Prayer*. Greenwillow, 1989, 19 pp. This book depicts a series of good-night prayers for children. IL: 6–7.

Theme/subject: Prayers

Tompert, Ann. *Just a Little Bit*. Houghton Mifflin, 1993, 29 pp. When Elephant and Mouse try the seesaw, Mouse needs the help of other animals to balance the weight of Elephant. A number of animals help out, but the seesaw doesn't budge until a small brown beetle adds her weight. Cumulative tale. IL: 6–8.

Theme/subject: Cumulative animal tale; Every little bit of help counts; Humor

Torres, Leyla. *Subway Sparrow*. Farrar, Straus, Giroux, 1993, 28 pp. A sparrow trapped in a subway train is rescued by four riders. Can be used to reinforce predicting and problem solving and using context to guess what Polish and Spanish speakers are saying. Text is partially multilingual. IL: 6–10.

Theme/subject: Cooperation; Animals: rescue; Multilingual

Trapani, Iza. *The Itsy Bitsy Spider*. Whispering Coyote Press, 1993, 26 pp. This traditional rhyme includes having the spider climb up a wall, a pail, a rocking chair, and a maple tree, at which point the spider weaves a web and rests in the sun. Repeated lines provide opportunities for choral singing or reading. IL: 6–7.

Theme/subject: Traditional rhyme; Perseverance

Weiss, Leatie. *My Teacher Sleeps in School*. Puffin, 1984, 28 pp. Because their teacher is there when they arrive and leave, some of the children believe that she lives in the classroom. To show the children that this is not so, she invites them to her home for a party. IL: 6–7. Available in paperback.

Theme/subject: School: teacher as a person

Welsh-Smith, Susan. *Andy, An Alaskan Tale*. Cambridge, 1988, 22 pp. Villagers in Alaska have fun with Andy, an Old English Sheepdog. They admire his shaggy hair and believe it is a wonderful parka. Even after he has moved away, they still smile when they remember his gentle spirit. Has brief glossary of Alaskan words. IL: 6–9.

Theme/subject: Pets: dogs; Life in Alaska

Westcott, Nadine Bernard. *Skip to My Lou.* Little, Brown, 1989, 28 pp. In this version of a traditional song, a young boy is asked to look after the farm, which is beset by many difficulties, so he skips to my Lou. After an uproarious afternoon skipping to my Lou, he and the farm animals clean up just before his parents return. Repeated lines provide opportunities for choral singing or reading. IL: 6–9.
Theme/subject: Traditional song; Dancing; Having fun

Westcott, Nadine Bernard. *I've Been Working on the Railroad.* Hyperion, 1996, 27 pp. This traditional song tells of working on the railroad: "I've been working on the railroad, Just to pass the time away. Don't you hear the whistle blowing, Rise up so early in the morn." Repeated lines provide opportunities for choral singing or reading. IL: 6–9. Available in paperback.
Theme/subject: Traditional song; Having fun; Transportation: railroads

Williams, Sherley Anne. *Working Cotton.* Harcourt, 1992, 26 pp. Although she is too small to carry her own sack, Shelan helps her family pick cotton. Shelan admires the speed with which her daddy picks cotton and believes she could pick 50 or 100 pounds of cotton if she were as big as her sisters. Although she is a willing worker, Shelan reflects that "It's a long time to night." IL: 6–9.
Theme/subject: Farming: migrant workers

Williamson, Stan. *The No-Bark Dog.* Modern Curriculum Press, 1962, 30 pp. Timothy's new dog won't bark. As time passes, Timothy becomes more and more concerned. Can be used to predict what the dog will do and problem solving. IL: 6–8. Available in paperback.
Theme/subject: Pets; Dogs: caring for

Wong, Herbert Yee. *Eek! There's a Mouse in the House.* Houghton Mifflin, 1992, 24 pp. A cat is sent in the house to get rid of a mouse, but the cat knocks over a lamp, so a dog is sent in to get rid of the cat. Because the dog breaks a dish, a hog is sent in to get rid of the dog. The story continues until an elelphant is sent in to get rid of all the animals, but this creates a surprise problem. Can be used to explore problem solving. IL: 6–8.
Theme/subject: Solution is worse than problem; Humor

Wood, Audrey. *The Napping House.* Harcourt, 1984, 30 pp. The bite of a flea starts a chain reaction that awakens the creatures and people sleeping in the napping house. IL: 6–9. Has sequel: *The Napping House Wakes Up.* Available in big-book format.
Theme/subject: Cumulative tale; Sleep; Humor

Wood, Don. *Quick as a Cricket.* Child's Play, 1982, 31 pp. Many animal similies are used to describe a young boy: quick as a cricket, happy as a lark, loud as a lion, quiet as a clam, brave as a tiger. Introduces use of similies. IL: 6–9.
Theme/subject: Personal description; Similies

Young, Ruth. *Golden Bear.* Viking, 1992, 26 pp. Golden Bear and the little boy are good friends. They make a snowman, play pirates, rock in the chair, and even make mud pies together. IL: 6–7.
Theme/subject: Song; Teddy bears

Ziefert, Harriet. *The Three Little Pigs.* Puffin, 1995, 30 pp. The smartest of the three pigs builds his house out of bricks and so the wolf is unable to blow it down. Repeated lines provide opportunities for choral or shared reading. IL: 6–7. Available in paperback.
Theme/subject: Traditional tale; Outwitting enemies

BEGINNING D

Abercrombie, Barbara. *Michael and the Cats*. Simon & Schuster, 1993, 18 pp. When Michael tries too hard to befriend his aunt's cats, they stay away from him, but when he watches to see what they like and acts accordingly, they become friendly. IL: 6–8.
Theme/subject: Pets; Cats: making friends with

Ahlberg, Allan. *The Pet Shop*. Greenwillow, 1990, 22 pp. Fed up with their pet skeleton dog who barks too much and digs up the yard, Little Skeleton and Big Skeleton try out a variety of pets who are even more trouble than the dog. In the end, they decide that a dog is the best pet for them. All the characters in the Funny Bones series are skeletons. Part of Funnybones series. Readers may need some help with British expressions and spellings: *miaow, cheeky*. Repeated lines provide opportunities for choral or shared reading. IL: 7–9. Available in paperback (Mulberry).
Theme/subject: Pets: choosing; Appreciating what one has; Humor

Alda, Arlene. *Sheep, Sheep, Sheep, Help Me Fall Asleep*. Doubleday, 1992, 28 pp. Advised to count sheep when he couldn't fall asleep, a young boy counts other animals instead: an itchy cow, a gorilla tickling his toes, a talking horse, a smiling rhino, and, finally, a very long line of sheep. IL: 6–7. Available in paperback.
Theme/subject: Sleep: difficulty falling asleep; Humor

Aliki. *Best Friends Together Again*. Greenwillow, 1995, 28 pp. In this sequel to *We Are Best Friends* in which Peter and Robert were separated by Peter's move, Peter and Robert have a joyful reunion when Peter comes to visit. When it's time for Peter to leave, the two are consoled by the memories they will have and the prospect of future visits. Reinforces letter writing. IL: 6–7.
Theme/subject: Friendship; Reunion; Letter writing

Allen, Jonathan. *Who's at the Door*. Tambourine, 1992, 23 pp. The three little pigs foil the big bad wolf's attempts to trick them. When the wolf disguises himself as a pig, they disguise themselves as a wolf. IL: 6–9.
Theme/subject: Outwitting enemies

Anholt, Catherine, & Anholt, Laurence. *Come Back, Jack*. Candlewick, 1993, 32 pp. A little girl who doesn't like books literally gets into a book when Jack, the little boy she is supposed to be watching, crawls into one and she follows. Jack and the little girl meet a number of nursery rhyme characters and then find themselves being chased by the giant from Jack and the Beanstalk. They mangage to run out of the book just in time. IL 6–8.
Theme/subject: Nursery rhymes; Fairy tales; Reading

Anholt, Laurence. *The New Puppy*. Western, 1994, 30 pp. After finally persuading her dad to let her have a puppy, Anna becomes upset when it chews up most of the things in her room, and she wants to get rid of it. She changes her mind that night when she hears it crying. IL: 6–8.
Theme/subject: Pets; Dogs: caring for

Anton, Tina. *Sharks, Sharks, Sharks*. Raintree Press, 1989, 31 pp. Drawings and easy-to-read text describe a variety of sharks and their major physical characerstics. Behavior of sharks is also explored. IL: 6–10. Available in paperback.
Theme/subject: Sharks

Babbitt, Natalie. *Bub or the Very Best Thing*. HarperCollins, 1994, 27 pp. Seeking information about what is the very best thing for the prince, the king and queen are told that vegetables, sleep, sunshine, and music are important. With the help of the cook, they finally discover what is really most important of all: love. IL: 6–8. Available in paperback.
Theme/subject: Love; Raising children

Baer, Gene. *Thump, Thump, Rat-a-Tat-Tat*. Atheneum, 1989, 30 pp. A marching band is depicted as it approaches from a distance and then comes closer so it is like "thunder coming, Getting louder, THUMP, THUMP, THUMP, THUMP." Lends itself to choral, partner, or shared reading. Reinforces *-at* and *-ump* patterns. IL: 6–7. Available in paperback.
Theme/subject: Music: marching bands

Baker, Barbara. *Digby and Kate*. Dutton, 1988, 48 pp. Although Digby is a dog and Kate is a cat and they have disagreements and misadventures, their friendship endures. Part of Digby and Kate series. Reinforces letter writing. IL: 6–8. Available in paperback.
Theme/subject: Friendship; Letter writing

Baker, Barbara. *Digby and Kate Again*. Dutton, 1988, 48 pp. Digby, a dog, and Kate, a cat, help each other meet the challenges of growing up and coping with everyday events and problems. Part of Digby and Kate series. IL: 6–8.
Theme/subject: Friendship; Letter writing; Riding a bike

Ballard, Robin. *Cat and Alex and the Magic Flying Carpet*. HarperCollins, 1991, 32 pp. After Cat tells him about a magic carpet that he found, Alex expresses a desire to go for a ride. The two of them lie down on the magic carpet and take a trip to the moon. Provides possible writing topic: Where would you go on a magic carpet? IL: 6–8. Out of print.
Theme/subject: Travel: fantasy; Magic carpet; Adventure

Barracca, Debra, & Barracca, Sal. *The Adventures of Taxi Dog*. Dial, 1990, 30 pp. A stray dog, Maxi is overjoyed when Jim takes him home, feeds him, and lets him ride along in his taxi. Maxi thoroughly enjoys being a taxi dog and even entertains passengers by wearing a Groucho Marx nose, mustache, and glasses. Part of Taxi Dog series. IL: 6–10.
Theme/subject: Pets: dog; Transportation: cabs; Humor

Bauman, A. F. *Guess Where You're Going, Guess What You'll Do*. Houghton Mifflin, 1989, 32 pp. The reader is given a series of visual and verbal clues and asked to: "Guess where you're going. Guess what you'll do." The reverse page provides the answers. Fosters predicting based on clues. IL: 6–8.
Theme/subject: Riddles, puzzles, games; Guessing based on clues

Bayer, Jane. *A, My Name Is Alice*. Dial, 1984, 26 pp. In this ball-bouncing rhyme, alliterative names, locations, and occupations are created for each letter of the alphabet: "A my name is Alice and my husband's name is Alex. We come from Alaska and we sell ants." Reinforces initial sounds. Lends itself to having students create verses using their names. IL: 6–7. Available in paperback.
Theme/subject: Play rhymes

Becker, Bonny. *The Quiet Way Home*. Holt, 1995, 24 pp. A little girl and her father take the quiet way home. Instead of going where the dog growls or the cars roar, they go where they can hear the skittle skattle of a kitten's paw or the squeak creak of a bicycle. IL: 6–8.
Theme/subject: Observing one's surroundings; Quiet

Benchley, Nathaniel. *Oscar Otter.* HarperCollins, 1966, 64 pp. Failing to heed his father's warning, Oscar Otter builds a slide that goes deep into the woods. Chased by a fox, Oscar is saved by a beaver. IL: 6–8. Available in paperback.
Theme/subject: Disobeying parents; Escape from enemies; Being helped by others

Benjamin, A. H. *What If?* Green Tiger Press, 1996, 24 pp. Farm animals worry that the new animal will take their places. As it turns out, the new animal, which is a kangaroo, is a very kindly creature who carries the farm animals' children in her pouch and takes them on a tour of the farm. IL: 6–8.
Theme/subject: Fear or distrust of others; Getting along with others

Berlan, Kathryn Hook. *Andrew's Amazing Monsters.* Maxwell, 1993, 28 pp. Fond of monsters, Andrew covered his walls with his drawings of strange creatures. Having drawn party hats on his monsters, Andrew was awakened that night by strange noises. The monsters were having a party in the attic. IL: 6–8.
Theme/subject: Monsters; Party

Bliss, Corinne Demas. *The Shortest Kid in the World.* Random House, 1994, 48 pp. Bothered by being the shortest kid in the class, Emily is even more upset when someone shorter than she transfers into her class. Eventually, the two become friends. IL: 6–9. Available in paperback.
Theme/subject: Growing up; Being short

Brenner, Barbara. *Beavers Beware!* Bantam, 1991, 32 pp. Beavers take over a family's diving dock and use it as a base for their new lodge. Although they lose their dock, the family gets a lesson in the ways of beavers. IL: 6–9. Available in paperback.
Theme/subject: Animals: beavers; People versus animals

Brenner, Barbara, & Hooks, William H. *Ups and Downs of Lion and Lamb.* Bantam, 1991, 48 pp. Despite difficulties with club membership and moving away, Lion and Lamb's improbable friendship thrives. In fact, when Lion is so frightened by a wolf that he is unable to roar, Lamb comes to his aid. Part of Lion and Lamb series. IL: 6–9. Available in paperback.
Theme/subject: Friendship; Courage; Moving

Bridwell, Norman. *Clifford's Puppy Days.* Scholastic, 1989, 30 pp. Although Clifford grew to be a giant dog, he was not much bigger than a mouse as a puppy, and so had a lot of misadventures. Part of Clifford series. IL: 6–8. Available in paperback.
Theme/subject: Pets: dogs; Fantasy; Humor

Brown, Craig. *Tractor.* Greenwillow, 1995, 24 pp. The tractor pulls machines that prepare the soil for planting, plant seeds, cultivate the soil, and help with the harvesting. All these machines are clearly shown in the text and explained more fully in the glossary. IL: 6–9.
Theme/subject: Farming: tractor and other farm machines

Brown, Margaret Wise. *The Diggers.* Hyperion, 1958, 1995, 29 pp. This book portrays all kinds of digging from a mole digging a hole and a boy digging for pirate treasure to workers digging a train tunnel through the side of a mountain. IL: 6–7.
Theme/subject: Construction: digging; Tunnels

Brown, Ruth. *Ladybug, Ladybug.* Dutton, 1988, 26 pp. In this version of a nursery rhyme, a lady bug hears that her house is on fire and her children are gone. After

a somewhat perilous journey home, she finds that they are all snug in their nest. Repeated lines provide opportunities for choral or shared reading. IL: 6–7. Available in paperback (Puffin).
Theme/subject: Nursery rhyme; Family: mother caring for young

Bulla, Clyde Robert. *The Christmas Coat*. Knopf, 1989, 36 pp. Believing that it was a gift for one of them, two quarrelsome brothers rip a coat in two. After finding out that the coat was a gift for a neighbor's child, they use their savings to have the coat mended and in the process learn how to get along with each other, which proves to be a wonderful gift for their mother. Reinforces problem solving. IL: 7–10. Out of print.
Theme/subject: Peers: getting along; Christmas gifts

Burton, Virginia. *The Little House*. Houghton Mifflin, 1942, 1969, 40 pp. Built in the country and surrounded by trees and flowers, the little house was quite content. As the years passed, a city grew up around the little house, and it grew old and shabby. Then the grandaughter of one of the little house's early occupants discovers the little house. Can be used to reinforce sequence. IL: 6–8. Available in paperback.
Theme/subject: Homes; Environment

Byars, Betsy. *Hooray for the Golly Sisters*. HarperCollins, 1990, 64 pp. As they travel across late nineteenth-century America putting on shows, the humorous Golly sisters encounter dangerous river crossings, swamps, and difficulty with their acts, especially when May-May substitutes pigs for rabbits in her magic act and Rose attempts to sing while waltzing on the high wire. Part of Golly Sisters series. IL: 6–9. Available in paperback.
Theme/subject: Show business; Pioneer days; Humor

Camp, Lindsay. *Keeping up with Cheetah*. Lothrop, Lee & Shepard, 1993, 24 pp. Abandoned as a friend by Cheetah because he runs too slow, Hippo tries to learn to run faster, but finally realizes that he was meant for waddling in the mud rather than running. Meanwhile, Cheetah comes to value Hippo for other qualities. IL: 6–8.
Theme/subject: Friendship; Being oneself

Carlson, Nancy. *Arnie and the New Kid*. Viking, 1990, 28 pp. While teasing Philip, who is wheelchair bound, Arnie falls down the steps and ends up on crutches. Temporarily disabled, Arnie starts befriending Philip and the two become good buddies. IL: 6–8. Available in paperback.
Theme/subject: Understanding others; Disabilities: wheelchairs

Caseley, Judith. *Grandpa's Garden Lunch*. Greenwillow, 1990, 20 pp. Sarah helps her grandpa plant and take care of his large garden. The plants grow and grow until one day grandma invites Sarah for lunch. Much of the food for the lunch comes from the garden. IL: 6–7.
Theme/subject: Grandparents; Gardening

Cauley, Lorinda Bryan. *Treasure Hunt*. Putnam's, 1994, 30 pp. A group of kids follow a series of clues hidden inside a book, under furniture, in a garden, and under a log. The clues lead to a special surprise. Reinforces following directions and predicting what the surprise is. IL: 6–8.
Theme/subject: Games/activities: treasure hunt; Picnic

Celsi, Teresa. *The Fourth Little Pig*. Steck Vaughn, 1990, 1992, 23 pp. Finding her brothers afraid to leave their brick home lest they be attacked by a wolf, the fourth lit-

tle pig convinces them to forget their fear of wolves and to go out into the world and live. Compare/contrast with original. IL: 6–9. Available in paperback.
Theme/subject: Fairytale; Fear: overcoming

Clifton, Lucille. *Everett Anderson's Friend*. Holt, 1976, 1992, 20 pp. When a family of girls moves into the apartment next door, Everett Anderson wishes they were boys. However, when Everett loses his key and the family invites him in, he and one of the girls become friends. Includes some Spanish words. IL: 6–8.
Theme/subject: Friends: making new; Multicultural; Partly multilingual

Clifton, Lucille. *Three Wishes*. Doubleday, 1992, 28 pp. Finding a penny on New Year's Day, Nobie takes it as a sign of good luck and makes three wishes. When her friend returns after an argument, she believes the last of her good luck wishes has come true. Possible writing topic: three wishes. IL: 7–9.
Theme/subject: Friendship

Coffelt, Nancy. *Tom's Fish*. Harcourt, 1994, 30 pp. Tom's favorite birthday present is a goldfish. There is only one problem: The fish swims upside down. Reinforces problem solving. IL: 6–9.
Theme/subject: Pets: goldfish; Humor

Cole, Joanna. *Bony-Legs*. Scholastic, 1983, 44 pp. With the help of creatures she befriended, Sasha escapes from the witch, Bony-legs. Reinforces *r* vowels. IL: 8–10. Available in paperback.
Theme/subject: Witches; Outwitting enemies

Cole, Joanna. *Hungry, Hungry Sharks*. Random House, 1986, 48 pp. This book highlights the many different kinds of sharks and their interesting behavior. IL: 6–10. Available in paperback.
Theme/subject: Animals: sharks

Cosgrove, Stephen. *The Fine Family Farm*. Forest House, 1991, 22 pp. Finding no fun in their work, the members of the Fine family stop doing their chores, including feeding the farm animals. Driven by hunger, the animals make a terrible clatter as they search through the farm house kitchen for food. Seeing the mess that's been made, the Fines start doing their chores once more, but also find that working together can be fun. Provides possible writing topic: chores. IL: 6–8.
Theme/subject: Farm; Responsibilities; Work: chores

Cowen-Fletcher, Jane. *It Takes a Village*. Scholastic, 1994, 28 pp. Feeling very proud that she has been entrusted with her little brother's care, Yemi is dismayed when he slips away while she purchases peanuts at the marketplace. Fortunately, Kokou is well cared for as he wanders through the village whose inhabitants put into practice their belief that it takes a village to raise a child. Repeated lines provide opportunities for choral or shared reading. IL: 6–9.
Theme/subject: Babysitting; Younger sibling; Multicultural: culture of a small African village

Crews, Donald. *Bigmama's*. Greenwillow, 1991, 30 pp. Illustrator Donald Crews recalls the summers that he spent on his grandmother's farm in Cottondale, Florida. There was fishing and swimming and lots of relatives. IL: 7–10. Available in paperback and audiotape (Varsity Readers Service).
Theme/subject: Autobiography; Grandparents; Farm life

Deetlerfs, Renee. *Tabu and the Dancing Elephants*. Dutton, 1995, 27 pp. When Tabu is carried off by elephants, his father chases after them with a spear, but the elephants pretend to be rocks and he does not see them. Tabu's mother uses music

to persuade the elephants to return her baby. Reinforces sequence and comparison/contrast between mother and father. IL: 6–8.
Theme/subject: Parents; Rescuing child; Using persuasion

Demarest, Chris L. *Kitman and Willy at Sea.* Simon & Schuster, 1991, 28 pp. The cat and mouse team of Kitman and Willy trick a hunter who is attempting to capture animals on an island and ship them to a zoo. Creating footprints for an imaginary creature, they lure the hunter into a trap. Reinforces sequence. IL: 6–8. Available in paperback.
Theme/subject: Escaping from enemies; Tricking enemies; Humor

Demarest, Chris L. *My Little Red Car.* Boyds Mill Press, 1992, 28 pp. A little boy imagines where he might go in his little red car: spiral up mountains, zoom down deep valleys, zig-zag toward the ocean. Suggests possible writing topic: Where would you go if you had a little red car? IL: 6–7. Available in paperback.
Theme/subject: Travel; Fantasy

De Regniers, Beatrice Schenk. *It Does Not Say Meow.* Seabury Press, 1972, 40 pp. Readers are given a number of clues to help guess the identity of common animals. IL: 6–8.
Theme/subject: Riddles

DeSaix, Deborah Durland. *In the Back Seat.* Farrar, Straus, Giroux, 1993, 28 pp. Sitting in the back seat of a car while traveling to Aunt Penelope's, Ariel and her little brother are transported into an imaginary world where they have a series of adventures, including an attack by snapping turtles and a giant hawk. The little brother is relieved when he arrives safely at his aunt's farm. IL: 6–9.
Theme/subject: Car trip; Imaginary adventures

Dinardo, Jeffrey. *The Wolf Who Cried Boy.* Grossett & Dunlap, 1989, 30 pp. A bored wolf creates excitement when he claims that a boy is after him. Shop owners, tired of being interrupted at work, dress up as a boy and give the wolf a good scare. Readers would need knowledge of the boy who cried wolf to understand this story. Readers can compare/contrast original version with this newer one. Provides possible writing topic: a lesson one has learned. IL: 6–8. Out of print.
Theme/subject: Telling the truth; False warnings; Humor: spoof

Dobkin, Bonnie. *Truck Stop.* Children's Press, 1994, 30 pp. A variety of trucks are seen doing a number of different jobs: dump trucks, cement trucks, moving vans, pick-ups, garbage trucks, delivery vans, and tow trucks for "when a car breaks down at night." IL: 6–8. Available in paperback.
Theme/subject: Transportation: trucks

Donaldson, Julia. *A Squash and a Squeeze.* Simon & Schuster, 1993, 24 pp. In this rhyming folktale, an old woman complained to a wise man that her house is a squash and a squeeze. He suggested that she take in her farm animals and later suggested that she put them out. After the crowding caused by taking animals in, her home felt roomy when it was just her in the house. IL: 6–8.
Theme/subject: Being satisfied with what one has; Folktale

Douglas, Barbara. *Good as New.* Lothrop, Lee & Shepard, 1982, 26 pp. K.C., a young cousin, demolishes Grady's beloved teddy bear, but grandfather comes to the rescue. He fixes the teddy bear so that it is better than new. Can be used to reinforce sequence. IL: 6–8. Available in paperback.
Theme/subject: Favorite possessions; Teddy bears; Grandparents

Dubanevich, Arlene. *Pig William*. Bradbury, 1985, 28 pp. Pig William takes so much time getting ready that he misses the bus that's taking the pigs to the picnic. However, because of rain, the other pigs are sent home, and later when the sun comes out, the pigs have a picnic in the backyard. Reinforces cause-effect: why Pig was late. IL: 6–7. Available in paperback (Aladdin).
Theme/subject: Family Life: being on time; Getting ready; Humor

Ehlert, Lois. *Mole's Hill: A Woodland Tale*. Harcourt, 1994, 30 pp. When told that her hill had to go to make way for a path to the pond, Mole devised a plan to save her home. She would make her hill so beautiful that no one would want to destroy it. Lends itself to predicting what Mole was doing to save her home. IL: 6–7.
Theme/subject: Home: protecting one's home

Everitt, Betsy. *Frida the Wondercat*. Harcourt, 1990, 30 pp. After a blue collar is put on Frida the cat, she is able to cook, drive a school bus, and waltz. Unfortunately, the attention this brings leaves Frida little time to spend with her owner. Readers can compare Frida before and after she gets the collar. Provides possible writing topic: what I'd like my pet to be able to do. IL: 6–9. Available in paperback.
Theme/subject: Pets: bond between pet and owner; Humor; Fantasy

Faulkner, Matt. *Jack and the Beanstalk*. Scholastic, 1986, 48 pp. In this traditional foktale, Jack and his mother become rich after Jack climbs the beanstalk and robs the giant. Can be used to reinforce sequence. IL: 6–8.
Theme/subject: Fairytale; Good outsmarting evil; Giants

Field, Rachel. *If Once You Have Slept on an Island*. Boyds Mills Press, 1993, 32 pp. According to this poem, once you have slept on an island, you'll never be the same. The sight and sounds of your surroundings will change you for good. Provides possible writing topic: experiences that change you. IL: 7–10.
Theme/subject: Sea: island; Nature: island; Poetry

Flack, Marjorie. *The Story about Ping*. Viking, 1933, 1961, 32 pp. Ping, a duck who lives on a boat on the Yangtzee River in China, hides when he sees that he will be late returning and would receive a spank for being the last duck to board the boat. Captured by a family on a house boat, Ping is set free by a little boy. IL: 6–8. Available in paperback (Puffin).
Theme/subject: Escaping from danger; Adventure

Fowler, Susi Gregg. *Fog*. Greenwillow, 1992, 30 pp. When a thick fog rolls in, grandma says that the family must listen to it. Because of the quiet, they become aware of chores left undone. After the chores are finished, grandma declares that the fog came for music. After the family spends the morning having a good time playing music, the fog fades away. IL: 6–9.
Theme/subject: Family life: family having fun; Fog

Gackenbach, Dick. *Harry and the Terrible Whatzit*. Clarion, 1977, 32 pp. Although afraid of the basement and its unknown terrors, Harry overcame his fears when his mother failed to return from the basement and he went there to investigate. IL: 6–9. Available in paperback.
Theme/subject: Fears: overcoming; Monsters

Gackenbach, Dick. *Dog for a Day*. Houghton Mifflin, 1987, 30 pp. With the help of a change machine that he invented, Sidney and his dog trade places. IL: 6–9.
Theme/subject: People becoming animals; Humor

Gackenbach, Dick. *Where Are Momma, Poppa, and Sister June?* Clarion, 1994, 32 pp. Because the dog had chewed up a note left by his family explaining that they had gone for pizza, a worried young boy imagines all the things that might have befallen his parents and sister. IL: 6–10.
Theme/subject: Family life: worrying about missing members

Gàg, Wanda. *Millions of Cats.* Putnam, 1928, 32 pp. Searching for the prettiest cat, the elderly peasant returned home with billions of cats. Fighting among themselves, the cats destroyed each other, except for a single kitten, which the man and his wife took in. IL: 6–8. Available in paperback.
Theme/subject: Pets: cats; Tall tale

Galdone, Paul. *The Three Little Pigs.* Clarion, 1970, 37 pp. The smartest of the three pigs builds his house out of bricks and so the wolf is unable to blow it down. He also escapes the wolf's attempts to catch him while he is out of the house. Lends itself to shared or choral reading. IL: 6–8. Available in paperback and audiotape.
Theme/subject: Traditional tale; Outwitting enemies

Galdone, Paul. *The Little Red Hen.* Clarion, 1973, 38 pp. Because her three friends don't help her grow and harvest the wheat and make flour from it, Little Red Hen does not share a cake with them. Repeated lines provide opportunities for choral or shared reading. IL: 6–8. Available in paperback and audiotape.
Theme/subject: Folklore: fable; Those who don't share in the work don't share in the rewards

Galdone, Paul. *The Three Billy Goats Gruff.* Clarion, 1973, 30 pp. Although he intimidates the first two Billy Goats Gruff, the troll is no match for the third brother. Can be used to reinforce sequence. IL: 6–7. Available in paperback.
Theme/subject: Folktale; Overcoming bully

Galdone, Paul. *The Three Little Kittens.* Clarion, 1986, 30 pp. The three little kittens lose their mittens and have other problems as well. Repeated lines provide opportunities for choral or shared reading. IL: 6–7. Available in paperback.
Theme/subject: Nursery rhyme; Responsibility

Gantos, Jack. *Rotten Ralph's Show and Tell.* Houghton Mifflin, 1989, 30 pp. Although Sarah's cat, Ralph, is always doing something rotten, she loves him just the same. IL: 6–9. Available in paperback (Sandpiper).
Theme/subject: Pets: cats; Humor

Garten, Jan. *Alphabet Tale.* Greenwillow, 1994, 52 pp. Based on a rhymed clue and a drawing of a tail, the reader is asked to guess the identity of the mystery animal. Promotes drawing conclusions based on verbal and visual clues and using context and intial letters. IL: 6–7.
Theme/subject: Riddles

Gershator, Phillis. *Sambalena Show-Off.* Simon & Schuster, 1995, 21 pp. Besides being lazy, Sambalena, is a show-off. One day, to show off, he put a clay pot on his head, which became stuck. In gratitide for having the clay pot removed, which was stuck there over night, Sambalena begins helping others, especially his grandmother, who got the pot off. The story is based on a traditional song from the Caribbean. Provides possible writing topic: learning a lesson. IL: 7–10.
Theme/subject: Learning a lesson the hard way

Gibson, Betty. *The Story of Little Quack.* Little, Brown, 1990, 30 pp. All the animals on the farm are too busy to play with Jackie, the farmer's son. Then Jackie discovers Little Quack, a baby duck, and the two play together each day until Little Quack disappears. They become friends again when Jackie discovers why Little Duck disappeared. IL: 6–7. Out of print.

Theme/subject: Friendship; Changing circumstances

Gilman, Phoebe. *Something from Nothing*. Scholastic, 1992, 28 pp. When Joseph was a baby, his grandfather made him a blanket. As the blanket became frayed, he made Joseph a jacket, then a tie, and so on, until there was nothing to be made but a story. Compare with *Just My Size*. Repeated lines provide opportunities for choral or shared reading. Reinforces Sequence. IL: 6–9.

Theme/subject: Grandparents; Clothes: reusing

Goldish, Meish. *What Is a Fossil?* Raintree, 1989, 32 pp. Text and illustrations describe four types of fossils and explain how they were formed. Features easy-to-read explanations. Reinforces sequence. IL: 7–9.

Theme/subject: Fossils

Gordon, Gaelyn. *Duckat*. Scholastic, 1992, 22 pp. A duck and a cat have identity problems. IL: 6–9.

Theme/subject: Being oneself; Humor

Greenfield, Eloise. *She Come Bringing Me that Little Baby Girl*. HarperCollins, 1974, 1990, 28 pp. Initially resentful of his baby sister, Kevin's attitude changes after he holds her, and his mom asks for his help. IL: 6–9.

Theme/subject: New baby; Siblings: jealousy

Grejniec, Michael. *Who Is My Neighbor?* Knopf, 1994, 29 pp. When the boy downstairs asks his neighbor for some candles during a power outage, the man treats him to a magic show in which he rides a horse and a lion and swings on a trapeze. Before the boy leaves, the man gives him a star to light his way. IL: 6–9.

Theme/subject: Neighbors; Magic

Griffith, Helen V. *Plunk's Dreams*. Greenwillow, 1990, 29 pp. A young boy imagines what his dog is dreaming about: being chased by a giant cat, exploring, meeting aliens from outer space. IL: 6–8.

Theme/subject: Dreams: dog's; Pet: dog

Gross, Ruth Belov. *The Bremen-town Musicians*. Scholastic, 1974, 32 pp. Four aging animals outwit a band of robbers in this retold tale from the brothers Grimm. IL: 6–8. Available in paperback.

Theme/subject: Folktale; Outwitting evil characters

Halpern, Shari. *I Have a Pet*. Simon & Schuster, 1994, 30 pp. Five children show their pets and tell what is special about each one and how they care for each one. Lends itself to comparison/contrast of pets. Possible writing topic and model: writing about pets. IL: 6–8.

Theme/subject: Pets: what's special about different kinds of pets

Harper, Wilhelmina. *The Gunniwolf*. Dutton, 1967, 28 pp. While gathering flowers, a little girl wanders into the forest and is threatened by the Gunniwolf. She tricks the Gunniwolf by singing him to sleep. Repeated lines provide opportunities for choral or shared reading. IL: 6–9.

Theme/subject: Folktale; Escaping from danger; Outwitting evil creatures

Hartman, Gail. *As the Crow Flies: A First Book of Maps*. Bradbury, 1991, 32 pp. The journeys of an eagle, rabbit, crow, horse, and gull are depicted and then shown as maps. The gull's map shows a harbor, island, lighthouse, and ocean. Reinforces map reading. See also *As the Roadrunner Runs*, a sequel to this text. IL: 6–9. Available in paperback.

Theme/subject: Maps; Animals: habitats and routes

Harwayne, Shelley. *Jewels, Children's Play Rhymes.* Mondo, 1995, 21 pp. Features 20 play rhymes from around the world. Includes brief poems, action, game, jump rope, and song rhymes. IL: 6–9.

Theme/subject: Word play; Rhymes

Havill, Juanita. *Jamaica's Find.* Scholastic, 1986, 31 pp. Finding a hat and a stuffed dog at the park, Jamaica turns the hat into lost-and-found but takes the stuffed dog home. After thinking it over, Jamaica returns the stuffed animal. Later, she becomes friends with the little girl who lost the animal. Part of Jamaica series. IL: 6–7. Available in paperback.

Theme/subject: Returning lost objects; Honesty

Havill, Juanita. *Jamaica's Blue Marker.* Houghton Mifflin, 1995, 28 pp. When Jamaica criticized Russell's picture, Russell responded by ruining her drawing. Later, Jamaica was pleased to hear that Russell was moving away, but then felt saddened and gave him a special going-away gift. Part of Jamaica series. Lends itself to study of characterization. IL: 6–8.

Theme/subject: Tolerance for others; Kindness; Moving away

Haynes, Max. *Dinosaur Island.* Lothrop, Lee & Shepard, 1991, 28 pp. One day each year, an island of dinosaurs appears. Unfortunately, Maddy and Bing are unable to locate any dinosaurs when they explore Dinosaur Island. Readers are invited to find the dinosaurs hidden in the illustrations. Reinforces following directions and analyzing illustrations so as to locate hidden figures. IL: 6–8.

Theme/subject: Games/activities: finding figures in hidden pictures; Dinosaurs

Hazen, Barbara. *Fang.* Atheneum, 1987, 28 pp. Although Fang looks fierce, he is really a very fearful dog. To set a good example, his young master pretends not to be afraid of such things as monsters, thunderstorms, and big kids. IL: 6–8. See *Stay, Fang.* Available in paperback (Aladdin).

Theme/subject: Pets: dog; Fear: overcoming

Hazen, Barbara. *Good-Bye, Hello.* Atheneum, 1995, 28 pp. A young girl says good-bye to her city neighborhood and friends and then greets her new suburban neighborhood. But she doesn't forget her old friends. Provides possible writing topic: moving. IL: 6–8.

Theme/subject: Moving

Hess, Debra. *Wilson Sat Alone.* Simon & Schuster, 1994, 27 pp. Wilson was a loner until a new girl entered the class. Wilson watched as she joined in the other children's work and play. And when the new girl, who was playing a game of monsters, roared at Wilson, Wilson roared back, and from that day on, joined in with the other children. IL: 6–8.

Theme/subject: Making friends; Being part of the group

Hewett, Joan. *Rosalie.* Lothrop, Lee & Shepard, 1987, 24 pp. A little girl tells about her pet dog, Rosalie. Although Rosalie is 16 and has grown deaf, everybody still loves her. IL: 6–8.

Theme/subject: Pets: dogs: growing old

Hoban, Lillian. *Arthur's Funny Money.* HarperCollins, 1981, 64 pp. Violet, Arthur's little sister, helps him come up with a way for earning money to buy a shirt and cap for his Frisbee team. Along with earning money by washing children's toys, Arthur learns some valuable math lessons. Reinforces adding and subtracting

and word problems. IL: 6–8. Available in paperback and audiotape (Caedmon).
Theme/subject: Humor; Earning money; Family life: sibling relationships
Hoff, Syd. *Duncan the Dancing Duck*. Clarion Books, 1994, 32 pp. After he bcomes
famous for his dancing, Duncan returns to his family for just one more dance.
He dances for his mom and then goes back to just being a duck. IL: 6–9.
Theme/subject: Fame; Humor
Hoff, Syd. *The Lighthouse Children*. HarperCollins, 1994, 32 pp. Living in a lighthouse,
Sam and Rose treated the seagulls as their children. After moving away, Sam
and Rose missed the seagulls but found a way to get them to visit. IL: 6–9. Avail-
able in paperback.
Theme/subject: Animals: sea gulls; Loneliness; Caring for others
Hoff, Syd. *Sammy the Seal*. HarperCollins, 1959, 64 pp. Despite having fun at school
during a vacation from the zoo, Sammy the seal decides that the zoo is really the
place that is home. IL: 6–9. Available in paperback.
Theme/subject: Home; Finding one's place in the world
Hooks, William H. *Feed Me*. Bantam, 1992, 32 pp. In this retelling of an Aesop's fable,
a mother lark realizes that her babies are safe in their cornfield nest until the
farmer decides not to rely on the help of friends and neighbors to harvest the
corn but depends on his own efforts. Reinforces *r* vowel and other vowel pat-
terns. Repeated lines provide opportunities for choral or shared reading. Avail-
able in paperback.
Theme/subject: Fable; Depending on oneself
Howard, Elizabeth Fitzgerald. *The Train to Lulu's*. Bradbury Press, 1988, 30 pp. Beepy
and Babs take a train trip from Boston to Baltimore where they stay with their
Great-Aunt Lulu during summer vacation. Reinforces map reading. IL: 6–9.
Available in paperback.
Theme/subject: Taking a trip by oneself; Transportation: trains
Howard, Ellen. *The Big Seed*. Simon & Schuster, 1993, 27 pp. Bess, the smallest girl in
her class, grows the biggest plant. When the children choose seeds to grow, Bess
believes she will be growing little yellow flowers and is surprised when sun-
flowers appear. IL: 6–8.
Theme/subject: Gardening; Accepting oneself
Howard, Jane R. *When I'm Sleepy*. Dutton, 1985, 22 pp. A young girl imagines what it
might be like to sleep the way animals do. She imagines herself sleeping in a
swamp, a cave, a hollow log, a nest, underwater, and other places. Companion
to *When I'm Hungry*. IL: 6–8.
Theme/subject: Sleeping: humans and animals; Humor
Howard, Jane R. *When I'm Hungry*. Dutton, 1992, 22 pp. A young boy imagines what
it might be like to eat like the animals. He imagines himself doing such things as
lapping up a bowlful of milk with puppies, swinging through the trees eating
bananas, sipping nectar from a flower. Companion to *When I'm Sleepy*. IL: 6–8.
Theme/subject: Eating: humans and animals; Humor
Howe, James. *There's a Dragon in My Sleeping Bag*. Atheneum, 1994, 26 pp. When his
big brother's attention is monopolized by an imaginary dragon, Simon begins to
feel left out and invents an imaginary camel. IL: 7–9.
Theme/subject: Siblings; Friendship; Imaginary playmates
Hubbard, Patricia. *My Crayons Talk*. Holt, 1996, 24 pp. Lively crayons express their
thoughts: Brown says, "Play, Mud-pie day." Purple shouts, "Yum! Bubble gum!"

Repeated lines provide opportunities for choral or shared reading. IL: 6–8.
Theme/subject: Drawing; Coloring

Hurwitz, Johanna. *New Shoes for Silvia*. Morrow, 1993, 28 pp. Silvia receives a gift of a beautiful pair of new shoes, but is unable to wear them because they are too big. The months pass and, finally, the shiny red shoes with the gleaming silver buckles fit. Uses some Spanish words. IL: 6–7.
Theme/subject: Gifts: clothing; Patience; Growing up; Partially bilingual

Ivimey, John W. *Three Blind Mice*. Clarion, 1987, 30 pp. In this altered version of the three blind mice, the mice lose their sight but regain it with the help of Dr. Hare's Magic Salve. Having regained their sight, they built a home and each learned a trade. Lends itself to partner, choral, or shared reading of repeated lines. IL: 6–8. Available in paperback.
Theme/subject: Traditional song; Traditional story

Jensen, Kiersten. *Possum in the House*. Gareth Stevens, 1989, 31 pp. When a possum gets loose in a house, it creates havoc in every room. It knocks over pots and pans, pushes books off shelves, and squeezes toothpaste out of the tube. Finally, it reaches a bedroom where it falls sound asleep. Repeated lines provide opportunities for choral or partner reading. IL: 6–9.
Theme/subject: Wild animals loose in house; Animal mischief

Johnson, Angela. *When I Am Old with You*. Orchard, 1990, 28 pp. A grandchild promises to spend lots of time with Grandaddy "when I am old with you." They will rock and talk, play cards, go fishing, and just enjoy being with each other. Repeated lines provide opportunities for choral or partner reading. IL: 6–8.
Theme/subject: Grandparents: spending time with

Johnson, Angela. *The Leaving Morning*. Orchard Books, 1992, 28 pp. A family says good-bye to their friends, relatives, and neighbors as they prepare to move from their city apartment. IL: 6–8.
Theme/subject: Moving; City life

Johnson, Crockett. *Harold and the Purple Crayon*. HarperCollins, 1955, 1993, 61 pp. Using his magic purple crayon, Harold creates objects and creatures as he takes an evening walk. Since there is no moon, he draws one. He also draws a path, a picnic lunch of pies, and a hot air balloon to carry him home. IL: 6–8. Available in paperback.
Theme/subject: Magic; Adventure; Journey

Johnson, Paul Brett, & Lewis, Celeste. *Lost*. Orchard, 1995, 32 pp. This book tells the true story of Flagg, a beagle who was lost in the desert. A little girl and her father searched and searched but were unable to find him. Finally, a prospector finds him. Reinforces sequence. IL: 6–10.
Theme/subject: Pets: dogs; Lost dogs

Jones, Rebecca C. *Matthew and Tilly*. Dutton, 1991, 28 pp. Matthew and Tilly are best friends and have fun together. After a quarrel over a broken crayon, they find that it's not much fun to play alone and so make up. Provides possible writing topic: making up after a quarrel. IL: 6–8.
Theme/subject: Friendship; Quarrels; Making up after a fight

Jordan, Helene J. *How a Seed Grows*. HarperCollins, 1960, 1992, 30 pp. This book explains what seeds are and how they grow. It also provides step-by-step directions for planting seeds and watching plants grow. Reinforces sequence/process: how seeds grow. IL: 6–8. Available in paperback.
Theme/subject: Seeds: growing

Kamen, Gloria. *Second-Hand Cat.* Atheneum, 1992, 30 pp. Going to the vet and riding in a car upset Louie, a cat that has just been given to Nathan. Much to Nathan's dismay, Louie runs away and disappears for a while but comes home when it starts to rain. Provides possible writing topic: pets running away. IL: 6–8.
Theme/subject: Pets: cats: likes and dislikes, running away

Kasza, Keiko. *The Rat and the Tiger.* Putnam, 1993, 29 pp. After Tiger fails to play fair or share, and then kicks down Rat's castle, Rat shouts that Tiger is not his friend anymore. Tiger reforms and the problem seems solved until a new kid moves in. Lends itself to comparison/contrast of Tiger and Rat and predicting what will happen next. IL: 6–7.
Theme/subject: Friendship: playing fair; Bullies

Keats, Ezra Jack. *The Snowy Day.* Viking, 1962, 32 pp. Peter enjoys playing in the snow so much that he attempts to save some of the snow by putting it in his pocket and taking it home. IL: 6–9. Available in paperback.
Theme/subject: Snow: playing in

Keats, Ezra Jack. *Louie.* Greenwillow, 1975, 32 pp. Louie is so captivated by the puppets at a show put on by neighborhood children that he speaks for the first time that anyone can remember. IL: 6–9.
Theme/subject: Overcoming difficulty; Puppets

Kent, Jack. *The Caterpillar and the Polliwog.* Simon & Schuster, 1982, 28 pp. A caterpillar and a polliwog are delighted when they turn into a beautiful butterfly and a handsome frog. IL: 6–9. Available in paperback.
Theme/subject: Stages of animal change; Chrysalis

Kessler, Ethel, & Kessler, Leonard. *Stan the Hot Dog Man.* HarperCollins, 1990, 64 pp. Stan, who has recently retired, opens up a hot dog stand and supplies hot dogs for students stranded by a snowstorm. IL: 6–9. Available in paperback.
Theme/subject: Helping others; Snowstorm; Retirement

Kessler, Leonard. *Here Comes the Strikeout.* HarperCollins, 1966, 64 pp. Desperate to get a hit after striking out 21 times in a row, Bobby seeks help from his friend Willy. Willy's advice and Bobby's hard work pay off. Provides possible writing topic: overcoming difficulty. IL: 6–9. Available in paperback.
Theme/subject: Sports: baseball; Overcoming difficulty; Friendship

Kessler, Leonard. *Kick, Pass, and Run.* HarperCollins, 1966, 64 pp. Animals learn how to play football by watching humans play. When a football lands in the woods, the animals play with it. In addition to being an amusing tale, the story provides background in the fundamentals of football. IL: 6–8. Available in paperback.
Theme/subject: Sports: football

Kessler, Leonard. *Super Bowl.* Greenwillow, 1980, 56 pp. Although disappointed that they lost the Super Bowl to the Animal Champs, the Super Birds decide that they will play better next year. Lends itself to choral reading or readers' theater. Students not assigned other parts can chant cheers. IL: 6–8. Available in paperback.
Theme/subject: Sports: football; Humor

Kessler, Leonard. *The Big Mile Race.* Greenwillow, 1983, 47 pp. With the help of Owl's coaching, the animals get ready for and run in the Big Mile Race. Because he hopped, Frog was last but is pleased that he finished and vows to hop faster next time. IL: 6–8. Available in paperback.
Theme/subject: Sports: running; Humor

Ketteman, Helen. *Not Yet, Yvette.* Whitman, 1992, 22 pp. Yvette and her dad prepare a surprise party for Mom. IL: 6–8. Available in paperback.
Theme/subject: Birthday party; Parents

Kimmel, Eric A. *Anansi and the Moss-Covered Rock.* Holiday House, 1988, 28 pp. Anansi, the spider, uses the power of a moss-covered rock to steal food from his friends. Observing from the forest, Bush Deer uses the rock to teach Anansi a lesson. IL: 6–8. Available in paperback.
Theme/subject: Trickster tale; Honesty; Teaching a lesson

Kimmel, Eric A. *I Took My Frog to the Library.* Viking, 1990, 24 pp. Bridgett brings a group of unusual pets, including a giraffe and an elephant, to the library with hilarious results. IL: 6–8.
Theme/subject: Library; Fantasy; Humor

Kimmel, Eric A. *The Old Woman and Her Pig.* Holiday, 1992, 30 pp. In this traditional tale, an old woman buys a pig but it won't go over a stile so she can't get it home. It takes a chain of events—beginning with feeding hay to a cow and ending with a dog nipping the pig—to get the pig to go over the stile. Reinforces sequence. IL: 6–8.
Theme/subject: Folktale; Chain story

Kraus, Robert. *Phil the Ventriloquist.* Greenwillow, 1989, 28 pp. Phil, the rabbit, gets on his parents' nerves when he uses his ability to throw his voice to make his father's shoes sing and his mother's hat tell jokes. But all is forgiven when Phil uses his special talent to scare off a burglar. Lends itself to readers' theater. IL: 6–10.
Theme/subject: Family life; Scaring off burglars; Humor

Krensky, Stephen. *Lionel at Large.* Dial, 1986, 56 pp. Lionel has a series of problems: dealing with his sister's runaway snake, making room for dessert, sleeping over, helping a friend get ready for a baby brother or sister, and visiting the doctor. IL: 6–8. Part of Lionel series. Available in paperback (Puffin).
Theme/subject: Growing up; Family life; Facing fears; Sibling relationships

Lee, Huy Voun. *At the Beach.* Holt, 1994, 26 pp. Xiao Ming's mother teaches him a series of Chinese characters by drawing them in the sand with a stick. She also explains why the characters are formed in a certain way: the character for a person, for example, looks like someone walking. Contains Chinese words. IL: 6–8.
Theme/subject: Family life; Language: Chinese; Multilingual

Lewis, Kim. *The Shepherd Boy.* Simon & Schuster, 1990, 26 pp. James learns to be a shepherd boy. Reinforces sequence. IL: 6–9.
Theme/subject: Animals: sheep; Occupations; Farms: sheep; Growing up

Lillegard, Lee. *My Yellow Ball.* Dutton, 1993, 29 pp. A little girl throws a ball so hard that it flies over the mountains, across the desert, to the jungle, over the ocean, and into space where it strikes a star. Wishing upon the star, the little girl gets her ball back and a puppy. Provides a possible writing topic: what I would wish for. IL: 6–8.
Theme/subject: Tall tale; Pets: getting a puppy

* Lobel, Arnold. *Frog and Toad Together.* HarperCollins, 1971, 64 pp. While having a series of lighthearted adventures, Frog and Toad discover the value of friendship. Part of Frog and Toad series. Highly recommended. IL: 6–8. Available in paperback.
Theme/subject: Friendship; Humorous adventures

Lobel, Arnold. *Owl at Home*. HarperCollins, 1975, 62 pp. While in or near his warm little home, Owl has a series of lighthearted but heart-warming adventures. IL: 6–8. Available in paperback.
Theme/subject: Humororous adventures

Lobel, Arnold. *Mouse Soup*. HarperCollins, 1977, 62 pp. A mouse uses his story-telling ability to trick a weasel out of making mouse soup. IL: 6–8. Available in paperback and audiotape.
Theme/subject: Telling stories; Outwitting enemies

* Lobel, Arnold. *Days with Frog and Toad*. HarperCollins, 1979, 64 pp. Frog and Toad experience the joys of friendship, including celebrating a birthday, flying a kite, sharing a scary story, being alone, and being together. Part of Frog and Toad series. Highly recommended. IL: 6–8. Available in paperback and audiotape (Caedmon).
Theme/subject: Friendship

London, Jonathan. *Froggy Gets Dressed*. Viking, 1992, 28 pp. Forgetting time after time to put on an article of clothing, Froggy has to stop playing in the snow and return home to get dressed all over again. Finally, tired of getting dressed, Froggy resumes hibernating. IL: 6–7. Available in paperback (Puffin).
Theme/subject: Getting dressed; Snow

Lucas, Barbara M. *Snowed In*. Bradbury, 1993, 27 pp. Wisely, a father living on the range in Wyoming in 1915 stocks up on pencils, paper, and books before the family is snowed in for the winter. During the long winter, the children play and read and are given lessons by their parents. IL: 6–10.
Theme/subject: Family life: farm, long ago

Mangas, Brian. *Follow that Puppy!* Simon & Schuster, 1991, 29 pp. When he takes Puppy for a walk, Grandpa is taken on a wild chase that ends up on the uppermost part of a suspension bridge. After being rescued by a police helicopter, Grandpa and Puppy return home. Reinforces sequence. IL: 6–9. Available in paperback.
Theme/subject: Pets: walks; Humor: exaggerated events

Mann, Kenny. *I Am Not Afraid*. Bantam, 1993, 28 pp. In this adaptation of a Masai tale, Tipilit is a brave older brother, but Leyo is small and meek. Leyo runs away when the river roars at him for trying to fill his gourd and a tree shouts at him when he attempts to cut off a dead branch for firewood. After Tipilit rescues him from a demon, he teaches him how to stand up to the river and the tree. IL: 8–10. Available in paperback.
Theme/subject: Traditional tale; Growing up; Learning to be brave; Siblings

Marshall, James. *Fox Be Nimble*. Penguin, 1992, 48 pp. Fox has a series of misadventures, including helplessly watching the children he was supposed to be babysitting float away as they held onto their balloons. Luckily, a favorable wind carried the children back home just before their mother returned. IL: 7–9. Available in paperback.
Theme/subject: Babysitting; Humorous misadventures

Martin, Bill, Jr., & Archambault, John. *Chicka Chicka Boom Boom*. Simon & Schuster, 1989, 30 pp. The letters of the alphabet run up a coconut tree in this rhymed tale. Repeated lines provide opportunities for choral or shared reading. IL: 6–7.
Theme/subject: Word study: sounds of words

Marzollo, Jean. *Pretend You're a Cat*. Dial, 1990, 26 pp. Readers pretend that they are a variety of animals. Excellent for developing ability to follow written directions. IL: 6–7.

Theme/subject: Animals; Pretend

Marzollo, Jean. *Snow Angel*. Scholastic, 1995, 28 pp. Accidentally left behind by her mother during a snowstorm, Jamie discovers a snow angel who enables her to fly over the town and her mother's car. Repeated lines provide opportunities for choral or partner reading. IL: 6–8.

Theme/subject: Family: parents; Fantasy: angels; Snow

Mayer, Mercer. *There's an Alligator under My Bed*. Dial, 1987, 30 pp. Using a trail of food, a clever little boy lures an alligator from under the bed to the garage, which he quickly locks. IL: 6–7.

Theme/subject: Outwitting dangerous creatures

McCully, Emily Arnold. *The Grandma Mix-up*. HarperCollins, 1988, 64 pp. Pip finds himself being cared for by two grandmas, one who is too easy and one who is too strict. Reinforces compound words. Part of Grandma series. Available in paperback.

Theme/subject: Grandparents

McDermott, Gerald. *Anansi the Spider: A Tale from the Ashanti*. Holt, 1972, 34 pp. When Anansi the spider got lost and fell into trouble, his six sons rescued him. Finding a great globe of light in the woods, Anansi planned to give it to one of his sons. Because Anansi was unable to decide which son deserved it most, the globe was put into the sky by Nyame, the god of all things, and it became the moon. IL: 6–9. Available in paperback.

Theme/subject: Pourquoi tale: creation of the moon; Anansi tale; Working together

McDermott, Gerald. *Zomo the Rabbit: A Trickster Tale from West Africa*. Harcourt, 1992, 30 pp. To obtain wisdom from the Sky God, Zomo must complete three virtually impossible tasks: obtain the scales of Big Fish, the milk of Wild Cow, and the tooth of Leopard. IL: 6–8. Available in paperback.

Theme/subject: Trickster tale; Wisdom

Moore, Inga. *Six-Dinner Sid*. Simon & Schuster, 1991, 28 pp. Until Sid gets sick and the vet blows the whistle on him, Sid, the cat, pretends to belong to six different families so that he can get six dinners. Lends itself to comparison/contrast of owners. IL: 6–8. Available in paperback.

Theme/subject: Pets: cats; Humor

Morris, Ann. *On the Go*. Lothrop, Lee & Shepard, 1990, 29 pp. People around the world travel in many different ways. Some go by foot with baskets on their heads. Others use horses, donkeys, or camels, and wheeled vehicles of many kinds. Others go by boat, plane, or even monorail. IL: 6–9. Available in paperback (Mulberry).

Theme/subject: Transportation: different kinds of in different places; Multicultural

* Mozelle, Shirley. *Zack's Alligator*. HarperCollins, 1989, 64 pp. Zack's uncle sent him Bridget, an alligator on a keychain that grows to full size when watered. Zack and his friend Turk create quite a stir when they take Bridget for a walk. After having the tire of his truck bitten by Bridget, the mail carrier complains about putting up with alligators as well as dogs. A police officer reminds Zack of a law

that says alligators must be on leashes. Highly recommended. IL: 6–10. Available in paperback.

Theme/subject: Pets: unusual: alligators; Fantasy; Humor

Mullins, Patricia. *Dinosaur Encore*. HarperCollins, 1992, 23 pp. Dinosaurs are compared with today's animals: Which one would be faster than an ostrich? Which one would eat more than four hungry horses? Which one would be smaller than a Dalmatian dog? Lends itself to comparison/contrast. Glossary phonetically respells dinosaur names. IL: 6–9.

Theme/subject: Dinosaurs

Murphy, Jill. *A Quiet Night In*. Candlewick, 1994, 24 pp. Because it's their dad's birthday, the Large children are giving him a quiet night in. However, their dad falls asleep early, as does their mom. The children tuck their parents in and go quietly to bed. IL: 6–7.

Theme/subject: Birthday; Bedtime; Family life

Narahashi, Keiko. *I Have a Friend*. Simon & Schuster, 1987, 27 pp. A little boy has a friend who sits with him on the steps and follows him down the street and stays with him all day, but disappears into the darkness. It is his shadow. IL: 6–7.

Theme/subject: Shadows

Neitzel, Shirley. *The Bag I'm Taking to Grandma's*. Greenwillow, 1995, 30 pp. A little boy attempts to pack many of his most prized possessions in preparation for a trip to Grandma's. Provides possible topic for writing: what would I pack for an overnight trip. IL: 6–7.

Theme/subject: Grandparents; Prized possessions

Nerlove, Miriam. *Christmas*. Whitman, 1990, 22 pp. In rhymed couplets, a little girl rejoices in the coming of Christmas. She delights in decorating the tree, wrapping presents, the coming of Santa Claus, exchanging presents, going to church, and celebrating the nativity. Readers would need background knowledge of nativity to understand story. IL: 6–7. Available in paperback.

Theme/subject: Christmas; Nativity

Ness, Caroline. *Let's Be Friends*. HarperCollins, 1995, 16 pp. Although Zack the cat is initially hostile, he and Lucy the dog become friends. IL: 6–7.

Theme/subject: Friendship; Making friends

Nones, Eric Jon. *Angela's Wings*. Farrar, Straus & Giroux, 1995, 27 pp. Angela wakes up one morning to find that she has grown wings. At first, Angela is embarrassed by the wings and stays to herself. After her grandmother advises her to make the best of the situation, she starts to enjoy her wings. They are an advantage on the basketball court and when viewing fireworks. Provides possible writing topics: if I had wings. IL: 7–10.

Theme/subject: Flying: person; Being oneself; Appreciating one's talents

Novak, Matt. *Mouse TV*. Orchard, 1994, 27 pp. A family of mice argue about what they should watch on TV. Then one night the TV breaks and the family discovers they can play games, sing songs, act out plays, make things, and read and have stories read to them. Best of all, there are no commercials. Provides possible writing topic: TV turnoff. IL: 6–9.

Theme/subject: Family: TV turnoff

Numeroff, Laura Joffe. *If You Give a Mouse a Cookie*. HarperCollins, 1985, 30 pp. Giving a mouse a cookie could set off a chain of events that include providing it with milk, a straw, a napkin, and so on. Provides possible model for writing. See

sequel: *If You Give a Moose a Muffin.* IL: 6–9. Available in paperback and CD-ROM.
Theme/subject: Food: snacks; Humor
Oppenheim, Joanne. *Left & Right.* Harcourt, 1989, 29 pp. Two brothers, Left and Right, who are cobblers have a series of arguments and decide to go their separate ways. Soon their customers begin to complain. The boots that were purchased after the brothers split up are hurting their feet. It seems Left was good at making boots for the left foot but not the right and Right was an expert cobbler of right-footed boots but not not left-footed ones. The problem is solved when the brothers agree to work together. IL: 6–8.
Theme/subject: Folktale; Cooperating
Parish, Peggy. *Amelia Bedelia Helps Out.* Greenwillow, 1979, 64 pp. Strange things happen when literal-minded Amelia Bedelia works in the garden. Bean plants are given steaks, bugs are dusted with a feather duster, and sowing bare spots with seeds is translated into sewing seeds together and using strings of sewn-together seeds to cover bare spots. Reinforces understanding of figurative language, homophones, and homographs. Part of Amelia Bedelia series. IL: 7–9. Available in paperback.
Theme/subject: Playing with language; Figurative language; Homophones; Humor
Paul, Ann Whitford. *Shadows Are About.* Scholastic. 1992, 29 pp. Two children observe the shadows that are about. The shadows "drive with cars and sway with trees." They also "clap with hands" and "paint dark pictures on the walls." IL: 6–7.
Theme/subject: Shadows
* Penner, Lucille. *Dinosaur Babies.* Random House, 1991, 32 pp. This book shows what dinosaur babies might have looked like, how they were cared for, and how they grew up. Reinforces *r* vowels and other vowels. Highly recommended. IL: 6–9. Available in paperback.
Theme/subject: Dinosaurs
Pickett, Anola. *Old Enough for Magic.* HarperCollins, 1989, 64 pp. When Peter's older sister plays with the magic kit that he got for his birthday, she turns herself into a frog. Finding a puzzling direction for turning a frog back into a person, Peter asks neighbors and the librarian for advice and finally finds the solution in a storybook: He must kiss the frog. Lends itself to prediction and problem solving. Possible writing topic: how I solved a problem. IL: 6–8.
Theme/subject: Magic; Peer relationships; Humor
Prater, John. *Once Upon a Time.* Candlewick, 1993, 24 pp. Fairytale characters pass by the house of a little boy who complains that there is "Not much to do. Not much to see." Requires knowledge of common fairytales. IL: 6–8. Available in paperback.
Theme/subject: Fairytales; Fantasy; Family life
Raffi. *Baby Beluga.* Crown, 1990, 30 pp. This song celebrates the life of a baby beluga whale. Lends itself to choral singing or reading. Part of Raffi Songs to Read series. IL: 6–8.
Theme/subject: Animals: beluga whales; Songs
Reiser, Lynn. *The Surprise Family.* Greenwillow, 1994, 28 pp. In this unique family, a chick adopts a boy as her mother. As a hen, she hatches duck eggs and raises a family of ducklings. Although, at first she is upset when they go swimming, she

realizes the ducklings are different from her and learns to accept them for what they are. Lends itself to comparison/contrast. IL: 6–8.

Theme/subject: Families: appreciating differences

Rey, H. A. *Curious George*. Houghton Mifflin, 1941, 54 pp. Captured by the man in the yellow hat, Curious George has series of hilarious adventures. Part of Curious George series. IL: 6–8. Available in paperback.

Theme/subject: Humorous misadventures

Rotner, Shelley, & Kreisler, Ken. *Nature Spy*. Simon & Schuster, 1992, 26 pp. In this photo essay, a young girl is a nature spy. She looks closely at plants and animals. She notices the feathers of a bird, the golden eye of a frog, and the seeds of a sunflower. IL: 6–9.

Theme/subject: Nature: noticing things in; Observation

Rounds, Glen. *The Three Billy Goats Gruff*. Holiday House, 1993, 29 pp. Although he intimidates the first two Billy Goats Gruff, the troll is no match for the third brother. IL: 6–8.

Theme/subject: Folktale; Overcoming bully

Russo, Martisabina. *Alex Is My Friend*. Greenwillow, 1992, 30 pp. Because of a birth defect, Alex is smaller than Ben even though Alex is a year older. As he grows older, Alex needs an operation and is unable to be very active. Even so, the two boys remain friends. They play games and tell stories and Alex tells funny jokes. IL: 6–8.

Theme/subject: Friendship; Disabilities

* Rylant, Cynthia. *Henry and Mudge: The First Book*. Simon & Schuster, 1990, 40 pp. As a puppy, Mudge comes to live with Henry and grows into a 180-pound companion. Part of Henry and Mudge series. Highly recommended. IL: 6–8. Available in paperback.

Theme/subject: Pets: dogs

Rylant, Cynthia. *Henry and Mudge and the Bedtime Thumps*. Simon & Schuster, 1991, 40 pp. Staying at his grandparents, Henry hears strange sounds in the night. Worse, Mudge is sleeping on the porch and so is unable to protect Henry from bears, bobcats, or other creatures that might happen by. Reinforces predicting what Henry will do. Provides possible writing topic: nightime fears. Part of Henry and Mudge series. IL: 6–8. Available in paperback.

Theme/subject: Pets: dogs; Fears: nightime

Sendak, Maurice. *Where the Wild Things Are*. HarperCollins, 1964, 36 pp. Sent to bed for misbehaving, Max imagines himself as the king of wild creatures. IL: 6–7. Available in paperback.

Theme/subject: Monsters; Misbehavior; Imagination

Serfozo, Mary. *Who Wants One?* Simon & Schuster, 1992, 32 pp. Going through the numbers one to ten, a little girl waves her magic wand and makes all sorts of wonderous things appear: "four goats in boats, six jolly dolphins doing tricks, seven swans on sky-blue lakes." Repeated lines provide opportunities for choral or partner reading. Model for creating a counting book. Uses question and answer format, which readers might try in their writing. IL: 6–7. Available in paperback.

Theme/subject: Counting; Pets: dog

Sharmat, Marjorie. *Mitchell Is Moving*. Simon & Schuster, 1978, 46 pp. Tired of living in the same old house, Mitchell the dinosaur decides to move, even though his

friend Margo objects. Mitchell is very happy with his new home and happier still when Margo builds a house next door to his. Provides practice for use of prefix *un*. Reinforces letter writing. IL: 6–9. Available in paperback.
Theme/subject: Friends: moving away

Sharmat, Marjorie. *I'm the Best*. Holiday House, 1991, 29 pp. Having had a series of owners, Dudley Dog is adopted by a young boy and his family. Little by little, the dog and the family learn to love each other. The story is told from the dog's point of view. Models writing technique: telling a story from an animal's point of view. IL: 6–8.
Theme/subject: Pet: dogs; New home for pet

Sharratt, Nick. *My Mom and Dad Help Me Laugh*. Candlewick, 1994, 26 pp. While a little boy has a preference for gray, his mom prefers spots and his dad stripes. Provides possible writing topic: favorite color. Offers opportunity for comparison/contrast of family members. IL: 6–9.
Theme/subject: Color; Clothes; Individual differences; Family life

Shelby, Anne. *The Someday House*. Orchard, 1996, 27 pp. Children dream about the kinds of houses they might live in someday: a houseboat on a river, one above a bakery, a house underground, a house in space, or one with secret passages where they could play hide-and-go-seek. Provides model for writing: "Someday we'll live in a house…. " IL: 6–9.
Theme/subject: Houses; Dream homes; Fantasy

Showers, Paul. *The Listening Walk*. HarperCollins, 1961, 1991, 30 pp. A little girl talks about all the sounds she hears as she takes a walk along a city street and a path in the woods. Provides practice in using phonics to decipher sounds phonetically spelled in story. Provides model for including sounds in writing. IL: 6–8.
Theme/subject: Listening; Noise; Environmental sounds

Simms, Laura. *The Squeaky Door*. Crown, 1991, 27 pp. In this adapted folktale from Puerto Rico, a small boy is frightened by a squeaky door. Hoping to quell his fears, the grandmother puts a cat in bed with him. When that doesn't work, she tries a dog, a cat, a snake, and finally a horse. The problem is solved when the house collapses and a new one is built—one that doen't have a squeaky door. Repeated lines provide opportunities for choral or partner reading. IL: 6–8. Out of print.
Theme/subject: Cumulative tale; Fears: noises at night; Humor; Solutions that are worse than the problem

Simon, Norma. *Cats Do, Dogs Don't*. Whitman, 1986, 29 pp. Contrasts cats and dogs: cats climb, dogs don't; cats purr when they're happy, dogs wag their tail; dogs act ashamed when they've been bad, cats don't. Both cats and dogs need love. Lends itself to comparison/contrast. IL: 6–9.
Theme/subject: Pets: cats and dogs

Siracusa, Catherine. *No Mail for Mitchell*. Random House, 1990, 32 pp. Sad because he never gets any mail, Mitchell the mail carrier is happily surprised when, during an illness, he receives a whole bag of mail from the people on his route. Reinforces writing letters. IL: 6–8. Available in paperback.
Theme/subject: Mail; Kindness; Humor

* Slepian, Jan, & Seidler, Ann. *The Hungry Thing*. Scholastic, 1967, 30 pp. One morning the Hungry Thing appears in town with a sign that says "Feed me." The creature demands shmancakes, tickles, and hookies. The townspeople and the

reader have to figure out what the Hungry Thing really wants. Promotes use of context and consonant substitution to figure out what the creature wants. If read aloud to students, can also be used to reinforce phonemic awareness of initial sounds. See *The Hungry Thing Returns* and *The Hungry Thing Goes to a Restaurant.* Highly recommended. IL: 6–9. Available in paperback.

Theme/subject: Language play: distortion of words; Humor

Slepian, Jan, & Seidler, Ann. *The Hungry Thing Returns.* Scholastic, 1990, 28 pp. One morning, the Hungry Thing and a small Hungry Thing appear in the school yard with signs that say "Feed Me" and "Me Too." The creatures ask for flamburger, bellyjeans, and crackeroni and sneeze. The headmaster, cook, students, and the reader have to figure out what the Hungry Thing and the Small Hungry Thing really want. Promotes use of context and consonant substitution to figure out what the creatures are requesting. If read aloud to students, can also be used to reinforce phonemic awareness of initial sounds. Sequel to *The Hungry Thing.* See also *The Hungry Thing Goes to a Restaurant.* IL: 6–9. Available in paperback.

Theme/subject: Language play: distortion of words; Humor

Stadler, John. *The Adventures of Snail at School.* HarperCollins, 1993, 64 pp. Snail has a series of humorous adventures at school, including meeting creatures from another planet. IL: 6–9.

Theme/subject: Adventure; School; Humor

Stevenson, James. *"Could Be Worse!"* Greenwillow, 1977, 29 pp. Whenever the grandchildren complain about a mishap like a flat tire on their bike or a splinter in their finger, Grandpa replies that it "could be worse." Then one morning, Grandpa explains what happened to him during the night. His misadventure includes being pulled from his bed by a giant bird and encountering such creatures as the abominable snowman, an enormous goldfish, and a giant lobster. IL: 6–10. Part of Grandpa series. Available in paperback (Mulberry).

Theme/subject: Grandparents; Adventure; Tall tale; Humor

Stevenson, James. *Monty.* Greenwillow, 1979, 28 pp. When Monty, the alligator, takes an unexpected vacation, three animal children who floated to school on his back have to find another way to cross the stream. Provides practice with predicting and problem solving. IL: 6–9. Available in paperback (Mulberry).

Theme/subject: Gratitude; Humor

Stevenson, James. *Will You Please Feed Our Cat?* Greenwillow, 1987, 30 pp. Grandpa tells about the time when he and his little brother Wainey agreed to feed the neighbor's cat and found themselves responsible for also feeding a hamster, a parakeet, a turtle, a rabbit, and all the cats in the neighborhood. They also had to water all the plants in a greenhouse. Part of Grandpa series. IL: 7–9.

Theme/subject: Pets: feeding; Humor: exaggeration; Grandparents

Sykes, Julie. *This and That.* Farrar, Straus and Giroux, 1996, 24 pp. When a cat begins borrowing items from the animals, they ask her what she is going to use them for. She responds "for this and that." Later, they learn that she used the items to build a nest for her new kittens whom she named "This" and "That." IL: 6–8.

Theme/subject: Birth of kittens; Animal home: nest

Thomas, Abigail. *Pearl Paints.* Holt, 1994, 29 pp. When Pearl got a set of paints for her birthday, she began painting. She painted during playtime and dinner and after dinner. She painted oceans, jungles, forests. She even painted in her dreams. Pro-

vides possible writing topic: things students like to do. IL: 6–9.
Theme/subject: Talents and abilities; Hobbbies; Interests

Van Leeuwen, Jean. *Tales of Amanda Pig*. Dial, 1983, 56 pp. In a series of five warm-hearted tales, Amanda Pig faces the joys and challenges of growing up, including dealing with imagined monsters and an older brother. Part of Amanda Pig series. IL: 6–8. Available in paperback.
Theme/subject: Growing up; Monsters; Sibling relationships

Walsh, Ellen Stoll. *You Silly Goose*. Harcourt, 1992, 30 pp. Even though flipped into a pond by a silly goose because he was mistaken for a fox, George Mouse helps save the geese from the real fox. Can be used to foster critical thinking: not drawing hasty conclusions based on insufficient evidence. IL: 6–8. Available in paperback.
Theme/subject: Escape from enemies; Hasty conclusions

Wheeler, Cindy. *Bookstore Cat*. Random House, 1994, 32 pp. Mulligan, the cat, works in a bookstore. He feels he helps the owner by knocking books off the shelves and entertaining customers. He also makes sure no birds get in the bookstore. When a pigeon flies into the shop, Mulligan goes into action. Although he wrecked the shop, he got rid of the pigeon. IL: 6–8. Available in paperback.
Theme/subject: Pets: cats; Humor

Whybrow, Ian. *Quacky Quack-quack*. Simon & Schuster, 1991, 24 pp. A little boy causes chaos when he eats the bread crumbs that he was supposed to feed to the animals and they noisily protest. An older brother finally helps put an end to the racket. Lends itself to readers' theater. There are many brief reading parts. IL: 6–7.
Theme/subject: Sharing; Humor

Wilcox, Cathy. *Enzo the Wonderfish*. Ticknor & Fields, 1983, 30 pp. Wanting a horse, a dog, or a cat for a pet, a young girl settles for a goldfish. She attempts to teach Enzo the kinds of tricks usually taught to a dog, but Enzo doesn't learn any of them, except going for a walk (while in its bowl) and playing dead. IL: 6–8.
Theme/subject: Pets: goldfish: teaching tricks to; Humor

Wildsmith, Brian. *Goat's Trail*. Knopf, 1986, 30 pp. A lonely goat descends from his mountain home to experience the excitement of the town. Along the way, he persuades other animals to follow him. Cutout windows add to the appeal of the book. IL: 6–7. Theme/subject: Exploring one's environment; Traveling

Wilson, Sarah. *Good Zap, Little Grog*. Candlewick, 1995, 24 pp. Little Grog is off to see strange creatures: the glipneep, the smibblet, the ooglet, the zoof, and the floom. Promotes use of phonics to decipher the names of strange creatures and their actions. IL: 6–8.
Theme/subject: Strange creatures; Fantasy

Winthrop, Elizabeth. *Maggie and the Monster*. Holiday House, 1987, 28 pp. Unable to get rid of the monster in her room. Maggie asks her what she wants and finds out that the monster is looking for her mother. After helping the monster find her mother, Maggie goes back to bed. IL: 6–8. Available in paperback.
Theme/subject: Families: searching for mothers; Monsters; Humor

Wolff, Patricia Rae, & Root, Kimberley. *The Toll-Bridge Troll*. Harcourt, 1995, 21 pp. To get to school, Trigg has to trick the troll that guards the bridge. The troll's mother is so impressed with the way Trigg uses riddles to trick her son, that she directs her son to go to school with Trigg so that he will get smart, too. Fosters understanding riddles. IL: 6–9.

Theme/subject: Outwitting enemies: trolls

Wormel, Mary. *Hilda Hen's Search*. Harcourt, 1994, 28 pp. Unable to use the henhouse because it is full, Hilda Hen has difficulty finding a place where she can lay her eggs. Reinforces suffix *y*. See *Hilda Hen's Happy Birthday*. IL: 6–7.

Theme/subject: Animals: hens; Nests; Home

Wormel, Mary. *Hilda Hen's Happy Birthday*. Harcourt, 1995, 28 pp. Believing that they have been left for her as birthday presents, Hilda Hen eats the horse's oats, the gardener's apples, and the farmer's cookies. IL: 6–7.

Theme/subject: Birthday; Gifts; Humorous misunderstanding

Yoshi. *Who's Hiding Here?* Picture Book Studio, 1987, 32 pp. Readers use verbal and visual clues, including cutouts, to guess who is hiding. Reinforces using visual and verbal clues to predict identity of creatures hiding. IL: 6–9. Available in paperback.

Theme/subject: Animals: protecting themselves by using camouflage

Young, Ed. *Seven Blind Mice*. Scholastic, 1992, p. 36. Six blind mice examining a strange something speculate that it is a pillar, a snake, a spear, a rope, a cliff, and a fan. The seventh mouse examining the whole beast reports that the strange something is an elephant. Demonstrates drawing conclusions based on all the evidence. IL: 6–8.

Theme/subject: Fable; Need to look at the whole, not just the parts

Ziefert, Harriet. *Pete's Chicken*. Tambourine, 1994, 32 pp. Although the other children made fun of the chicken he drew in art class, Pete Rabbit decided it was beautiful because no one else would draw a chicken in exactly the same way. IL: 6–8.

Theme/subject: Art; Individuality

Zimmerman, Andrea, & Clemesha, David. *The Cow Buzzed*. HarperCollins, 1993, 28 pp. When the farm animals catch a cold, they also begin making the sound of the animal from whom they caught the cold, so that the duck oinks and the rooster barks. IL: 6–8. Available in paperback.

Theme/subject: Animal sounds: switching; Humor

Zion, Gene. *Harry the Dirty Dog*. HarperCollins, 1956, 28 pp. Harry, who hates baths, gets so dirty that his family doesn't recognize him. Part of Harry the Dirty Dog series. IL: 7–9 Available in paperback.

Theme/subject: Pets: dogs: baths; Not being recognized; Humor

* Zion, Gene. *No Roses for Harry*. HarperCollins, 1958, 28 pp. Trying to get rid of a rose-covered sweater that he hates, Harry is helped by a bird who unravels the sweater and uses the yarn to make a nest. Part of Harry series. IL: 6–9. Highly recommended. Available in paperback.

Theme/subject: Pets; Humor; Gifts

GRADE 2A

* Allard, Harry, & Marshall, James. *Miss Nelson Is Missing*. Houghton Mifflin, 1985, 32 pp. When Miss Nelson's class misbehaves, a mysterious substitute, Viola Swamp, who is really Miss Nelson in disguise, quickly whips the class into shape. Miss Nelson series. Highly recommended. IL: 7–10. Available in paperback.

Theme/subject: School: teachers; Student behavior; Humor

Arnosky, Jim. *Raccoons and Ripe Corn.* Lothrop, Lee & Shepard, 1987, 22 pp. A raccoon family pulls ripe ears of corn to the ground and eats them. Nature series. IL: 6–9. Available in paperback (Mulberry).
Theme/subject: Animals: raccoons; Feeding habits
Arnosky, Jim. *Otters Under Water.* Putnam, 1992, 24 pp. A mother otter watches as her cubs swim underwater. Fast swimmers, they hunt for fish. One otter chases a yellow perch; the other catches a silver minnow. Nature series. IL: 6–9. Available in paperback.
Theme/subject: Animals: Otters' living habits: Natural habitat
Arnosky, Jim. *Every Autumn Comes the Bear.* Putnam, 1993, 28 pp. A bear examines its surroundings before retiring to its cave for its long winter's sleep. Nature series.
Theme/subject: Animals: hibernation; Bears
Baehr, Patricia. *Mouse in the House.* Holiday, 1994, 29 pp. Seeking to get rid of a mouse who drank her tea and ate her cake, Mrs. Teapot acquires a cat, a dog, an owl, and a snake. Finding that the animals cause a lot of trouble, she gets rid of the creatures and solves the problem by giving the mouse its own tea and cake. IL: 6–9.
Theme/subject: Pest: getting rid of; Solutions that are worse than the problem; Humor
* Bang, Molly. *The Paper Crane.* Greenwillow, 1985, 29 pp. Treated to a fine meal by the owner of a restaurant that had few customers, an elderly stranger left a paper crane that would dance when the owner clapped his hands. Customers flocked to see the magic crane. Reinforces cause-effect relationships: why business fell off and why it improved. Highly recommended. IL: 6–9. Available in paperback (Mulberry).
Theme/subject: Kindness; Magic; Restaurant
Bang, Molly Garrett. *Wiley and the Hairy Man.* Simon & Schuster, 1976, 64 pp. With the help of his mom, Wiley tricks the Hairy Man three times in this adapted American folktale. IL: 8–11.
Theme/subject: Folktale; Outwitting one's enemies
Bemelmans, Ludwig. *Madeline.* Penguin, 1939, 44 pp. Madeline, who lives in a home for little girls, has an attack of appendicitis and has to be rushed to the hospital. Part of Madeline series. IL: 6–9. Available in paperback, audiotape, and big book.
Theme/subject: Illness; Hospital
Benjamin, Alan. *Buck.* Simon & Schuster, 1993, 24 pp. When her dog Buck grew lame, the narrator traded him for a rooster and a hen. Through a series of trades, the narrator acquired a palace but trades it for Buck because "life without him's not the same." IL: 7–10.
Theme/subject: Pets: dogs; Value of pets over riches
Boegehold, Betty D. *A Horse Called Starfire.* Bantam, 1991, 32 pp. Encountering a horse for the first time, Wolf Cub persuades his father that it is a tame animal. Riding the horse into his village, Wolf Cub is told that he has a brought his people a great gift. IL: 6–9. Available in paperback.
Theme/subject: Native Americans; Animals: first horses in America
Brenner, Barbara. *Wagon Wheels.* HarperCollins, 1978, 64 pp. In this true story of an African American pioneer family living in the 1870s, three boys and their dad endure the dangers and hardships of frontier life. IL: 7–10. Available in paperback.
Theme/subject: Family life; Pioneers in the West

Brown, Marc. *Arthur's Pet Business*. Little, Brown, 1990, 30 pp. Before he can get a puppy for a pet, Arthur has to prove that he is responsible, which he does by taking care of a variety of pets, including a boa constrictor. By happy coincidence, one of the pets that he cared for has puppies and Arthur is promised one. IL: 6–9. Available in paperback.

Theme/subject: Taking responsibility; Pets

Burton, Marilee Robin. *My Best Shoes*. Tambourine, 1994, 22 pp. For each day of the week, a boy or girl wears a special pair of shoes: on Monday, there are tie shoes; on Tuesday, tap shoes; on Wednesday, play shoes. Repeated lines provide opportunities for choral or partner reading. Writing topic: favorite shoes. IL: 6–8.

Theme/subject: Clothes: shoes

Chermayeff, Ivan. *Fishy Facts*. Harcourt Brace, 1994, 29 pp. Interesting fish facts are featured: The male toadfish is as loud as a subway train, the sawfish cuts up its food, the lantern fish glows in the dark. Reinforces compound words. Provides possible writing project: creating a fact book about animals. IL: 6–9.

Theme/subject: Fish: interesting facts

Christian, Mary Blount. *Swamp Monsters*. Dial, 1983, 56 pp. By dressing up like people, the swamp monsters spend a day with children and find them interesting but strange. IL: 6–9. Available in paperback.

Theme/subject: Monsters

Coerr, Eleanor. *The Josephina Story Quilt*. HarperCollins, 1986, 64 pp. Heading out West in a wagon train, Faith persuades her father to take her pet hen Josephina along. Although something of a pest, Josephina warns the family when robbers approach. IL: 7–10. Available in paperback and audiotape.

Theme/subject: Family life. Pets: hen; Westward movement: wagon trains

Coerr, Eleanor. *Chang's Paper Pony*. HarperCollins, 1988, 64 pp. Helping his grandfather who is a cook for workers in a gold mining camp, Chang dreams of owning a pony. With the help of a friendly miner and a little luck, Chang's dream comes true. Reinforces characterization and making predictions. IL: 7–10. Available in paperback.

Theme/subject: Pets: pony; Loneliness; Honesty; Prejudice

Costeau Society. *The Dolphins*. Simon & Schuster, 1991, 16 pp. Color photos and captions provide an overview of dolphins. IL: 6–9.

Theme/subject: Animals: dolphins

Cristaldi, Kathryn. *Baseball Ballerina*. Random, 1992, 48 pp. The main character would rather play baseball than take ballet lessons, but she begins to appreciate ballet a little more when she uses baseball and ballet skills to help out the lead dancer. Writing topic: favorite activities. IL: 6–9. Available in paperback.

Theme/subject: Learning skills; Parents

Cuyler, Margery. *That's Good! That's Bad!* Holt, 1991, 32 pp. A little boy has a lot of frightening misadventures, which turn out to be both good and bad. Repeated lines provide opportunities for choral or partner reading. Provides model for writing and possible topic: things that are both good and bad. IL: 6–9. Available in paperback.

Theme/subject: Adventure; Escape from danger

de Paola, Tomie. *Charlie Needs a Cloak*. Prentice-Hall, 1973, 27 pp. Charlie, the shepherd, needed a new cloak, so he sheared the sheep and then washed and carded

the wool. After spinning the wool into yarn and dyeing it, Charlie wove the yarn into cloth and sewed a beautiful red cloak for himself. Reinforces process sequence: making a cloak. IL: 6–8. Available in paperback.
Theme/subject: Making clothes
Disalvo-Ryan, Dyanne. *City Green.* Morrow, 1994, 30 pp. Marcia and her neighbors transform a vacant lot into a neighborhood garden that beautifies the surrounding area and cheers up a grumpy neighbor. Reinforces sequence. IL: 6–9.
Theme/subject: Gardening; Neighbors; Young and old working together
Dorflinger, Carolyn. *Tomorrow Is Mom's Birthday.* Whispering Coyote Press, 1994, 28 pp. A young boy can't figure out what to get his mother for her birthday, especially since he has only $5.95. He finally comes up with a sure-fire gift idea. Demonstrates problem solving. IL: 6–7.
Theme/subject: Family: parent's birthday; Gifts
* Dorros, Arthur. *Abuela.* Dutton, 1991, 34 pp. After asking herself, "What if I could fly?" Rosabella finds herself flying with her Abuela (grandmother) over New York City. The two have a conversation, which is partly in Spanish, about the many wonderous things that they see. Conversation could provide a good basis for a readers' theater presentation or partner reading. Highly recommended. IL: 7–10.
Theme/subject: Fantasy: people flying; Grandparents; Partially bilingual
Dorros, Arthur. *This Is My House.* Scholastic, 1992, 29 pp. This book depicts the many different kinds of houses built in the United States and in other countries. It also tells about the kinds of dwellings that were constructed thousands of years ago. Homes are described from a child's point of view. Builds awareness of other languages. Says "This is my house" in a number of languages. Multicultural. IL: 7–10.
Theme/subject: Houses; Shelter; Geography: countries, climate; Multicultural; Multilingual
Dorros, Arthur. *Radio Man.* HarperCollins, 1993, 32 pp. Diego, a young migrant worker, likes to listen to the radio as he and his family travel from job to job. The radio helps him keep track of where he is and where he has been. Through a call-in service, he can also keep in touch with old friends. Text is written in Spanish and English. Has a glossary of Spanish expressions.
Theme/subject: Family life; Migrant farmers; Friends: keeping in touch with; Bilingual: Spanish and English
Dubowski, Cathy East, & Dubowski, Mark. *Pretty Good Magic.* Random, 1987, 48 pp. Not satisfied at being just a pretty good magician, Presto learns a new trick in which he makes hundreds of rabbits appear. Unfortunately, he isn't able to make the rabbits disappear. IL: 6–10. Available in paperback.
Theme/subject: Magic tricks; Humor
Ehlert, Lois. *Red Leaf, Yellow Leaf.* Harcourt, 1992, 31 pp. A tree began with the falling of maple seeds. The tree grew until one day nursery workers dug it up and sold it. It was then transplanted and now is a home for birds. Has cutout pages. Reinforces sequence: steps in a process. IL: 6–9.
Theme/subject: Trees: growing and transplanting
Fowler, Alan. *The Biggest Animal Ever.* Children's Press, 1992, 30 pp. Photos and brief text describe the habits and physical characteristics of whales. Has an illustrated glossary to help readers with difficult terms. Rookie Read-About Science series.

IL: 6–9. Available in paperback.

Theme/subject: Animals: whales

Fowler, Alan. *Frogs and Toads and Tadpoles, Too.* Children's Press, 1992, 32 pp. The text and full-color photos describe frogs and toads and highlight some differences between the two. Part of Rookie Read-About Science series. IL: 6–9.

Theme/subject: Frogs; Toads; Tadpoles

Fowler, Alan. *The Upside-Down Sloth.* Children's Press, 1993, 32 pp. Color photos and brief text describe an unusual but fascinating animal. Has illustrated glossary. Rookie Read-About Science series. IL: 6–9. Available in paperback and big book.

Theme/subject: Animal: sloth

Fowler, Alan. *What Magnets Can Do.* Children's Press, 1993, 32 pp. Color photos and brief text describe magnets and show what they can do. Has illustrated glossary. Rookie Read-About Science series. IL: 6–9. Available in paperback.

Theme/subject: Magnets

Fowler, Alan. *Wooly Sheep and Hungry Goats.* Children's Press, 1993, 32 pp. Color photos and brief text provide an overview of sheep and goats. Has illustrated glossary. Rookie Read-About Science series. IL: 6–9.

Theme/subject: Animals: sheep and goats

Fowler, Alan. *The Best Way to See a Shark.* Children's Press, 1995, 31 pp. Color photos and brief text describe some major types of sharks and also explain physical features and habits of sharks. Rookie Read-About Science series. IL: 6–9. Available in paperback.

Theme/subject: Animals: sharks

Freeman, Don. *Corduroy.* Viking, 1968, 32 pp. Lonely because no one has bought him, Corduroy, a teddy bear in a department store, is finally purchased by a little girl. IL: 6–7. Available in paperback and audiotape (Live Oak).

Theme/subject: Toys: teddy bears; Loneliness

Galdone, Paul. *Little Red Riding Hood.* McGraw-Hill, 1974, 29 pp. Although forbidden to do so, Little Red Riding Hood wanders off the path on her way to see her grandmother. When she arrives, the wolf disguised as her grandmother swallows her. A passing hunter slices open the wolf and saves both Little Red Riding Hood and her grandmother. IL: 6–7.

Theme/subject: Fairytale; Obeying parents; Adventure: being rescued

Gibbons, Gail. *Farming.* Holiday House, 1988, 30 pp. This book explains what happens on a farm during the four seasons. IL: 6–9.

Theme/subject: Farming; Seasons

Giff, Patricia Reilly. *The Almost Awful Play.* Viking, 1985, 25 pp. With some timely improvisation, Ronald Morgan helps save the class play. Part of Ronald Morgan series. IL: 7–9. Available in paperback (Puffin) and audiotape (Live Oak).

Theme/subject: School: class play

* Giff, Patricia Reilly. *Today Was a Terrible Day.* Viking, 1985, 25 pp. Realizing that Ronald Morgan had a really bad day in school, his teacher writes a note to cheer him up. Ronald is delighted to get the note, especially when he discovers that he can read it on his own. Part of Ronald Morgan series. Highly recommended. IL: 7–9. Available in paperback (Puffin) and audiotape (Live Oak).

Theme/subject: School: having a bad day; Teacher: kind

Giff, Patricia Reilly. *Watch Out, Ronald Morgan.* Viking, 1985, 25 pp. Getting glasses solves some but not all of the difficulties Ronald Morgan has at school in this

warm-hearted but true-to-life tale. Promotes understanding of need for glasses. Part of Ronald Morgan series. IL: 7–9. Available in paperback (Puffin).
Theme/subject: Glasses

Haas, Jessie. *Chipmunk!* Greenwillow, 1993, 21 pp. A cat chases a chipmunk into the house. The chase overturns a plant, wrecks a castle made of blocks, and results in spilt food and overturned furniture. The terrified chipmunk finally takes refuge by sitting on the father's head. Reinforces sequence. IL: 6–9.
Theme/subject: Wild animals loose in house; Chimpmunks

Hadithi, Mwenye. *Baby Baboon.* Little, Brown, 1993, 28 pp. Mother Baboon escapes from Leopard but Baby Baboon is not quick enough. Vervet Monkey tricks Leopard into tossing Baby Baboon high into the air so that Mother Baboon from her perch in the trees catches him. Reinforces sequence. IL: 6–8.
Theme/subject: Trickster tale; Outwitting enemies; Pourquoi tale: why leopards lurk in trees

Hall, Katy, & Eisenberg, Lisa. *Sheepish Riddles.* Dial, 1996, 48 pp. This book features sheep-related riddles such as: "Why is it hard to talk to a ram? (He keeps butting in.)" IL: 7–9.
Theme/subject: Riddles

Hartman, Gail. *As the Roadrunner Runs: A First Book of Maps.* Bradbury, 1994, 30 pp. The journeys of desert animals are depicted and then shown as maps. The jackrabbit's map shows a railroad station, an old well, and tasty grass. Sequel to *As the Crow Flies.* Reinforces map reading. IL: 6–9. Available in paperback.
Theme/subject: Maps; Animals: habitats and routes

Hennessy, B. G. *Road Builders.* Penguin, 1994, 28 pp. Shows step-by-step how a road is built. Special attention is given to the equipment used in road construction. Reinforces sequence: steps in building a road. IL: 6–8.
Theme/subject: Construction: road building

Heo, Yumi. *Father's Rubber Shoes.* Orchard, 1995, 29 pp. Yearning for the way life was back in his native Korea and missing his father, who spends long hours at his store, Yungsu feels better after making a new friend while taking his dad a treat. IL: 6–9.
Theme/subject: Moving; Being in a strange land; Making friends; Multicultural

Himmelman, John. *The Clover County Carrot Contest.* Silver Burdett, 1991, 44 pp. The Wrights, a creative family, enter a carrot-growing contest. All but one carrot seem almost sure to win in at least one of the categories: largest carrot, crunchiest carrot, and so on. Noting that Belle's carrot is not doing very well, each of the other members of the family secretly supplies help with surprising results. IL: 6–8. Available in paperback.
Theme/subject: Contests; Family life: helping other members of the family

Hirsh, Marilyn. *I Love Hanukkah.* Holiday House, 1984, 28 pp. Grandfather tells a little boy the story of how Hanukkah came to be and explains how Hanukkah is celebrated. The family then celebrates Hanukkah. IL: 6–9. Available in paperback and audiotape (Live Oak).
Theme/subject: Religious celebrations: Hanukkah

* Hoban, Lillian. *Arthur's Pen Pal.* HarperCollins, 1976, 64 pp. Although he initially prefers his pen pal to his little sister, Arthur learns to appreciate his little sister. Reinforces letter writing. Highly recommended. IL: 6–8. Available in paperback and audiotape (Caedmon).
Theme/subject: Family life: siblings; Pen pals

* Hoban, Russell. *Bread and Jam for Frances.* HarperCollins, 1964, 31 pp. Concerned that Frances is eating only bread and jam, Mother Badger finds a way to entice her to eat a variety of foods. Frances series. Highly recommended. IL: 6–8. Available in paperback and big-book format.
Theme/subject: Family life: parents and children; Eating habits

Hoffman, Mary. *Boundless Grace.* Dial, 1995, 24 pp. Grace travels to Africa to visit her father, who has remarried and has a new family. Although feeling confused about the new family, she is happy to see her father and learns to like his family. She discovers that families are like stories—they are what you make them. Sequel to *Amazing Grace.* IL: 6–10.
Theme/subject: Families; Divorce

Hopkins, Lee Bennett (Ed.). *Surprises.* HarperCollins, 1986, 64 pp. This collection of 38 easy-to-read poems have a special appeal to young people. Some of the poems are very easy to read. IL: 6–10. Available in paperback.
Theme/subject: Poetry: varied subjects

Hopkins, Lee Bennett. *Questions, Poems Selected by Lee Bennett Hopkins.* HarperCollins, 1992, 64 pp. A collection of easy-to-read poems asks such questions as: "Who am I? Who has seen the wind? What is the opposite of two?" IL: 7–10. Available in paperback.
Theme/subject: Poetry: varied subjects

Jaffe, Nina. *Sing, Little Sack!* Bantam, 1993, 48 pp. A strange little man puts Marisol into a sack and plans to become famous by putting on shows with his singing sack. Discovering that Marisol is in the sack, her mother and the people of the village help her escape and fill the sack with garbage. Bilingual text: Spanish and English. Repeated lines provide opportunities for choral or partner reading. IL: 6–8.
Theme/subject: Puerto Rican folktale; Outwitting evil person; Bilingual

Johnson, Angela. *Julius.* Orchard, 1993, 30 pp. Julius, a cool pig from Alaska, brings fun and excitement to Maya and her family. IL: 6–9.
Theme/subject: Humor; Pets; Families: having fun

Johnson, Dolores. *What Kind of Baby-sitter Is This?* Simon & Schuster, 1991, 32 pp. Determined not to like his new baby-sitter, Kevin is surprised when she puts on a baseball cap, takes out a pennant, and starts watching a baseball game on television. As the evening wears on, she reads to Kevin from her baseball book and tells him jokes. Kevin has so much fun that he doesn't even notice his mother's return. Could be used to demonstrate characterization. IL: 6–8.
Theme/subject: Baby-sitters

Johnson, Doug. *Never Babysit the Hippopotamuses.* Holt, 1993, 28 pp. Babysitting the Hippopotamuses can pose special problems, not the least of which is getting them into their pajamas. IL: 6–9.
Theme/subject: Babysitting; Humor

Jones, Rebecca C. *Great Aunt Martha.* Dutton, 1995, 30 pp. When Great Aunt Martha came to visit, everyone is very quiet because Great Aunt Martha is old and needs her rest. Playmates are sent home and the TV is turned off. However, what Great Aunt Martha really wants is to have fun. IL: 6–9.
Theme/subject: Relatives: visits by; Older people

Kasza, Keiko. *Grandpa Toad's Secrets.* Putnam's, 1995, 30 pp. When Grandpa Toad shows Little Toad how to protect himself from enemies that lurk in the forest, Little Toad demonstrates that he has learned his lessons. IL: 6–8.
Theme/subject: Grandparents; Learning new skills

Keats, Ezra Jack. *Pet Show!* Simon & Schuster, 1972, 32 pp. Archie's cat disappears just before the start of the pet show. Reinforces making predictions. IL: 6–9. Available in paperback.
Theme/subject: Pets: cats; Sharing

Koontz, Michal Robin. *Chicago and the Cat.* Dutton, 1993, 30 pp. After fixing Chicago Rabbit carrot pancakes and lettuce juice, the cat, who was a brash univited guest, becomes Chicago's friend. However, the two have difficulty agreeing on the planting of a garden and acquiring a pet, with humorous results. Lends itself to comparing and contrasting characters. See also *Chicago and the Cat: The Family Reunion.* IL: 6–8.
Theme/subject: Friendship; Compromise; Humor

Kuskin, Karla. *Roar and More.* HarperCollins, 1956, 1990, 42 pp. This book features poems about the noises that animals make, including the roar of the lion, the honk of the elephant, and the hiss of the snake. IL: 6–8. Available in paperback.
Theme/subject: Poems: animals; Animal sounds

* Kuskin, Karla. *Something Sleeping in the Hall.* HarperCollins, 1985, 64 pp. A number of unusual animals appear in this collection of easy-to-read poems: a bird that can't tie its shoes, a parrot that squawks to a celery stalk, a lizard that loves ice cream. Highly recommended. IL: 7–10.
Theme/subject: Animals; Poetry; Humor

* Kuskin, Karla. *Soap Soup and Other Verses.* HarperCollins, 1992, 64 pp. This excellent collection of easy-to-read, lighthearted verses has special appeal to children. Highly recommended. IL: 6–10. Available in paperback.
Theme/subject: Poetry: various subjects

Kuskin, Karla. *City Dog.* Clarion, 1994, 27 pp. When the city dog was taken to the country, she found soft grass, warm ground, and "rabbit holes to paw and nose." IL: 7–10.
Theme/subject: Pets: dogs; Poetry

Legge, David. *Bamboozled.* Scholastic, 1994, 30 pp. Each week, a little girl visits her grandfather, whose home is full of such oddities and impossibilities as portraits whose figures drink milk from the table with a straw and an elephant who washes dishes by squirting them with water from its trunk. Sensing that there is something strange going on, the little girl finally figures it out: grandfather's socks don't match. Promotes carefully looking at illustrations to detect the many oddities contained in them. IL: 6–11.
Theme/subject: Games/activities: oddities in illustrations; Grandparents: visiting

Levy, Elizabeth. *Schoolyard Mystery.* Scholastic, 1994, 45 pp. After falling into a pool while exploring a cave with his parents, Chip Stone becomes invisible. Chip and his friends decide to use Chip's condition to help their classmates by solving mysteries. Reinforces drawing conclusions and predicting. IL: 7–9. Paperback.
Theme/subject: Mystery/adventure; Magical powers

Lionni, Leo. *Swimmy.* Knopf, 1963, 28 pp. Part of a school of red fish, Swimmy stood out because he was black and larger and faster than the red fish. After his school

is eaten by a hungry tuna, Swimmy joins another school of red fish but teaches them to swim as one giant fish so they won't be eaten. IL: 6–8. Available in paperback.
Theme/subject: Fish; Working together; Staying together for safety

Maestro, Marco, & Maestro, Giulio. *What Do You Hear When Cows Sing and Other Silly Riddles?* HarperCollins, 1996, 48 pp. This book features a number of riddles that play with language: "What do you call a train that sneezes? Ah-choo-choo train." Provides opportunity to apply phonics skills to distorted words: *moosic*. Reinforces homophones. IL: 6–9.
Theme/subject: Riddles

Marshall, James. *George and Martha Rise and Shine.* Houghton Mifflin 1976, 44 pp. George and Martha's friendship survives fibbing, a scientific experiment, scary movies, a picnic, and a secret club. Part of George and Martha series. IL: 6–9. Available in paperback.
Theme/subject: Friendship; Misadventures

Marzollo, Jean. *Soccer Sam.* Random, 1987, 48 pp. After experiencing some difficulty with basketball and other sports, Sam's cousin from Mexico introduces Sam and his second-grade classmates to the game of soccer. With his cousin's help, Sam's class forms a team and beats the third-graders. Multicultural. Includes some Spanish words. IL: 6–8. Available in paperback.
Theme/subject: Sports: soccer; Friendship; Multicultural; Partially bilingual

Marzollo, Jean. *I Spy, A Book of Picture Riddles.* Scholastic, 1992, 28 pp. In color photographs containing many objects, readers are challenged to locate a series of items: "I spy a snake, a three-letter word, And flying underneath, a great white bird . . . ." Text also provides suggestions for writing riddles. IL: 6–9.
Theme/subject: Riddles: visual; Games and activities: finding objects in photo

McConnachie, Brian. *Elmer and the Chickens vs. the Big Leagues.* Crown, 1992, 30 pp. While tossing the ball against the side of the barn, Elmer imagines that he is pitching against baseball's best. Backing up Elmer are the chickens. Provides possible writing topic: writing about daydreams. IL: 7–9.
Theme/subject: Baseball: imaginary game; Daydreaming

McDonald, Megan. *Is This a House for Hermit Crab?* Orchard, 1990, 26 pp. Rejecting a rock, an old tin can, a piece of driftwood, a plastic pail, and a fishing net as possible homes, a hermit crab finally finds a shell that is just right. And it does so just in time to hide from the pricklepine fish, its deadly enemy. IL: 6–8. Available in paperback.
Theme/subject: Hermit crab; Keeping safe from enemies

* McGovern, Ann. *Stone Soup.* Scholastic, 1968, 32 pp. A hungry young man tricks a selfish woman into making soup. Highly recommended. IL: 6–9. Available in paperback.
Theme/subject: Fairytales; Greed; Outwitting selfish person

McKean, Thomas. *Hooray for Grandma Jo!* Crown, 1994, 28 pp. Having lost her glasses, Grandma Jo mistakes a runaway lion for her grandson. Because he is treated so well, the lion becomes fond of Grandma Jo and aids in the capture of a thief who is burglarizing her home. IL: 6–9.
Theme/subject: Mistaken identity; Grandparents; Humor

Meddaugh, Susan. *Tree of Birds.* Houghton Mifflin, 1990, 30 pp. Harry rescues Sally, an injured bird, but is followed by Sally's flock when he fails to release Sally after she recovers. Reinforces problem solving. IL: 6–9. Available in paperback. Theme/subject: Animals: caring for injured; Releasing captive wild animals; Humor

Miller, Montzalee. *My Grandmother's Cookie Jar.* Price/Stern/Sloan, 1987, 26 pp. At night, Grandma would take the top off the Indian head cookie jar, give her granddaughter some cookies, and tell her stories about buffalo hunts, fireside chants, and the coming of the strangers. After Grandma's death, Grandpa gives the jar to the granddaughter so that one day she can tell her children about the days of old. IL: 7–10. Out of print.
Theme/subject: Grandparents; Passing on one's heritage

Moss, Marissa. *Mel's Diner.* Troll, 1994, 30 pp. Mabel enjoys helping out in her parents' diner. She likes finding lost treasures, dancing to the music of the juke box, talking to and helping the customers, and eating the food served there. Can be used to demonstrate importance of setting in a story. Provides possible writing topic: favorite places. IL: 7–10. Available in paperback.
Theme/subject: Family life: working together; Helping others; Restaurants: diners

Most, Bernard. *A Dinosaur Named after Me.* Harcourt, 1991, 32 pp. Children describe their favorite dinosaurs ands tell what these dinosaurs' names would be if they were named after them. For instance, Zach's favorite dinosaur is Brachiosaurus, a very tall creature. Zach likes it because he is tall and would have named it ZACH-iosaurus. Reinforces multisyllabic words. Names of dinosaurs are phonetically respelled. Provides possible writing topic: writing about favorite dinosaur. IL: 6–9. Available in paperback.
Theme/subject: Dinosaurs

Noll, Sally. *I Have a Loose Tooth.* Greenwillow, 1992, 30 pp. Molly tries to tell everyone about her loose tooth, but no one listens until she makes a card for greeting grandma. Promotes phonemic awareness: story has several substitutions for *loose* and *tooth.* Provides possible writing format: writing a greeting card. IL: 6–7.
Theme/subject: Loose tooth; Grandparents

Numeroff, Laura Joffe. *If You Give a Moose a Muffin.* HarperCollins, 1989, 30 pp. If you give a visiting moose a muffin, it will want jam, and then more muffins, which means going to the store for muffin mix, and getting a sweater for the moose to wear to the store. The chain of events goes on and on. Sequel to *If You Give a Mouse a Cookie.* IL: 6–9.
Theme/subject: Food: snacks; Humor

O'Connor, Jane. *Eek! Stories to Make You Shriek.* Grossett & Dunlap, 1992, 48 pp. Three stories of the supernatural are featured: a monster is mistaken for a friend dressed up in a Holloween costume, a dog disappears into a picture, and a spoiled child is given a doll that demands to be taken back to the store. Available in paperback.
Theme/subject: Scary stories; Monsters

Oechsli, Kelly. *Mice at Bat.* HarperCollins, 1986, 64 pp. The Mighty Mites and the Boomers, baseball teams of mice, play in the Big Game. The game is close, so the Boomers call in a surprise pinch hitter. The Mighty Mites smell a rat. IL: 6–9. Available in paperback.
Theme/subject: Sports: baseball; Mice

Oppenheim, Joanne. *"Uh-Oh!" Said the Crow.* Bantam, 1993, 32 pp. Crow is sent to investigate when mysterious thumps are heard on the barn roof in the middle of the night. Lends itself to readers' theater. There are many speaking parts. Reinforces /aw/ pattterns. IL: 6–8. Out of print.

Theme/subject: Fable; Fear of the unknown; Spreading fear

Parish, Peggy. *Thank You, Amelia Bedelia.* HarperCollins, 1964, 30 pp. Taking instructions literally, Amelia Bedelia attempts to make a jelly roll by rolling jelly and puts check marks on clean clothes when asked to check the laundry. Reinforces understanding of figurative language, homophones, and homographs. Part of Amelia Bedelia series. IL: 7–10. Available in paperback and audiotape.

Theme/subject: Playing with language; Figurative language; Homographs; Humor

Parkinson, Curtis. *Tom Foolery.* Bradbury, 1993, 30 pp. Hearing a fish splash, Tom Foolery, a cat aboard a boat, investigates and falls overboard. Luckily, Tom is able to swim to shore. With the help of a barking dog, Tom Foolery's owners find him. IL: 6–9.

Theme/subject: Pets: cats; Lost pets; Rescue

Pilkey, Dav. *When Cats Dream.* Orchard, 1992, 29 pp. When cats fall asleep, they dream of flying through the air, wearing shoes and a tie, and stalking through the jungle. IL: 6–8.

Theme/subject: Pets: cats; Cats: dreams

* Platt, Kin. *Big Max.* HarperCollins, 1965, 64 pp. Big Max, who bills himself as the world's geatest detective and who travels by umbrella, helps the king of Pooka Pooka find his missing elephant. Fosters making inferences based on clues. Big Max series. Reinforces / $\overline{oo}$ / patterns. Highly recommended. IL: 7–10. Available in paperback.

Theme/subject: Detective; Mystery; Humor

Platt, Kin. *Big Max and the Mystery of the Missing Moose.* HarperCollins, 1977, 64 pp. Despite a series of humorous mistakes, Max helps the zoo keeper track down Marvin, the missing moose, who escaped so that he could be with his family. Fosters making inferences based on clues. Big Max series. IL: 7–10.

Theme/subject: Detective; Mystery; Humor

Reneaux, J. J. *Why Alligator Hates Dog: A Cajun Folktale.* August House, 1995, 26 pp. Dog teases Alligator but falls down a hole one day and finds itself snout to snout with Alligator. Since the alligator "thinks with his stomach," Dog is able to trick him out of having him for lunch by promising him a bucket of table scraps. Dialog lends itself to readers' theater dramatization. IL: 6–9.

Theme/subject: Folktale; Outwitting enemies; Multicultural

Rotner, Shelley. *Wheels Around.* Houghton Mifflin, 1995, 29 pp. Photos and captions depict the many ways in which wheels are used. They help us work and play and get around. Buses carry us to school. Tractors help farmers. Trucks deliver food and carry cars, fuel, and logs. IL: 6–8.

Theme/subject: Transportation: wheeled vehicles

Ryder, Joanne. *The Snail's Spell.* Scholastic, 1982, 28 pp. The reader is asked to imagine what it would be like to be a snail: You have no bones, arms, or legs; you cannot run or walk; and your teeth are on your tongue. Lends itself to imaging. IL: 6–9.

Theme/subject: Animals: snails

Rylant, Cynthia. *The Relatives Came*. Bradbury, 1985, 28 pp. When the relatives came from Virginia, there was a lot of hugging, and laughing, and talking. The relatives stayed for weeks and ate all the strawberries and melons, but they tended the garden and fixed any broken things they could find. Provides possible writing topic: visit by relatives. IL: 6–9. Available in paperback.
Theme/subject: Family: relatives coming for a visit

Sanfield, Steve. *Bit by Bit*. Philomel, 1995, 28 pp. When his fine winter coat wears out, Zundel the tailor salvages what is left and makes it into another article of clothing. And when that wears out, he does the same thing again. Repeated lines provide opportunities for choral or partner reading. IL: 6–9.
Theme/subject: Clothing: recycling; Making new clothing out of old

Sendak, Maurice. *Chicken Soup with Rice*. HarperCollins, 1962, 32 pp. A little boy marks special activities as he goes through the months but always includes eating chicken soup with rice. IL: 7–9.
Theme/subject: Months of the year

Sharmat, Marjorie Weinman. *Nate the Great*. Dell, 1972, 32 pp. Boy detective Nate the Great helps Annie solve the case of the missing picture. Reinforces looking for clues and drawing conclusions. Nate the Great series. IL: 6–9. Available in paperback.
Theme/subject: Detective: young person

Sharmat, Marjorie Weinman. *Nate the Great and the Musical Note*. Coward-McCann, 1990, 48 pp. Boy detective Nate the Great helps Pip decipher a phone message from his mother but put into a secret code by his piano teacher. Through careful investigation, Nate discovers that the key to deciphering the message is to use the names of musical notes. Reinforces looking for clues and drawing conclusions. Part of Nate the Great series. IL: 6–9. Available in paperback (Dell).
Theme/subject: Detective: young person

Sharmat, Marjorie Weinman. *Nate the Great and the Tardy Tortise*. Delacorte, 1995, 42 pp. With the help of his dog Sludge, Nate the Great solves the case of the runaway tortise. Although he reunites the tortise with its owner, he finds that he will miss having the little creature around. Reinforces looking for clues and drawing conclusions. Part of Nate the Great series. IL: 6–9.
Theme/subject: Detective: young person; Pets: tortise

Slote, Elizabeth. *Nellie's Grannies*. Tambourine Books, 1993, 30 pp. Nelly enjoys visiting her two grandmothers. One lives on a farm, and the other lives in an apartment house in the city. The grandmothers plan different but special activities for Emily. Lends itself to comparison/contrast of city and farm and two grandmothers. IL: 6–9. Theme/subject: Grandparents: differences

Smith, Mavis. *A Snake Mistake*. HarperCollins, 1991, 28 pp. To encourage his hens to lay more eggs, a farmer plants fake eggs in the form of lightbulbs in the hens' nests. A snake searching for hens' eggs swallows two of the light bulbs and is rushed to the vet by the kindly farmer. Based on a true story. IL: 6–11. Out of print.
Theme/subject: Animals: helping; Snakes; Amazing happenings

Spier, Peter. *Bored—Nothing to Do*. Doubleday, 1978, 42 pp. Bored because they have nothing to do, two boys make and then fly an airplane. Later, because they used various parts from the family car, TV, fence, baby carriage, and other items to make their plane, they must take the airplane apart and "put it all back where it belongs." IL: 7–10. Out of print.
Theme/subject: Play: finding things to do; Boredom; Airplanes

Stevenson, James. *We Hate Rain!* Greenwillow, 1988, 30 pp. When his grandchildren complain about two days of rain, Grandpa describes the month of rain that he and Uncle Wainey experienced in which friends and sea creatures floated in and out of the boys' home. Part of Grandpa series. IL: 6–9.
Theme/subject: Rain; Humor: exaggeration

Stevenson, James. *Fun, No Fun.* Greenwillow, 1994, 30 pp. The author depicts in words and drawings things that were fun and not fun as he was growing up. Provides model for writing: listing things that are fun and not fun. IL: 7–10.
Theme/subject: Autobiography; Fun; Personal interests

Teague, Mark. *The Field Beyond the Outfield.* Scholastic, 1992, 30 pp. Fearing that Ludlow was becoming obsessed with monsters, his parents signed him up for baseball. Playing deep in right field, Ludlow discovered just beyond the trees a baseball game that was being played by monsters. IL: 7–11. Available in paperback.
Theme/subject: Sports: baseball; Monsters; Fantasy

Teague, Mark. *Pigsty.* Scholastic, 1994, 30 pp. Wendell's messy room becomes a pigsty when pigs come to live there. IL: 6–10.
Theme/subject: Cleaning: rooms; Animals acting like people; Humor

Turner, Ann. *Dust for Dinner.* HarperCollins, 1995, 64 pp. A family leaves the Dust Bowl of the 1920s and heads west for California in hopes of finding a better life. Along the way, they must choose between getting rid of their dog and dad's temporary job. IL: 7–11.
Theme/subject: Family life: facing hard times; History: Dust Bowl, Depression

Viorst, Judith. *Alexander and the Terrible, Horrible, No Good, Very Bad Day.* Atheneum, 1972, 28 pp. From the time he wakes up until he falls asleep, everything seems to go wrong for Alexander. Provides possible writing topic: bad day. Models inclusion of supporting examples. IL: 6–8. Available in paperback.
Theme/subject: Bad day

Waber, Ira. *Ira Sleeps Over.* Scholastic, 1972, 46 pp. For his first sleepover with his friend Reggie, Ira decides to leave his teddy bear at home but later regrets his decision. IL: 6–7. Available in paperback and audiotape (Live Oak).
Theme/subject: Growing up: being away from home overnight

Waggoner, Karen. *The Lemonade Babysitter.* Little, Brown, 1992, 29 pp. Hoping to get rid of her elderly babysitter, Molly asks him to do a series of things that she thinks he won't like to do, like dance and go to the zoo. Mr. Herbert, the babysitter, enjoys dancing and has fun at the zoo. The two become good friends. Because of extensive dialog, the story lends itself to readers' theater. IL: 6–9.
Theme/subject: Babysitters; Understanding others

Welch, Willy. *Playing Right Field.* Scholastic, 1995, 29 pp. A discouraged young fielder takes a renewed interest in baseball when he accidentally makes an important catch. IL: 6–10.
Theme/subject: Sports: baseball; Self-esteem; Daydreams

Wells, Rosemary. *Lucy Comes to Stay.* Dial, 1994, 26 pp. Lucy learns to love and care for her new puppy. Provides possible topic for writing: caring for and learning about a pet. Also models first-person writing. IL: 6–9.
Theme/subject: Pets: new: caring for

Wildsmith, Brian. *The Owl and the Woodpecker.* Oxford University Press, 1971, 30 pp. Quarreling because Owl makes noise at night when Woodpecker is trying to sleep and Woodpecker makes noise during the day when Owl is trying to sleep. Owl and Woodpecker become friends after Woodpecker warns Owl that his tree is about to fall. Lends itself to predicting what Woodpecker will do and problem solving. IL: 6–8. Available in paperback.
Theme/subject: Getting along with others

Winter, Susan. *My Shadow.* Doubleday, 1994, 29 pp. Waking up and finding that her shadow has disappeared, a little girl searched for it outside. She asked all the animals, but they couldn't help. At last, the sun popped out from behind the hills and her shadow appeared. IL: 6–8.
Theme/subject: Shadows

Wolff, Ferida. *Seven Loaves of Bread.* Tambourine, 1993, 29 pp. Each day Milly bakes seven loaves of bread, several of which go to animals and people who help out on the farm or supply goods. When Milly becomes ill and Rose takes over the baking, she doesn't bake as many loaves because she feels it is too much work. Rose soon learns that without their bread, the animals and people won't help out. Lends itself to exploration of causes and effects. IL: 6–8.
Theme/subject: Rewarding those who help you

Wu, Norbert. *Fish Faces.* Holt, 1993, 28 pp. Color photos and captions depict a variety of fish. Some are beautiful, some are ugly or strange, and some are downright frightening. IL: 6–10.
Theme/subject: Animals: fish

Yardley, Joanna. *The Red Ball.* Harcourt, 1991, 29 pp. When a dog snatches Joanie's red ball and takes it up into the attic, Joanie discovers that the red ball has found its way into an old photo. When Joanie reaches for the ball, it goes from photo to photo, with each photo showing an older version of the baby in the first photo. The person in the photos turns out to be her grandmother. IL: 6–9. Available in paperback.
Theme/subject: Grandparents: grandmother; Strange happening

Yee, Wong Herbert. *Mrs. Brown Went to Town.* Houghton Mifflin, 1996, 28 pp. In this humorous rhyming tale, when Mrs. Brown ends up in the hospital after a fall from her bike, the animals take over the home with consequences so disastrous that they all have to be taken to the hospital. IL: 6–9.
Theme/subject: Animals taking over house; Humor

Yolen, Jane. *Commander Toad and the Planet of the Grapes.* Coward-McCann, 1982, 64 pp. Landing on a strange planet, Commander Toad is swallowed by a grape. Noting that one crew member is allergic to the planet, Doc Peeper devises a way to rescue the commander. Contains much word play. Commander Toad series. IL: 6–10. Available in paperback.
Theme/subject: Science fiction; Humor

Zoehfeld, Kathleen Weidner. *What Lives in a Shell?* HarperCollins, 1994, 26 pp. A number of different kinds of animals live in shells: snails, turtles, crabs, clams, and oysters. One of the most unusual shell dwellers is the hermit crab, which takes up residence in other creatures' shells. IL: 6–9. Available in paperback.
Theme/subject: Animals: shells

Appendix A

Primary Readability Index

The purpose of the Primary Readability Index is to estimate the difficulty levels of beginning reading books, which include books from the very beginning level up through the first half of second grade. The levels and major criteria used to determine them are listed below.

Picture Level

Overview: A single word or phrase is depicted with an illustration. The word *lion*, for instance, is accompanied by a drawing of a lion; the word *three* is accompanied by the numeral three and three dots. The text is so fully and clearly depicted that no reading is required.
Length: 12 to 24 pages
Number of lines of text per page: 1 word per page
Illustrations: 1 per page; depict all of text
Hard words: All words are depicted.
Language: Familiar
Content: Familiar
Examples: *Colors* by John Burningham
 Numbers by Guy Smalley
 Up to Ten and Down Again by Lisa Campbell Ernst

Caption/Frame Level

Overview: The text is illustrated so that the reader can use pictures to identify most but not all of the words. Caption-level books frequently feature frame sentences, which are easy sentences such as: "I can _____, I am _____, or _____ can swim" that are repeated throughout the text. The name of the object, animal, or person that completes the frame is usually depicted. The reader would need to know initial consonants and a few sight words.

Length: 12 to 24 pages
Number of lines of text per page: 1 to 2
Illustrations: 1 per page; depict most of text
Hard words: Most words will be familiar. They would be found on the Primary High-Frequency Word List (found later in this chapter) or would be depicted by an illustration.
Language: Familiar; often contains repeated phrases or sentences
Content: Familiar
Examples: *Cat on the Mat* by Brian Wildsmith
My Barn by Craig Brown
The Cat Sat on the Mat by Alice Cameron

Easy Sight Word

Overview: This level is similar to the caption level but there are a greater number of different words used and more reading is required. The reader would need to know initial consonants and a number of sight words.
Length: Fewer than 100 words
Number of lines of text per page: 1 to 2
Illustrations: 1 per page; usually depict some or much of text
Hard words: Words are mostly easy sight words. From 4 to 6 words out of 100 are not on the Primary High-Frequency Word List.
Different words: No more than 35 different words
Language: Brief sentences and familiar vocabulary
Content: Familiar
Examples: *Brown Bear, Brown Bear, What Do You See?* by Bill Martin
Bugs by Patricia and Fredrick McKissack
Who Is Who? by Patricia McKissack

Beginning Reading A

Overview: This level is similar to the sight-word level but the text is usually longer and there are a greater number of different words. The reader would need to know short-vowel patterns and a number of high-frequency words. There are 35 to 50 different words.
Length: Up to 100 to 150 words
Number of lines of text per page: 1 to 3
Illustrations: 1 per page; usually depict some of text
Hard words: Approximately 7 to 8 words per 100 are not on the Primary High-Frequency Word List.
Different words: 35 to 50 different words
Language: Brief sentences and familiar vocabulary
Content: Familiar
Examples: *The Ant and the Dove* by Mary Lewis Wang
　　　　　 The Foot Book by Dr. Seuss
　　　　　 Sleepy Dog by Harriet Ziefert

Beginning Reading B

Overview: The vocabulary is becoming more diverse and the illustrations are less helpful. The stories contain more than 50 different words. The reader would need to know short-vowel and long-vowel patterns.
Length: Up to 150 to 200 words
Number of lines of text per page: Up to 5 or more
Hard words: From 9 to 10 words per 100 are not on the Primary High-Frequency Word List.
Different words: More than 50 different words
Language: Brief sentences but becoming longer; familiar vocabulary
Content: Familiar
Examples: *And I Mean It, Stanley!* by Crosby Bonsall
　　　　　 Jason's Bus Ride by Harriet Ziefert
　　　　　 The Cake that Mack Ate by Rose Robart

Beginning Reading C

Overview: Selections are becoming longer and more complex. Books may be divided into very brief chapters. The reader would need to know short-, long-, other-vowel (*-ow, -oy, -oo, $\overline{oo}$, -aw*), and r-vowel patterns.
Length: 200 to 300 words or more
Number of lines of text per page: Up to 6 or more
Illustrations: 1 per page; support text but may depict a hard word or two
Hard words: Approximately 11 to 12 words are not on the Primary High-Frequency Word List.

Language: Brief sentences but becoming longer; familiar vocabulary
Content: Familiar
Examples: *Little Bear's Visit* by Else Minark
   Clifford the Small Red Puppy by Norman Bridwell
   Yoo Hoo, Moon! by Mary Blocksma

Beginning Reading D

Overview: Selections are longer with more involved plots or more detailed explanations. Books are usually divided into chapters. The reader would need a grasp of basic vowel patterns. Texts have a number of multisyllabic words.
Length: 300 to 500 words or more
Number of lines of text per page: Up to 10 or more
Illustrations: 1 per page; support text
Hard words: From 13 to 14 words are not on the Primary High-Frequency Word List.
Language: Sentences becoming longer and more varied; text may contain 1 or 2 unfamiliar words
Content: May introduce new concepts
Examples: *Henry and Mudge, the First Book* by Cynthia Rylant
   Frog and Toad at Home by Arnold Lobel
   Feed Me by William Hooks

Grade 2A

Overview: There is a noticeable increase in the number of words not on the Primary High-Frequency Word List. There is also an increase in multisyllabic words.
Length: Up to 64 pages
Number of lines of text per page: Up to 20 lines
Illustrations: 1 per page; may be supportive
Hard words: About 15 to 20 words are not on the Primary High-Frequency Word List.
Language: Sentences becoming longer and more complex; text may contain several unfamiliar words
Content: May introduce new concepts
Examples: *Bread and Jam for Frances* by Russell Hoban
   Thank You, Amelia Bedelia by Peggy Parish
   Stone Soup by Ann McGovern

Figure A.1
Primary Readability Index

Title of text _____

_____ Number of pages
_____ Approximate number of words
_____ Number of lines per page
_____ Estimated number of different words
_____ Hard word score (average number of words per 100 not on the
Primary High-Frequency Word List). If more than one passage has
been sampled, obtain an average of the hard word scores yielded.

Picture	All words depicted by illustrations
Caption	Most words depicted by illustrations
Easy sight word	4–6
Beginning A	7–8
Beginning B	9–10
Beginning C	11–12
Beginning D	13–14
Grade 2A	15–20

Number of hard words depicted by illustrations

_____ None   _____ Some   _____ Most   _____ All

_____ Number of different words

Easy sight word	35 or less
Beginning A	35–50
Beginning B	More than 50

_____ Number of illustrations per page

Relationship of illustrations to text (check one)
_____ Depict all of text
_____ Depict most of text
_____ Depict much of text
_____ Depict some of text
_____ Are simply supportive

Difficulty of vocabulary and concepts
_____ Familiar vocabulary and concepts
_____ One or two unfamiliar words or concepts
_____ Several unfamiliar words or concepts

(Continued)

Figure A.1
(Continued)

Structural aids to understanding
_____ Little or no repetition
_____ Repetition of a phrase or sentence
_____ Repetition of a phrase or paragraph
_____ Use of rhyme

Estimated interest level

_____ Low   _____ Medium   _____ High

Familiarity of topic or story line

_____ Low   _____ Medium   _____ High

Estimated difficulty level

_____

DETERMINING DIFFICULTY LEVEL
OF BEGINNING READING BOOKS

The Primary Readability Index (see Figure A.1) uses both objective and subjective factors to estimate the difficulty level of beginning reading books. The key objective factor that determines the difficulty level of early reading materials is vocabulary, or the difficulty that the novice reader will experience when pronouncing the words in a book. Stories that use a few common words should prove easier to read than those that use a variety of words, including some that do not occur with high frequency. Vocabulary difficulty is measured by counting the number of words that do not appear on the Primary High-Frequency Word List (see Figure A.2). This listing is a compilation of the 500 words that occur with the highest frequency in first-grade textbooks and children's books that are on a first-grade level. It is based on *The Educator's Word Frequency Guide* (Zeno, Ivens, Millard, & Rajduvvuri, 1995). In tryouts, in which teachers assessed the difficulty levels of beginning reading materials, those who used the number of hard words as an aid were much more accurate than those who used only subjective factors (Gunning, 1996).

To determine the number of hard words, select a 100-word sample and count the number of words not on the Primary High-Frequency Word List. When counting words, consider hyphenated words (e.g., twenty-seven) to be one word. Also count initials (e.g., CBS) and numerals (e.g., 1,357) as one

Figure A.2
Primary High-Frequency Word List

a	bikes	day	fish
about	bird	did	fix
across	birthday	didn't	floor
afraid	black	different	flower
after	blue	do	fly
again	boat	doctor	follow
air	book	does	food
all	both	dog	for
alone	box	don't	found
along	boy	door	four
always	bring	down	fox
am	brother	drink	friend
an	brown	drop	frog
and	bus	duck	from
animal	but	each	front
another	by	ear	fun
answer	cake	earth	funny
any	call	eat	game
anybody	came	egg	gave
anything	can	end	get
are	can't	enough	girl
arm	cannot	even	give
around	car	ever	go
as	care	every	gone
ask	cat	everyone	good
at	catch	everything	got
away	change	eye	grandfather
baby	children	face	grandma
back	city	fall	grandmother
bad	clean	family	grandpa
bag	climb	far	grass
ball	close	farm	great
be	cloud	farmer	green
bear	cold	fast	ground
because	come	father	grow
bed	cook	feel	guess
been	could	feet	had
before	couldn't	fell	hair
began	cow	felt	hand
behind	cried	few	happen
bell	cry	find	happy
best	cut	fine	hard
better	dad	fire	has
big	dark	first	hat

(Continued)

Figure A.2
(Continued)

have	keep	minute	paper
he	kept	mom	park
head	kid	money	part
hear	kind	moon	party
heard	king	more	people
held	kitten	morning	pet
hello	knew	mother	pick
help	know	mountain	picture
hen	lake	mouse	piece
her	last	move	pig
here	late	much	place
high	laugh	must	plant
hill	learn	my	play
him	leave	name	please
himself	left	near	pond
his	leg	need	pretty
hit	let	never	pull
hold	let's	new	push
hole	letter	next	put
home	light	nice	quick
horse	like	night	quiet
hot	line	no	rabbit
house	lion	noise	race
how	listen	not	rain
hurt	little	nothing	ran
I	live	now	reach
I'll	long	of	read
I'm	look	off	ready
I've	lost	oh	real
idea	lot	old	really
if	love	on	red
in	lunch	once	remember
inside	made	one	rest
into	make	only	ride
is	man	open	right
isn't	many	or	river
it	mark	other	road
it's	may	our	rock
its	maybe	out	room
jeep	me	outside	run
job	mean	over	sad
jump	men	own	said
just	might	paint	same

(Continued)

Figure A.2
(Continued)

sat	stand	through	week
saw	star	time	well
say	start	tired	went
school	stay	to	were
sea	step	toad	wet
see	stick	today	what
seeds	still	together	what's
seem	stood	told	wheel
seen	stop	too	when
set	store	took	where
she	story	top	which
sheep	street	town	while
ship	sun	train	white
shoe	sure	tree	who
shop	surprise	tried	why
short	swim	truck	wife
should	table	try	will
shout	take	turn	wind
show	talk	turtle	window
sick	tall	two	wish
side	tell	uncle	with
sign	ten	under	without
sing	than	until	wolf
sister	thank	up	woman
sit	that	us	won't
sky	that's	use	wood
sleep	the	very	word
slowly	their	voice	work
small	them	wait	would
smile	then	walk	write
snow	there	want	year
so	these	warm	yell
some	they	was	yellow
someone	thing	wasn't	yes
something	think	watch	you
sometime	this	water	you'll
soon	those	way	your
sound	thought	we	you're
spot	three	we'll	

word. Consider as familiar those words on the list to which *s, es, d, ed, ing, ly, er,* and *est* have been added (e.g., comparative degree such as *faster, slower* but not *worker* or *helper*). Also include as familiar those words that undergo a change of letters as a result of adding *ing, ed,* or *s* (e.g., *running, hoping, planned, cities*). Do not count as hard words proper names of people (e.g., *William Reynolds* or *Maria Lopez*). However, titles, even if used with names, are considered as hard words (e.g., *Captain Johnson, Aunt May*). Also count as unfamiliar those names of animals not on the list that are used as proper names (e.g., *And so* Alligator *and* Panther *became friends*). Abbreviations (e.g., *St., lbs.*) are counted as being unfamiliar unless they are on the list.

If the book being analyzed has fewer than 100 words, divide the number of hard words by the number of words in the book (7 ÷ 77 = 9 hard words). Keep in mind that passages with fewer than 100 words are less reliable. Many of the easiest children's books have only 30 or 40 words. The hard word score is less useful for these books. Careful subjective judgment will be required.

For brief books, those with 300 or fewer words, analyze the entire work in 100–word segments. For longer texts, analyze as many samples as you can. Analyze at least three samples, selected from the beginning, middle, and end of the book. The more samples you analyze, the more valid and reliable is the estimate of difficulty. Many children's books increase in difficulty so that the latter part of the book has far more hard words than the beginning portions. Average the hard words scores of the passages sampled. Figure A.1 provides estimated levels based on the proportion of hard words per 100 words. However, the hard word score should *never* be used as the sole determining factor in estimating difficulty level. Subjective factors should be carefully considered. In tryouts of the Primary Readability Index, when subjective factors were considered, changes were made in estimated difficulty levels about one-third of the time. In most instances, the estimated difficulty level was lowered.

The number of different words can also be used as a factor in estimating difficulty level. Differentiating among the easy sight word level and beginning A and beginning B requires making fine discriminations. Calculating or estimating the number of different words can be used to assist in differentiating among these levels. Some children's books provide a listing of the number of different words. If such a list is not provided and if the book is brief, count the number of different words. An easy way to do this is to list each different word in alphabetical order. If the text is long, estimate the number of different words. Figure A.1 provides estimated levels based on the number of different words in a selection. Beyond beginning reading level B, the number of different words loses its value as an indicator of level of difficulty.

Using the hard word score as an anchor, consider the subjective factors listed in Figure A.1. If some of the hard words are depicted by illustrations, lower the difficulty estimate. Lower the estimate, too, if the words listed as being difficult are easy to decode. For instance, words such as *bat* and *pot* are not on the Primary High-Frequency Word List but are easy to sound out. On the other hand, increase the estimate if the hard words are multisyllabic words or are words that might not be in the reader's listening vocabulary.

Also consider the length of the text. Short pieces are easier to read than longer ones. Consider, too, how helpful the illustrations are. Books that have illustrations that provide an overview of the text or that depict significant portions of the text are easier than those that do not. Also note the overall interest of the selection, familiarity of the topic and language, repetition of elements, use of rhyme, and such format factors as number of lines per page. Above all, note whether the average beginning reader would have the background of information necessary to read the text. A book about the Vietnam War, no matter how simply written, would be beyond most beginning readers. Watch out, too, for the use of figurative language and allusions that are beyond beginning readers. Use the description provided for each level as a guide for determining difficulty but be flexible. Use one of the benchmark books provided at each level as a kind of holistic summary of factors. Ask yourself: Which one of these benchmark books is the target book most like? If a benchmark book is not available, use the passages presented in Figures 1.1 through 1.8 in Chapter 1 or use the selections from the Reading Passages Inventory (Appendix B) as a guide. When estimating difficulty level, be conservative. If you are undecided whether a book is a beginning C or a beginning D, for instance, place it at the higher level. It is better to give a student a book that is on the easy side rather than one that is too difficult.

CONSTRUCTION OF THE PRIMARY READABILITY INDEX

A preliminary Primary Readability Index was constructed by surveying classical readability research (Chall & Dale, 1995; Klare, 1984) and recent work on leveling books through the use of subjective methods (Peterson, 1991; Weaver, 1992). A checklist of possible factors was assembled. Factors assessed include the following: reader background and interest, familiarity of subject matter, familiarity of language, complexity of syntax, use of illustrations, predictability of text, length of text, format of text, decodability of text, and special skills needed to read text. In addition, because, according to classical readability research, vocabulary load is the major factor in estimating difficulty level, a tally was made of words whose printed forms might be difficult for beginning readers. Difficult words were defined as those not appearing on the Primary High-Frequency Word List.

To refine the Primary Readability Index, a preliminary analysis of approximately 100 children's book's was conducted. Both the objective factors of number of different words in a selection and number of words not on the Primary High-Frequency Word List were combined with such subjective factors as use of illustrations and reader's background to produce a description of each level of difficulty and to choose benchmark books for each level that would serve as examples of the key characteristics of texts at that level. Based on an analysis of the 100 books, it was decided to set up eight levels of difficulty, ranging from picture reading to beginning second grade. After being refined, the Primary Readability Index was then used to estimate the difficulty levels of approximately 2,000 children's books.

STATISTICAL VALIDITY

To assess statistical validity, correlations between books analyzed and those contained on the Reading Recovery (Peterson, 1991) and Weaver booklists (Story House, 1996) were calculated. Levels yielded by the Spache Readability Formula (Spache, 1974) were also compared with those yielded by the Primary Readability Index. In addition, note was made of characteristics of text that seemed to make a book easier or harder to read. The correlation between the Primary Readability Index and the Reading Recovery Booklist is $r = .68$ ($n = 76$) (Spearman), which is significant at the .001 level. Correlation between the Primary Readability Index and the Weaver Booklist is $r = .61$ ($n = 32$) (Spearman), which is significant at the .001 level. The correlation between the Primary Readability Index and Spache is $r = .56$ ($n = 80$) (Spearman), which is significant at the .001 level.

GOODNESS OF FIT

Goodness of fit was assessed in order to see how close the assessment devices were in their estimates of difficulty level. Degree of agreement between levels yielded by the Primary Readability Index was compared with those yielded by the Spache, Reading Recovery Book List, and the Weaver listing. To make the instruments comparable, the 20 levels of Reading Recovery were collapsed into 7 levels and levels from all three instruments were translated into grade equivalents. The Primary Readability Index yielded the same levels as the Reading Recovery Booklist 41/76, or 74 percent, of the time. The two devices were within one level of each other 67/76, or 88 percent, of the time. In no instance was there a difference of more than two levels. The Primary Readability Index yielded the same levels as the Weaver Booklist 18/32, or 56 percent, of the time. The two devices were within one level of each other 24/32, or 75 percent, of the time. In no instance was there a difference of more than two levels.

PRACTICALITY AND RELIABILITY

To assess reliability and practicality, two experiments were conducted. In the first, a group of nine advanced graduate students enrolled in a summer literacy laboratory course were asked to assign readability levels to six text samples. Before making their judgments, they were provided with subjective criteria only. Four weeks later, eight of these same students, plus one who had been absent for the initial assessment, were provided with criteria that included the subjective factors used in the first assessment and also one objective factor: number of hard words per 100. When given only subjective criteria, teachers experienced some difficulty assigning readability levels. Graduate students' assessments agreed with the designated level only 20.8 percent of the time. However, their assessments were within one level 60.4 percent of the time. When provided with the objective criteria of number of hard words, the percentage of agreement increased substantially. There was exact agreement 66.6 percent of the time and agreement within one level 100 percent of the time.

In a second study, 12 pairs of teachers were asked to rank seven selections from easiest to most difficult using subjective criteria only. The pairs of teachers were then asked to rank the selections again. This time, they were given two objective criteria: number of different words in the lower-level selections and number of hard words in each selection. Before being given objective criteria, the evaluators misplaced 26.1 percent of the selections. However, all of the misplacements, except for one, were within one level of the designated level. When objective criteria were used, the percentage of misplacements was reduced to 11.9 percent. All of the misplacements were within one level of the designated level.

┌ Appendix B ───────────┐

Graduated Word Lists and Primary Reading Passages Inventory

$\mathbf{T}$he purpose of the Graduated Word Lists and the Primary Reading Passages Inventory is to help you determine the students' reading levels. The Word Lists and the Primary Reading Passages Inventory yields three levels: independent, instructional, and frustration.

The *independent level* is the point at which students can read on their own, without any help from teachers, parents, or peers. They recognize 98 to 99 percent of the words and their comprehension is nearly perfect. At the *instructional level,* students can read at least 95 out of 100 words and they recall at least 75 percent of what they read. If given instructional assistance, they can read with confidence and competence. At the *frustration level,* the material is simply too difficult for the student to read, even with assistance. Students miss 10 or more words out of 100 and/or remember only half of what they read. Students may exhibit lip movement during silent reading, may be easily distracted, or may engage in hair twisting, grimacing, or other stress-signaling behaviors (Johnson, Kress, & Pikulski, 1987).

GRADUATED WORD LISTS

The Graduated Word Lists consist of five sets of words that gradually become more difficult. Testing begins with the first list and continues until the student misses 10 on any one list.

Before administering the Graduated Word Lists, explain their nature and purpose to the child. For example, say, "I am going to ask you to read some words for me. As you go through the lists of words, they will become harder, but do the best you can." As the the student reads from the Student Copy of the Graduated Word Lists, you record the child's performance on the Teacher's Marking Copy. Use a check (✓) to indicate that a word has been read correctly. Use a check with a tail (✓) to indicate that the student made an error or failed to respond within about 5 seconds. If you have enough time, record the student's errors. This will help you better understand the processes the student is using and will provide information about the kinds of elements the student has mastered and those she or he is having difficulty with. If the student mispronounces or substitutes a word, write the mispronunciation or substitution. If the student says, "I don't know," write *dk* in the blank. Write *o* if the student makes no response. A sample-marked Graduated Word Lists is presented in Figure B.1. Figure B.2 is the Student Copy of the Graduated Word Lists and Figure B.3 is the Teacher's Marking Copy of the Graduated Word Lists.

Before administering the Graduated Word Lists, photocopy the Teacher's Marking Copy so that you can record students' performances. Permission is granted to users of this text to make as many copies of the Teacher's Marking Copy as are needed to assess their students.

After you have finished administering the Graduated Word Lists, enter the results on the Reading Inventory Summary Sheet. (Figure B.6 on page 166 shows a sample-marked Reading Inventory Summary Sheet; Figure B.7 on page 167 is a copy of the blank form.) Tally the total number of words read correctly and then use Table B.1 (page 162) to help you determine the student's reading level. Although the Graduated Word Lists can be used to obtain a reading level, using the Primary Reading Passages Inventory will provide a more reliable and valid estimate because it assesses comprehension as well as the ability to read words. However, if time or circumstances do not permit administration of the Primary Reading Passages Inventory, the Graduated Word Lists should yield a reasonably accurate level.

Figure B.1
Graduated Word Lists: Sample Marked Copy

Name _Mark S._   Grade _1_   Date _12–11_

1. I	✓		1. ball	✓
2. see	✓		2. sleep	✓
3. is	✓		3. laugh	✓
4. can	✓		4. morning	✓
5. go	✓		5. rabbit	run
6. big	bad ✓		6. today	✓
7. man	✓		7. because	✓
8. got	get		8. children	✓
9. saw	✓		9. gave	✓
10. dog	do		10. should	✓
11. stop	✓		11. money	0
12. cat	✓		12. rain	ran
13. am	✓		13. paper	0
14. who	✓		14. afraid	dk
15. run	ran ✓		15. swim	✓
16. book	✓		16. listen	I–
17. jump	j–		17. surprise	sheep
18. bird	✓		18. story	✓
19. night	dk		19. together	✓
20. give	got		20. shout	✓

Number Correct _15_   Number Correct _11_

Figure B.2
Graduated Word Lists: Student Copy

List A	List B	List C
1. I	1. ball	1. funny
2. see	2. sleep	2. everyone
3. is	3. laugh	3. remember
4. can	4. morning	4. warm
5. go	5. rabbit	5. noise
6. big	6. today	6. might
7. man	7. because	7. follow
8. got	8. children	8. river
9. saw	9. gave	9. different
10. dog	10. should	10. guess
11. stop	11. money	11. mountain
12. cat	12. rain	12. party
13. am	13. paper	13. trouble
14. who	14. afraid	14. giant
15. run	15. swim	15. garden
16. book	16. listen	16. owl
17. jump	17. surprise	17. scare
18. bird	18. story	18. beautiful
19. night	19. together	19. strong
20. give	20. shout	20. wonder

List D	List E
1. hungry	1. chicken
2. tomorrow	2. understand
3. believe	3. promise
4. summer	4. pretend
5. strange	5. yesterday
6. caught	6. library
7. round	7. treasure
8. angry	8. problem
9. machine	9. instead
10. breakfast	10. whisper
11. question	11. hospital
12. forest	12. station
13. weather	13. energy
14. middle	14. explore
15. threw	15. favorite
16. country	16. practice
17. important	17. meadow
18. straight	18. announce
19. branch	19. language
20. engine	20. measure

Figure B.3
Graduated Word Lists: Teacher's Marking Copy

Name_____ Grade _____ Date _____

List A		List B	
1. I	_____	1. ball	_____
2. see	_____	2. sleep	_____
3. is	_____	3. laugh	_____
4. can	_____	4. morning	_____
5. go	_____	5. rabbit	_____
6. big	_____	6. today	_____
7. man	_____	7. because	_____
8. got	_____	8. children	_____
9. saw	_____	9. gave	_____
10. dog	_____	10. should	_____
11. stop	_____	11. money	_____
12. cat	_____	12. rain	_____
13. am	_____	13. paper	_____
14. who	_____	14. afraid	_____
15. run	_____	15. swim	_____
16. book	_____	16. listen	_____
17. jump	_____	17. surprise	_____
18. bird	_____	18. story	_____
19. night	_____	19. together	_____
20. give	_____	20. shout	_____

Number Correct _____   Number Correct _____

(*Continued*)

Figure B.3
(Continued)

List C		List D	
1. funny	_____	1. hungry	_____
2. everyone	_____	2. tomorrow	_____
3. remember	_____	3. believe	_____
4. warm	_____	4. summer	_____
5. noise	_____	5. strange	_____
6. might	_____	6. caught	_____
7. follow	_____	7. round	_____
8. river	_____	8. angry	_____
9. different	_____	9. machine	_____
10. guess	_____	10. breakfast	_____
11. mountain	_____	11. question	_____
12. party	_____	12. forest	_____
13. trouble	_____	13. weather	_____
14. giant	_____	14. middle	_____
15. garden	_____	15. threw	_____
16. owl	_____	16. country	_____
17. scare	_____	17. important	_____
18. beautiful	_____	18. straight	_____
19. strong	_____	19. branch	_____
20. wonder	_____	20. engine	_____

Number Correct_____   Number Correct _____

(*Continued*)

Figure B.3
(Continued)

List E

1. chicken   _____

2. understand   _____

3. promise   _____

4. pretend   _____

5. yesterday   _____

6. library   _____

7. treasure   _____

8. problem   _____

9. instead   _____

10. whisper   _____

11. hospital   _____

12. station   _____

13. energy   _____

14. explore   _____

15. favorite   _____

16. practice   _____

17. meadow   _____

18. announce   _____

19. language   _____

20. measure   _____

Number Correct   _____   Estimated Grade Level   _____

Total Number Correct   _____

PRIMARY READING PASSAGES INVENTORY

In the Primary Reading Passages Inventory, the student reads a series of passages that grow in difficulty. The levels of difficulty of the passages match the levels of difficulty of the books listed in this text: picture, caption, easy sight, beginning A, beginning B, beginning C, beginning D, and Grade 2A.

If you have administered the Graduated Word Lists, use the student's performance to determine the starting point on the Primary Reading Passages Inventory. Table B.1 shows starting points as indicated by scores on the Graduated Word Lists. If you have not administered the Graduated Word Lists, start with the easiest passage. Continue testing until the material is obviously too difficult for the student. This will be the point where the student reaches her or his frustration level (unable to read at least 90 percent of the words or cannot answer at least half the comprehension questions asked about the selection).

Before administering the passages, put the student at ease. Explain to the student that you would like her or him to read some stories to you so that you can better tell what kinds of books might be best for her or him. Tell the student that as she or he reads, you will be making little notes about the reading. Also tell the student that after she or he has read the selection, you will be asking questions about it.

To determine a student's reading levels, assess both word recognition in context—which is the ability to read the words in the Reading Passages Inventory—and comprehension—which is the ability to answer a series of questions about the passages that have been read. As the student reads aloud, use a series of symbols to describe her or his reading behavior. Note mispronounced words, omitted words, inserted words, and words supplied by the examiner. The examiner supplies words when the student requests him or her to do so or it is clear that the student will not be able to read the

Table B.1
Estimated Reading Levels

Number of Words Read Correctly	Estimated Reading Level
0–5	Picture
6–10	Caption
11–20	Sight
21–35	Beginning A
36–50	Beginning B
51–65	Beginning C
66–80	Beginning D
81–90	Grade 2A
91–100	Beyond Grade 2A

Figure B.4
Inventory Marking Symbols

young the y~~ell~~ow bird	Mispronounced word
the yell~~ow~~ bird	Omitted word
big the ʌ yellow bird	Inserted word
the ⟨yellow⟩ bird	Word supplied by examiner
young ✓ the y~~ell~~ow bird	Self-corrected error

word independently. Self-corrections do not count as errors. Using the symbols shown in Figure B.4, note all errors and self-corrections. A sample marked-up inventory selection is presented in Figure B.5. The student reads from the Student Copy of the Primary Reading Passages Inventory. You mark the Teacher's Marking Copy of the inventory.

Before administering the Primary Reading Passages Inventory, photocopy the Teacher's Marking Copy so that you can record students' performances. Permission is granted to users of this text to make as many copies of the Teacher's Marking Copy as are needed to assess their students.

Comprehension Check

After the student has read a passage, comprehension is checked. Students' responses to questions should be recorded so you can take time later to examine any responses about which you are unsure. If the student has not supplied enough information for you to make a determination as to whether the answer is right or wrong, you can ask the student to tell you more.

Determining Levels

Continue testing until the student's word recognition falls below 90 percent. That is the frustration level. Then enter the student's word recognition in context and comprehension scores on the form provided in Reading Inventory Summary Sheet (page 167). (If you have not already done so, enter the scores from the Graduated Word Lists but do not use these to calculate word recognition in context.) Using both word recognition in context and comprehension scores, establish the student's reading levels: independent (98 to 99 percent word recognition, 90 to 100 percent comprehension), instructional

Figure B.5
Sample Marking Sheet

Easy Sight Word Level

Directions: Say to the student: "This story tells about an interesting animal. Read the story to find out what this animal is and what it does."

Marking: Using the symbols listed in Figure B.4, note the student's reading performance.

The Red Kangaroo

Hop! Hop! Hop! The red kangaroo likes to hop. The red kangaroo can hop over you. It can hop ten feet.

The red kangaroo is big. It is bigger than a man. Baby red kangaroos are very little. A baby red kangaroo could (fit) in your hand.

✓ 1. What does the red kangaroo like to do?   Hop.

✓ 2. How far can the red kangaroo hop?   10 feet.

✓ 3. How big is the red kangaroo when it is fully grown?   Bigger than a man.

✓ 4. How big is the red kangaroo when it is first born?   Could fit in your hat.

Word Recognition _____94_____ %

Comprehension _____100_____ %

Word Recognition Conversion Table (47 words in selection)

Number of errors

1   2   ③   4   5   6

Percentage correct

98   96   ⑨④   92   90   88

(95 to 97 percent word recognition and 75 to 89 percent comprehension), or frustration (50 percent word recognition or 50 percent comprehension). Each page of the Teacher's Marking Copy contains a chart at the bottom for the rapid determination of percentage of word recognition. Levels obtained should be considered as estimates and should be verified by carefully observing students as they read children's books and other materials. Make

whatever adjustments are necessary. A sample-marked Reading Inventory Summary Sheet is presented in Figure B.6. Figure B.7 is a blank form of this summary that may be photocopied by users of this text in order to assess their students. Immediately following these two figures are Figures B.8 through B.15, the students' copies of reading passages, and Figures B.16 through B.23, the teacher's marking copies.

Constructing Your Own Inventory

The Primary Reading Passages Inventory is provided here for your convenience. You can also use an actual book from each level to estimate students' reading levels. For instance, you might use the following, each of which is published in paperback:

Picture level	*Colors*
Caption	*Cat on the Mat*
Sight word	*Who Is Who?*
Beginning A	*Sleepy Dog*
Beginning B	*And I Mean It, Stanley!*
Beginning C	*Little Bear's Visit*
Beginning D	*Frog and Toad at Home*
Grade 2A	*Thank You, Amelia Bedelia*

Proceed just as you would when administering the Primary Reading Passages Inventory. Give the Graduated Word Lists in order to find a starting point. Then have the students read from the appropriate-level books. Have them read sample passages of approximately 50 words at the lowest levels and up to 150 to 200 words at the beginning D and Grade 2A levels. After a student has orally read a selection, you might ask her or him to retell it and use the retelling to assess comprehension, or compose a series of four to five questions.

Need for Ongoing Assessment

As with any placement device, reading inventories are fallible. Carefully monitor the students' performances as they read. If they seem to be stumbling over every fourth or fifth word, or do not seem to know what they have read, the book is probably too hard. If, on the other hand, they are zipping through the books, they may need more challenging fare. Keep in mind, too, that students vary in their tolerance for errors. Some are very cautious and become discouraged when they encounter difficult words. These children might do better if they are given material that is closer to their independent levels. As their confidence grows, they can be given more challenging books.

Figure B.6
Reading Inventory Summary Sheet: Sample-Marked Copy

Name __Mark S._____ Age __7_____ Date ___12–11___

Grade __1____ School __P.S. 132_____ Examiner __Thomas G._____

<u>**Word Lists Scores**</u>   <u>**Passage Scores**</u>

		Word Recognition in Context	Comprehension
List A __15__	Picture Level	__100__	__100__
List B __11__	Caption Level	__100__	__100__
List C __6__	Sight Word	__97__	__100__
List D _____	Beginning A	__96__	__80__
List E _____	Beginning B	__90__	__40__
Total __32__	Beginning C	_____	_____
	Beginning D	_____	_____
Estimated Level __Beg. A__	Grade 2A	_____	_____

(Word Lists)

Levels (Passage Inventory)   **Summary of Strengths and Needs**

Independent ___Caption___   __Knows beginning consonants__

Instructional ___Beg. A___   __and short vowel patterns.__

Frustration ___Beg. B___   __Needs long vowel patterns.__

<u>**Scoring Criteria**</u>

<u>**Word List Scores**</u>   <u>**Passage Scores**</u>

Level	Score
Picture	0 – 5
Caption	6 – 10
Sight	11 – 20
Beg. A	21 – 35
Beg. B	36 – 50
Beg. C	51 – 65
Beg. D	66 – 80
2A	81 – 90
Beyond 2A	91 – 100

	Word Recognition in Context		Comprehension
Independent	99%	and	90%
Instructional	95%	and	75%
Frustration	90%	or	50%

Figure B.7
Reading Inventory Summary Sheet

Name _____ Age _____ Date _____
Grade _____ School _____ Examiner _____

Word List Scores	**Passage Scores**	
(Word Inventory)	**Word Recognition in Context**	**Comprehension**
List A _____	Picture Level _____	_____
List B _____	Caption Level _____	_____
List C _____	Sight Word _____	_____
List D _____	Beginning A _____	_____
List E _____	Beginning B _____	_____
Total _____	Beginning C _____	_____
Estimated Level _____	Beginning D _____	_____
	Grade 2A _____	_____
(Word Lists)		

Levels (Passage Inventory)   **Summary of Strengths and Needs**

Independent _____   _____

Instructional _____   _____

Frustration _____   _____

Scoring Criteria

Word List Scores		**Passage Scores**		
		Word Recognition in Context		**Comprehension**
Level	**Score**			
Picture	0–5	Independent	99% and	90%
Caption	6–10	Instructional	95% and	75
Sight	11–20	Frustration	90% or	50
Beg. A	21–35			
Beg. B	36–50			
Beg. C	51–65			
Beg. D	66–80			
2A	81–90			
Beyond 2A	91–100			

Figure B.8
Primary Reading Passages Inventory—
Cats: Student Copy

Cats

One cat.   Two cats.

Three cats.

Four cats.

Figure B.9
Primary Reading Passages Inventory—
Seals: Student copy

I see a seal.

I see a seal in the zoo.

(Continued)

Figure B.9
(Continued)

I see six seals.

I see six seals in the zoo.

Figure B.10
Primary Reading Passages Inventory—
Kangaroo: Student Copy

The Red Kangaroo

Hop! Hop! Hop! The red kangaroo likes to hop. The red kangaroo can hop over you. It can hop ten feet.

The red kangaroo is big. It is bigger than a man. Baby red kangaroos are very little. A baby red kangaroo could fit in your hand.

Figure B.11
Primary Reading Passages Inventory—
Giraffe: Student Copy

The Tallest Animal

The giraffe is the tallest animal of all. A baby giraffe is six feet tall. When it is fully grown, a giraffe can be 18 feet tall.

The giraffe's long neck and long legs make it tall. Its legs are six feet long. And so is its neck. The giraffe has the longest legs and longest neck of any animal. Giraffes eat a lot of food. With their long necks, giraffes can eat from the tops of trees.

Figure B.12
Primary Reading Passages Inventory—
Ben: Student Copy

Ben

Ann was sad. Ben had climbed up a tree. Ben is her cat. "Come down, Ben!" Ann ordered. "Come down right away!" Ben did not come down. He just climbed to a higher branch.

Ann did not know what to do, so she called her mom at the office. Her mom is a vet. "Put a dish of milk at the bottom of the tree," her mom said. Ann did just that. When Ben saw the dish of milk, he climbed down the tree as fast as he could.

Figure B.13
Primary Reading Passages Inventory—
Johnny Appleseed: Student Copy

Johnny Appleseed

John looked strange. He wore a tin pan for a hat, and he was dressed in rags. Even so, people liked John. He was kind to others, and he was kind to animals.

John loved apples. He left his home and headed West about 200 years ago. He wanted everyone to have apples. On his back he carried a pack that was full of apple seeds. At that time, there were few apple trees in many parts of our country. Traveling from place to place, John planted his apple seeds. As the years passed, the seeds grew into trees. After planting hundreds and hundreds of apple trees, John came to be called "Johnny Appleseed."

Figure B.14
Primary Reading Passages Inventory—
Puppy: Student Copy

Puppy Tails

Bob gets a new puppy almost every year. The puppy is not Bob's to keep. Bob only has the puppy for a year and then he must give it back.

Bob is in a club known as Puppy Tails. The boys and girls in Puppy Tails raise puppies for Seeing Eye. Seeing Eye trains guide dogs for blind people. A puppy is not ready for guide dog training until it is at least 14 months old. The boys and girls in Puppy Tails take care of the puppies until they are grown up enough to be taught by Seeing Eye.

Bob feels sad when the year is up and he has to give his puppy back to Seeing Eye. He will miss his pup. But in a way, Bob feels happy, too. He knows that his pup will help someone in need.

Figure B.15
Primary Reading Passages Inventory—
Clowns: Student Copy

Clowns

What do you like best about the circus? Many boys and girls like the clowns best of all.

Clowns wear funny costumes. Clowns might wear shoes that are so big that you could put two feet in one shoe. Their baggy pants and extra-large shirts may also be many sizes too big for them. And a clown king may wear a crown that is so big it covers his ears.

Clowns do funny tricks. They pretend that they are throwing pails of water at each other. But all that comes out are bits of paper. They may also drive tiny cars. It looks funny to see a very tall clown climb out of a very small car.

It is not easy to be a clown. Circus clowns spend much of their time on trains traveling to towns and cities around the country. Clowns also spend many hours painting their faces and practicing their tricks. Although being a clown is hard work, it is fun. It is fun to make children and grown-ups laugh.

Figure B.16
Primary Reading Passages Inventory—
Cats: Teacher Marking Copy

Picture-Level Marking Sheet   Cats

Directions: Say to the student: "These pictures show some cats. The words under the picture tell what is in the picture. Look at the first picture and read the words under it." If the student is able to read the first caption, proceed to the next one. If the student has difficulty, discuss the content of the picture and its relationship to its caption. For example, say: "It shows one cat and so the words under it say 'One cat.'" Watch to see whether the student is attending to the picture, the words, or both.

Marking: Using the symbols listed in Figure B.4, note the student's reading performance. Note whether the student seems to be using picture clues, word or letter clues, or both.

One cat.   Two cats.

Three cats.   Four cats.

1. How many cats were there in the first picture?
2. How many cats were there in the second picture?
3. How many cats were there in the third picture?
4. How many cats were there in the fourth picture?

Word Recognition _____%
Comprehension _____ %

Word Recognition Conversion Table (8 words in selection)

Number of errors

1   2   3   4

Percentage correct

88   75   62   50

Figure B.17
Primary Reading Passages Inventory—
Seals: Teacher Marking Copy

Directions: Say to the student: "This story tells about some things that a boy in a wheelchair sees. Read the story to find out what the boy sees."

Marking: Using the symbols listed in Figure B.4, note the student's reading performance. Note whether the student seems to be using picture clues, word or letter clues, or both.

Seals

I see a seal.

I see a seal in the zoo.

I see six seals.

I see six seals in the zoo.

1. What did the boy see first?
2. Where was the boy?
3. How many seals did he see all together?
4. What makes you think that the boy might have difficulty walking?

Word Recognition _____%
Comprehension _____ %

Word Recognition Conversion Table (22 words in selection)

Number of errors

| 1 | 2 | 3 |

Percentage correct

| 95 | 91 | 86 |

Figure B.18
Primary Reading Passages Inventory—
Kangaroo: Teacher Marking Copy

Easy Sight-Word Level Marking Sheet   The Red Kangaroo

Directions: Say to the student: "This story tells about an interesting animal. Read the story to find out what this animal is and what it does."

Marking: Using the symbols listed in Figure B.4, note the student's reading performance.

The Red Kangaroo

Hop! Hop! Hop! The red kangaroo likes to hop. The red kangaroo can hop over you. It can hop ten feet.

The red kangaroo is big. It is bigger than a man. Baby red kangaroos are very little. A baby red kangaroo could fit in your hand.

1. What does the red kangaroo like to do?
2. How far can the red kangaroo hop?
3. How big is the red kangaroo when it is fully grown?
4. How big is the red kangaroo when it is first born?

Word Recognition _____%
Comprehension _____ %

Word Recognition Conversion Table (47 words in selection)

Number of errors

| 1 | 2 | 3 | 4 | 5 |

Percentage correct

| 98 | 96 | 94 | 91 | 89 |

Figure B.19
Primary Reading Passages Inventory—
Giraffe: Teacher Marking Copy

Beginning Reading A-Level Marking Sheet   The Tallest Animal

Directions: Say to the student: "This story tells about a big animal. Read to find out about the big animal."

Marking: Using the symbols listed in Figure B.4, note the student's reading performance.

The Tallest Animal

The giraffe is the tallest animal of all. A baby giraffe is six feet tall. When it is fully grown, a giraffe can be 18 feet tall.

The giraffe's long neck and long legs make it tall. Its legs are six feet long. And so is its neck. The giraffe has the longest legs and longest neck of any animal. Giraffes eat a lot of food. With their long necks, giraffes can eat from the tops of trees.

1. How tall is a baby giraffe?
2. How tall is a fully grown giraffe?
3. What parts of the giraffe make it tall?
4. How much food does a giraffe eat?
5. How do giraffes use their long necks?

Word Recognition _____%
Comprehension _____ %

Word Recognition Conversion Table (78 words in selection)

Number of errors

| 1 | 2 | 3 | 4 | 5 | 6 | 7 | 8 | 9 |

Percentage correct

| 99 | 97 | 96 | 95 | 94 | 92 | 91 | 90 | 88 |

Figure B.20
Primary Reading Passages Inventory—
Ben: Teacher Marking Copy

Beginning Reading B-Level Marking Sheet Ben

Directions: Say to the student: "This story tells about a girl and her cat. Read to find out about the girl and her cat."

Marking: Using the symbols listed in Figure B.4, note the student's reading performance.

Ben

Ann was sad. Ben had climbed up a tree. Ben is her cat. "Come down, Ben!"

Ann ordered. "Come down right away!" Ben did not come down. He just climbed

to a higher branch.

Ann did not know what to do, so she called her mom at the office. Her mom

is a vet. "Put a dish of milk at the bottom of the tree," her mom said. Ann did just

that. When Ben saw the dish of milk, he climbed down the tree as fast as he could.

1. Why was Ann sad?
2. Whom did Ann call?
3. Why would Ann's mom know a lot about cats?
4. What plan did Ann's mom have for getting the cat down?
5. What did Ben do when he saw the milk?

Word Recognition _____%
Comprehension _____ %

Word Recognition Conversion Table (89 words in selection)

Number of errors

1	2	3	4	5	6	7	8	9	10

Percentage correct

99	98	97	96	94	93	92	91	90	89

Figure B.21
Primary Reading Passages Inventory—
Johnny Appleseed: Teacher Marking Copy

Beginning Reading C-Level Marking Sheet   Johnny Appleseed

Directions: Say to the student: "This story tells about a man by the name of John, who loved apples. Read to see what John did."

Marking: Using the symbols listed in Figure B.4, note the student's reading performance.

Johnny Appleseed

John looked strange. He wore a tin pan for a hat, and he was dressed in rags. Even so, people liked John. He was kind to others, and he was kind to animals.

John loved apples. He left his home and headed West about 200 years ago. He wanted everyone to have apples. On his back he carried a pack that was full of apple seeds. At that time there were few apple trees in many parts of our country. Traveling from place to place, John planted his apple seeds. As the years passed, the seeds grew into trees. After planting hundreds and hundreds of apple trees, John came to be called "Johnny Appleseed."

1. How did John dress?
2. Why did people like him?
3. About how many years ago did John leave home?
4. When he left home, what did he carry on his back?
5. Why was John called "Johnny Appleseed"?

Word Recognition _____%
Comprehension _____ %

Word Recognition Conversion Table (114 words in selection)

Number of errors

1	2	3	4	5	6	7	8	9	10	11	12

Percentage correct

99	98	97	96	96	95	94	93	92	91	90	89

Figure B.22
Primary Reading Passages Inventory—
Puppy Tails: Teacher Marking Copy

Beginning Reading D-Level Marking Sheet   Puppy Tails

Directions: Say to the student: "This story tells about a club called Puppy Tails. Read the story to find out about this club."

Marking: Using the symbols listed in Figure B.4, note the student's reading performance.

Puppy Tails

Bob gets a new puppy almost every year. The puppy is not Bob's to keep. Bob only has the puppy for a year and then he must give it back.

Bob is in a club known as Puppy Tails. The boys and girls in Puppy Tails raise puppies for Seeing Eye. Seeing Eye trains guide dogs for blind people. A puppy is not ready for guide dog training until it is at least 14 months old. The boys and girls in Puppy Tails take care of the puppies until they are grown up enough to be taught by Seeing Eye.

Bob feels sad when the year is up and he has to give his puppy back to Seeing Eye. He will miss his pup. But in a way, Bob feels happy, too. He knows that his pup will help someone in need.

1. What do the boys and girls in Puppy Tails do?
2. What do seeing Eye Dogs do?
3. How old should a puppy be before it is ready for Seeing Eye training?
4. How long does Bob keep a puppy?
5. Why does Bob feel both sad and happy when he has to give his puppy back?

Word Recognition _____%
Comprehension _____ %

Word Recognition Conversion Table (142 words in selection)

Number of errors

1	2	3	4	5	6	7	8	9	10	11	12	13	14	15

Percentage correct

99	99	98	97	96	96	95	94	94	93	92	92	91	90	89

Figure B.23
Primary Reading Passages Inventory—
Clowns: Teacher Marking Copy

Beginning Reading 2A-Level Marking Sheet   Clowns

Directions: Say to the student: "This story tells about clowns. Read the story to find out about clowns."

Marking: Using the symbols listed in Figure B.4, note the student's reading performance.

Clowns

What do you like best about the circus? Many boys and girls like the clowns best of all.

Clowns wear funny costumes. Clowns might wear shoes that are so big that you could put two feet in one shoe. Their baggy pants and extra-large shirts may also be many sizes too big for them. And a clown king may wear a crown that is so big it covers his ears.

Clowns do funny tricks. They pretend that they are throwing pails of water at each other. But all that comes out are bits of paper. They may also drive tiny cars. It looks funny to see a very tall clown climb out of a very small car.

It is not easy to be a clown. Circus clowns spend much of their time on trains traveling to towns and cities around the country. Clowns also spend many hours painting their faces and practicing their tricks. Although being a clown is hard work, it is fun. It is fun to make children and grown-ups laugh.

1. As told in the story, what kind of clothes do clowns wear?
2. As told in the story, how big are the shoes that they might wear?
3. As told in the story, what are some funny thing that clowns do?
4. As told in the story, why is it hard to be a clown?
5. As told in the story, why is it fun to be a clown?

Word Recognition _____%
Comprehension _____ %

Word Recognition Conversion Table (173 words in selection)

Number of errors

1	2	3	4	5	6	7	8	9	10	11	12	13	14	15	16	17	18	19

Percentage correct

99	99	98	98	97	97	96	95	95	94	94	93	93	92	91	91	90	90	89

Appendix C

Sets of Books for Beginning Readers Produced by Educational Publishers

In addition to the children's books listed in Chapter 4, there are several sets of books created by educational publishers that have been designed to foster reading development through the presentation of high-frequency words in predictable books written on beginning reading levels. Four of these are imports from New Zealand and Australia. The various series are described below. See Appendix D for publishers' addresses.

• Early Success (Houghton Mifflin)
Designed as an early intervention program for youngsters in grades 1 and 2 who are struggling to learn to read, the progam consists of 30 little story books on each of two levels, letter cards, and a teacher's manual.

• Learn to Read Science (Creative Teaching Press)
Features 24 well-illustrated, easy-to-read 16-page booklets on science topics. Booklets are written on caption/frame and easy sight-word levels.

• Literacy 2000 (Rigby)
The books gradually increase in difficulty from those that contain a single sentence or phrase per page to ones that contain five or more sentences per page. The program also contains a variety of books designed for shared reading. Included in the series are a number of informational texts. Although created for kindergarten, the program seems appropriate for first-graders or older youngsters reading on a first-grade level.

• Little Red Readers (Sundance)
Designed for kindergarten and grade 1, these books are published in five graduated sets of five books each.

• Read More Books (Dominie Press)
These 12-page informational books are written around themes (People at Work, At the Store, Where Do You Live?) or language patterns (I can _____, yes, no). Four-color photos on the left-hand page are accompanied by one- or two-line captions on the right-hand page. Sentences for most books are written in highly predictable patterns, but the degree of picture support varies. Although the photos support the text, it is not always possible to read the text on the basis of the photos.

• Reading Corners (Dominie Press)
This is a series of eight-page booklets designed to reinforce high-frequency sentence patterns. In the easiest texts, a full-page illustration is accompanied by a one-sentence caption that incorporates a basic sentence pattern: I like _____. Here is _____. I have _____.

• Ready Readers (Modern Curriculum Press)
Designed for the primary grades, Ready Readers consist of 200 booklets ranging in length from 8 to 24 pages. Booklets are arranged in five levels of difficulty from beginning-reading level to end-of-first-grade level. Sets of books are accompanied by big books, teacher's guides, word and picture cards, take-home stories, and audio cassettes. The program has a phonics emphasis.

• Ready to Read (Richard C. Owen)
These are designed to provide students in New Zealand with a graded series of children's books from the very beginning stage of reading through approximately the end of second grade. The series contains more than 40 titles. Divided into nine graded levels, according to ease of reading, each book has a small color wheel on the back cover, indicating the levels at which the book might be shared or used for guided or independent reading. Because Ready to Read was designed for students in New Zealand, some expressions may be unfamiliar to readers in the United States, so you may want to adapt some of the texts or use them selectively.

• Story Box (Wright Group)
Books are arranged in sets A through G, which gradually increase in difficulty. Each set contains eight titles for a total of 56 titles. There are also 25 books for shared reading. The A, or easiest, books present a repeated sentence with only the last word changing. The G, or most advanced, books have two to three lines per page.

• Sunshine at Home (Wright Group)
Although designed for use by parents, this 40-book set of emergent literacy reading books might also be used in the classroom and clinic. Each book contains three selections. Gradually growing in difficulty, the series is arranged in four sets of 10 books each. The series reinforces a group of 98 high-frequency words. Words introduced in earlier levels are reinforced in later levels. A Spanish version is available.

Appendix D

Publishers' Addresses

Addison-Wesley
1 Jacob's Way
Reading, MA 01867
800-447-2226

Annick Press
Ellicott Station
Buffalo, NY 143205
800-387-5085
(distributed by Firefly)

Arcade
141 Fifth Avenue
New York, NY 10010
800-343-9204

Astor-Honor
530 Fifth Avenue
New York, NY 10036
212-687-6190

Atheneum (*see* Simon & Schuster)

August House
Box 3223
Litttle Rock, AR 72203
800-284-89784

Bantam Doubleday Dell
1540 Broadway
New York, NY 10036
800-223-5780

Boyds Mill Press
815 Church Street
Honesdale, PA
800-949-7777

Bradbury (*see* Simon & Schuster)

Candlewick Press
2067 Massachussets Avenue
Cambridge, MA 02140
617-661-3330
(distributed by Penguin)

Carolrhoda (*see* Lerner)

Children's Press
Old Sherman Turnpike
Danbury, CT 06801
800-621-1115

Child's Play
67 Minot Avenue
Auburn, ME 04210
800-639-6404

Child's World
1730 James Drive
North Mankato, MN 56003
800-599-7323

Chronicle Books
275 Fifth Avenue
San Francisco, CA 94103
800-722-6657

Clarion Books
(*see* Houghton Mifflin)

Cool Kids
1098 NW Boca Raton Boulevard
Boca Raton, FL 33432
800-428-0578
(distributed by Atheneum)

Coward McCann (*see* Putnam)

Creative Teaching Press
10701 Holder Street
Cypress, CA 90630
714-995-7888

Crowell (*see* HarperCollins)

Crown (*see* Random House)

Dandelion Press
810 S. 12th Street
Laramie, WY 82070
307-745-4134

Delacorte
(*see* Bantam Doubleday Dell)

Dial Press (*see* Penguin Books)

Dodd, Mead (*see* Putnam)

Dominie Press
5945 Pacific Center Boulevard
San Diego, CA 92121
800-232-4570

Dorling Kindersley
1224 Heil Quaker Boulevard
La Vergne, TN 37086
800-937-5557

Dutton (*see* Penguin Books)

Doubleday
(*see* Bantam Doubleday Dell)

Farrar, Straus, Giroux
19 Union Square West
New York, NY 10003
800-788-6262

Forest House
P. O. 738
Lake Forest, IL 60045
800-394-7323

Four Winds (*see* Simon & Schuster)

Franklin Watts
95 Madison Avenue
7th FloorNew York, NY 10016
800-621-1115

Gareth Stevens
River Center Building
1555 N. River Center Drive
Suite 201
Milwaukee, WI 53212
800-3421-3569

Green Bark Press
Box 1108
Bridgeport, CT 06601
(distributed by Baker & Taylor)
800-775-1200

Green Tiger Press (*see* Simon &
Schuster)

Greenwillow (*see* Morrow)

Grosset & Dunlap (*see* Putnam)

Harcourt Brace Jovanovich
6277 Sea Harbor Drive
Orlando, FL 32887
800-543-1918

HarperCollins
1000 Keystone Industrial Park
Scranton, PA 18512
800-331-3761

Holiday House
425 Madison Avenue
New York, NY 10017
212-688-0085

Holt
151 Benigno Boulevard
Bellmar, NJ 08031
1-800-426-0462

Houghton Miflin
Wayside Road
Burlington, MA 01803
800-225-3362

Hyperion
114 Fifth Avenue
New York, NY 10011
800-343-9204

Kids Can Press (*see* Little, Brown)

Kingfisher Books
2150 N. Tenya Way
No. 1052
Las Vegas, NV 89128
702-242-9009

Knopf (*see* Random House)

Ladybird Books (*see* Penguin)

Lerner Group
241 First Avenue
Minneapolis, MN 55401
800-328-4929

Lippincott
227 E. Washington Square
Philadelphia, PA 19106
800-777-2295

Little, Brown
200 West Street
Waltham, MA 02154
800-759-0190

Live Oak Media
PO Box 652
Pine Plains, NY 12567
518-398-1010

Lothrop, Lee & Shepard
(*see* Morrow)

Macmillan (*see* Simon & Schuster)

Maxwell
200 Old Tappan Road
Old Tappan, NJ 07675
800-223-2336

McGraw-Hill
1212 Avenue of the Americas
New York, NY 10020
800-262-4729

Millbrook Press
2 Old New Milford Road
Brookfield, CT 06804
800-223-2336

Modern Curriculum Press
299 Jefferson Road
P. O. Box 480
Parsippany, NJ 07054-8655
800-321-3106

Mondo
1 Plaza Rd.
Greenvale, NY 11548
800-242-3650

Morrow
1350 Avenue of the Americas
New York, NY 10019
800-237-0657

Mulberry Books (*see* Morrow)

National Library Service
   for the Blind and
   Physically Handicapped
Library of Congress
Washington, DC 20542
800-424-9100

North-South Books
1123 Broadway
Suite 800
New York, NY 10016
800-282-8257

Orchard Books (*see* Franklin Watts)

Oxford University Press
2001 Evans Road
Cary, NC 27513
800-445-9714

Peachtree
495 Armour Circle NE
Atlanta, GA 30324
800-875-8909

Penguin Books
Box 120
Bergenfield, NJ 07621
800-331-4624

Philomel Books (*see* Putnam)

Picturebook Studio
   (*see* Simon & Schuster)

Prentice-Hall
   (*see* Simon & Schuster)

Price/Stern/Sloan (*see* Putnam)

Promotional Book Company
666 Fifth Ave.
New York, NY 10019
212-675-0364

Puffin Books (*see* Penguin Books)

Putnam
One Grosset Drive
Kirkwood, NY 13795
800-847-5515

R&S Books
Raintree Steck-Vaughn
310 Wisconsin Avenue
Milwaukee, WI 53203
800-531-5015

Random House
400 Hahn Road
Westminister, MD 21157
800-733-3000

Richard C . Owen
P. O. Box 585
Katonah, NY 10536
800-262-0787

Rigby
P. O. Box 797
Crystal Lake, IL 60039
800-822-8661

Rizzoli
300 Park Avenue South
New York, NY 10010
800-221-7945

Scholastic
P. O. Box 7501
Jefferson City, MO 65102
800-325-6149

School Zone
1819 Industrial Drive
P. O. Box 777
Grand Rapids, MI 49417
800-253-0564

Silver Burdett Press
P. O. Box 2649
Columbus, OH 43216
800-848-9500

Silver Press
  (*see* Silver Burdett Press)

Simon & Schuster
1230 Avenue of the Americas
New York, NY 10020
800-223-2336

Steck Vaughn (*see* R&S Books)

Sundance
P. O. Box 1326
Littleton, MA 01460
800-456-2419

Tambourine (*see* Morrow)

Ticknor & Fields
  (*see* Houghton Mifflin)

Tricycle
Divison of Ten Speed Press
P. O. Box 7123
Berkeley, CA 94707
800-841-2665

Troll Associates
100 Corporate Drive
Mahwah, NJ 07430
800-526-5289

Tundra Books
P.O. Box 1030
Plattsburgh, NY 12901
514-932-5434

Viking (*see* Penguin Books)

Walker
435 Hudson Street
New York, NY 10014
800-289-2553

Western Publishing
1220 Mound Avenue
Racine, WI 53404
800-558-5972

Whispering Coyote Press
480 Newbury Street
Suite 104
Danvers, MA 01923
800-929-6104

Whitman (*see* Western Publishing)

Willowwisp Press
801 94th Avenue North
Suite 100
St. Petersburg, FL 33702
800-877-8090

The Wright Group
19201 120th Avenue
Bothell, WA 98011
800-523-2371

References

Anderson, L. (1984). The environment of instruction: The function of seatwork in a commercially developed curriculum. In G. G. Duffy, L. R. Roehler, & J. Mason (Eds.), *Comprehension instruction: Perspectives and suggestions* (pp. 93, 96). New York: Longman.

Anderson, R. C. (1996). Research foundations to support wide reading. In V. Greaney (Ed.), *Promoting reading: Views on making reading materials accessible to increase literacy levels* (pp. 55–77). Newark, DE: International Reading Association.

Anderson, R. C., Wilson, P. T., & Fielding, L. G. (1988). Growth in reading and how children spend their time outside of school. *Reading Research Quarterly, 35,* 285–303.

Chall, J. S., Bissex, G. L., Conard, S. S., & Harris-Sharples, S. H. (1996). *Qualitative assessment of text difficulty: A practical guide for teachers and writers.* Cambridge, MA: Brookline.

Chall, J. S., & Dale, E. (1995). *Readability revisited: The new Dale-Chall Readability Formula.* Cambridge, MA: Brookline.

Clay, M. M. (1991). Introducing a new storybook to young readers. *The Reading Teacher, 45,* 264–273.

Clay, M. M. (1993). *Reading Recovery: A guidebook for teachers in training.* Portsmouth, NH: Heinemann.

Deford, D. E., Lyons, C. A., & Pinnell, G. S. (1991). *Bridges to literacy: Learning from Reading Recovery.* Portsmouth, NH: Heinemann.

Fielding, L. G. (1996). Choice makes reading instruction child centered. In C. M. Roller (Ed.), *Variability not disability: Struggling readers in a workshop classroom* (pp. 43–55). Newark, DE: International Reading Association.

Fielding, L. G. , Wilson, P. T., & Anderson, R. C. (1986). A new focus on free reading: The role of trade books in reading instruction. In T. E. Raphael (Ed.), *The contexts of school-based literacy* (pp. 149–160). New York: Random House.

Fountas, I., & Pinnell, G. S. (1996). *Guided reading: Good first teaching for all children.* Portsmouth, NH: Heinemann.

Fry, E. (1977). Fry's readability graph: Clarifications, validity, and extension to level 17. *Journal of Reading, 21,* 242–252.

Gunning, T. (1996, December). *Assessing the difficulty level of emergent and beginning reading children's books.* Paper presented at the annual meeting of the National reading Conference, Charleston, SC.

Guthrie, J. T., Schafer, W., Wang, Y. Y., & Afflerbach, P. (1995). Relationships of instruction to amount of reading: An exploration of social, cognitive, and instuctional connections. *Reading Research Quarterly, 30,* 8–25.

Gutkin, R. J. (1990). Sustained _____ reading. *Language Arts, 67,* 490–492.

Harris, A., & Jacobson, M. (1982). *Basic reading vocabularies.* New York: Macmillan.

Holdaway, D. (1979). *The foundations of literacy.* New York: Aston Scholastic.

Houle, R., & Montmarquette, C. (1984). An empirical analysis of loans by school libraries. *Alberta Journal of Educational Research, 30,* 104–114.

Johnson, M. S., Kress, R. A., & Pikulski, J. J. (1987). *Informal reading inventories* (2nd ed.). Newark, DE: International Reading Association.

Klare, G. R. (1984). Readability. In P. D. Pearson (Ed.), *Handbook of reading research* (pp. 681–744). New York: Longman.

Krashen, S. (1993). *The power of reading: Insights from research.* Englewood, CO: Libraries Unlimited.

Lauber, P. (1996, May). *Producing informational books for children is not as easy as it looks.* Paper presented at the International Reading Association annual convention, New Orleans, LA.

Learning Media. (1994). *Books for Ready to Read classrooms.* Katonah, NY: Richard C. Owen.

Morrow, L. (1982). Relationships between literature programs, library corner designs, and children's use of literature. *Journal of Educational Research, 76,* 221–230.

Morrow, L. (1993). *Literacy development in the early years: Helping children read and write* (2nd ed.). Boston: Allyn and Bacon.

Morrow, L., & Weinstein, C. (1982). Increasing children's use of literature through program and physical changes. *Elementary School Journal, 83,* 131–137.

Morrow, L., & Weinstein, C. (1986). Encouraging voluntary reading: The impact of a literature program on children's use of library centers. *Reading Research Quarterly, 21,* 330–346.

Neuman, S. (1986). The home environment and fifth-grade students' leisure reading. *Elementary School Journal, 86,* 335–343.

Osborn, J. (1984). The purposes, uses, and content of workbooks and some guidelines for publishers. In R. C. Anderson, J. Osborn, & R. J. Tierney (Eds.), *Learning to read in American schools: Basal readers and content texts* (pp. 51–67). Hillsdale, NJ: Lawrence Erlbaum.

Paul, T. D. (1996). *Patterns of reading practice.* Madison, WI: Institute for Academic Excellence.

Peterson, B. (1991). Selecting books for beginning readers. In D. E. DeFord, C. A. Lyons, G. S. Pinnell (Eds.), *Bridges to literacy: Learning from Reading Recovery* (pp. 111–138). Portsmouth, NH: Heinemann.

Spache, G. S. (1974). *Good reading for poor readers* (9th ed.). Champaign, IL: Garrard.

Story House. (1996). *Story House catalog.* Charlotteville, NY: Author.

Topping, K. (1987). Paired reading: A powerful technique for parent use. *The Reading Teacher, 40,* 604–614.

Topping, K. (1989). Peer tutoring and paired reading: Combining two powerful techniques. *The Reading Teacher, 42,* 488–494.

Weaver, B. M. (1992). *Defining literacy levels.* Charlotteville, NY: Story House.

Wilson, P. (1992). Among nonreaders: Voluntary reading, reading achievement, and the development of reading habits. In C. Temple & P. Collins (Eds.), *Stories and readers: New perspectives on literature in the elementary classroom* (pp. 157–169). Norwood, MA: Christopher-Gordan.

Zeno, S. M., Ivens, S. H., Millard, R. T., & Rajduvvuri (1995). *The educator's word frequency guide*. Brewster, NY: Touchstone Applied Science Associates.

Author Index

Title Index

Subject Index

Little Beaver and the Echo (MacDonald), 98
Very Lonely Firefly, The (Carle), 90
Wilson Sat Alone (Hess), 115
Loose tooth:
 I Have a Loose Tooth (Noll), 137
Lost animal or person:
 Have You Seen My Duckling? (Tafuri), 36
 Little Pink Pig (Hutchins), 53
 Lost! (McPhail), 78
 Where's Spot? (Hill), 53
Lost objects:
 Jamaica's Find (Havill), 115
 Spot Goes to the Circus (Hill), 74
 This Is the Bear (Hayes), 74
 Where Is It? (Lillegard), 43
Lost pets:
 Case of the Cat's Meow, The (Bonsall), 89
 Have You Seen My Cat? (Carle), 35
 Lost (Johnson & Lewis), 117
 Snow on Snow (Chapman), 91
 Tom Foolery (Parkinson), 138
 Where's Al? (Barton), 39
Love:
 Bub or the Very Best Thing (Babbitt), 107
 Which Horse Is William? (Kuskin), 97
Lullabies:
 Asleep, Asleep (Ginsburg), 41
 Hush Little Baby (Aliki), 66
 Once: A Lullaby (Nichol), 56

Magic:
 Paper Crane, The (Bang), 129
Magic carpet:
 Cat and Alex and the Magic Flying Carpet (Ballard), 107
Magic tricks:
 Pretty Good Magic (Dubowski & Dubowski), 131
Magnets:
 What Magnets Can Do (Fowler), 132
Mail:
 No Mail for Mitchell (Siracusa), 125
 Will Goes to the Post Office (Landstrom & Landstrom), 97
Maps:
 As the Crow Flies: A First Book of Maps (Hartman), 114
 As the Roadrunner Runs: A First Book of Maps (Hartman), 133

Math (*see also* Counting):
 Doorbell Rang, The (Hutchins), 74
 Monster Math (Maccarone), 77
Mistaken identity:
 Hooray for Grandma Jo! (McKean), 136
Monsters:
 Andrew's Amazing Monsters (Berlan), 108
 Field Beyond the Outfield, The (Teage), 140
 Go Away, Big Green Monster (Emberley), 60
 Harry and the Terrible Whatzit (Gackenbach), 112
 I Hear a Noise (Goode), 52
 Maggie and the Monster (Winthrop), 127
 Monsters! (Namm), 44
 Swamp Monsters (Christian), 130
 Tales of Amanda Pig (Van Leeuwen), 127
 Three-Star Billy (Hutchins), 96
 Where the Wild Things Are (Sendak), 124
Months of the year:
 Chicken Soup with Rice (Sendak), 139
Moods, grouchy:
 Crab Apple (Reese), 45
Moon:
 Does the Moon Change Shape? (Goldish), 93
 Moon, The (Stevenson), 104
 Moongame (Asch), 67
 Papa, Please Get the Moon for Me (Carle), 50
 Rabbit Moon (Rowe), 102
 Yoo Hoo, Moon! (Blocksma), 89
 You're a Genius, Blackboard Bear (Alexander), 66
Moving:
 Big Hello, The (Schulman), 102
 Dust for Dinner (Turner), 140
 Father's Rubber Shoes (Heo), 133
 Good-Bye, Hello (Hazen), 115
 Goodbye, House (Asch), 88
 I'm Not Moving, Mama (Carlstom), 90
 Josephina Story Quilt, The (Coerr), 130
 Leaving Morning, The (Johnson), 117
 Mitchell Is Moving (Sharmat), 124
 Ups and Downs of Lion and Lamb (Brenner & Hooks), 108
 We Are Best Friends (Aliki), 87
Multicultural:
 Coconut Mon (Milstein), 99
 Everett Anderson's Friend (Clifton), 110

Shapes:
  Color Zoo (Ehlert), 85
  Shape of Things to Come (Dodds), 60
  There's a Square: A Book about Shapes (Serfozo), 80
Sharing:
  Doorbell Rang, The (Hutchins), 74
  Floppy Teddy Bear (Lillie), 97
  If I Owned a Candy Factory (Stevenson), 81
  Little Red Hen, The (Barton), 67
  Little Red Hen, The (Galdone), 113
  Little Red Hen, The (Ziefert), 84
  Mister Momboo's Hat (Leemis), 54
  My New Sandbox (Jakob), 54
  Pet Show! (Keats), 135
  Quacky Quack-quack (Whybrow), 127
  Rat and the Tiger, The (Kasza), 118
  Who Took the Farmer's Hat? (Nodset), 56
Sharks:
  Best Way to See a Shark, The (Fowler), 132
  Hungry, Hungry Sharks (Cole), 110
  Sharks, Sharks, Sharks (Anton), 106
Sheep:
  Charlie Needs a Cloak (dePaola), 130
  Shepherd Boy, The (Lewis), 119
  Wooly Sheep and Hungry Goats (Fowler), 132
Shoes:
  Alligator Shoes (Dorros), 70
  My Best Shoes (Burton), 130
  Shoes Like Miss Alice's (Johnson), 96
  Shoes, Shoes, Shoes (Morris), 56
  Whose Shoe? (Miller), 38
Show and tell:
  Show and Tell Frog, The (Oppenheim), 79
Siblings:
  Arthur's Pen Pal (Hoban), 133
  Chang's Paper Pony (Coerr), 130
  Come Out and Play, Little Mouse (Kraus), 76
  Don't Tease the Guppies (Collins), 91
  My Brother Ant (Byars), 90
  Old Enough for Magic (Pickett), 123
  Pig William (Dubanevich), 112
  She Come Bringing Me that Little Baby Girl (Greenfield), 114
  There's a Dragon in My Sleeping Bag (Howe), 116
  With My Brother (Roe), 79

Sign language:
  Handtalk Zoo (Ancona & Ancona), 49
Sizes:
  Sizes (Smalley), 36
Sleep:
  Asleep, Asleep (Ginsburg), 41
  Can't Sleep (Raschka), 79
  Cock-A-Doodle-Doo (Runcie), 64
  Dark Night, Sleepy Night (Ziefert), 83
  Going to Sleep on the Farm (Lewison), 76
  Good Night, Gorilla (Rathmann), 36
  Horatio's Bed (Ashforth), 88
  "I'm Not Sleepy" (Cazet), 90
  Little Donkey, Close Your Eyes (Brown), 90
  Monster Can't Sleep (Mueller), 56
  Napping House, The (Wood), 105
  Night Zoo (Bernal), 37
  Noise Lullaby, The (Ogburn), 57
  Once: A Lullaby (Nichol), 56
  Rabbit Moon (Rowe), 102
  Rockabye Farm (Hamm), 52
  Say Good Night (Ziefert), 65
  Sheep, Sheep, Sheep, Help Me Fall Asleep (Alda), 106
  SHHHH (Henkes), 42
  Sleepy Book (Zolotow), 84
  So Sleepy, So Wide Awake (Paschkis), 63
  Ten in a Bed (Rees), 45
  There's a Nightmare in My Closet (Mayer), 77
  Time for Bed (Fox), 71
  Wake Up, Sun (Harrison), 73
  What a Noise: A Fun Book of Sounds (Morris), 99
  When I'm Sleepy (Howard), 116
  While I Sleep (Calhoun), 60
  Yoo Hoo, Moon! (Blocksma), 89
  You're a Genius, Blackboard Bear (Alexander), 66
Sleepover:
  Ira Sleeps Over (Waber), 140
Sloth:
  Upside-Down Sloth, The (Fowler), 132
Snails:
  Snail's Spell, The (Ryder), 138
Sneezing:
  One Day in the Jungle (West), 58
  Something's Coming (Edwards), 92
Snow:
  Footprints in the Snow (Benjamin), 48

Skills Index